Life as a Heavenly Tribal Messiah

Heavenly Tribal Messiah Collection 3

|LIFE SKILLS|

Life as a Heavenly Tribal Messiah

Heavenly Tribal Messiah Academy

PREFACE

If Adam and Eve had not fallen, all of humanity would have become one family under God and the world naturally would have inherited God's good lineage and traditions. Since all people would have been brothers and sisters, this would have been a peaceful ideal world without conflict. However, since the Fall, conflicts have arisen over differences of ideology, philosophy and religion, including the worldwide conflict between the democratic world and the communist world and border disputes between nations.

Heavenly Parent chose and prepared the nation of Korea and sent the Reverend Sun Myung Moon and his wife, Hak Ja Han, as the True Parents, Messiah and Saviors of humankind. They have devoted their entire lives to working for the salvation of humankind. As a result, it is finally possible for the world's people to begin dreaming a dream of peace. As humankind begins to follow the path of salvation, they can start to build a world of peace, without conflicts or struggles. The key to salvation and the world of peace is the Marriage Blessing, which re-creates families such as that which Adam and Eve would have had, if they had not fallen, and those families are the building blocks to a world of peace with Heavenly Parent as its center.

The original family is a family in which three generations live together in happiness with the grandparents in the position representing Heavenly Parent, the father and mother creating substantial love, and the children who are to be leaders of the future are singing joyfully. The family that follows the original model as envisioned by God is a family of three generations living together and singing with joy, with grandparents at the head, in a position to be respected like our Heavenly Parent, followed by the father and mother who give their unconditional love, and the children who are the joy and hope for the future. The family is a model of the kingdom of heaven, completing the four realms of heart, a place to exchange parental love, conjugal love, siblings' love and filial love. If the world were filled with blessed families built on this model, it truly would be one global village centered on Heavenly Parent.

But the very first family that was created to fulfill this ideal was lost. As Adam and Eve fell away from God and their two sons, Cain and Abel, fought, God's ideal family vanished from the earth. The elder son, Cain, came to represent evil, unable to approach God directly. Because God could not abandon this first family, despite their mistakes, He set up the second son, Abel, in the position of relative goodness, and began to lead humankind down the road of the providence of restoration. As families multiplied upon the earth, the population of the earth became polarized, following the division between the two brothers, into a Cain-type realm and an Abel-type realm. This has led to the individualistic, self-centered thinking that we see today, which is responsible for the conflicts in politics, the economy, religion, culture and every other area of life.

As a result, the world desperately needs True Parents, who have appeared in the role of Messiah, Savior and original ancestors of goodness. All of humankind must be engrafted onto their love and lineage of goodness in the world of the heart. Those who have received the Blessing of True Parents are transferred right away into the Abel tribe with Heavenly Parent as its center. These blessed families represent the desire of Heavenly Parent—the recovery of Adam's family and the creation of a world community under God—which is also the hope of all humankind. We have received the Blessing so that we can reach out to the Cain world, let them know about True Parents and Heavenly Parent, and bring them to receive the Blessing. When we have gone through the work of connecting a Cain tribe to our blessed family in this way, we can finally restore the separation between the two brothers in the family of Adam and Eve. The ideal relationship of brothers under Heavenly Parent finally will be manifested. This work is precisely the work of the heavenly tribal messiahs. It is the providence to restore the world that was divided in two realms of Cain and Abel because of one family's Fall, by reversing the process, into a community of families that matches Heavenly Parent's original model.

In the end, the restoration of a tribe is the providence to find the lost brothers and sisters and restore them to a position centered on Heavenly Parent. The heavenly tribal messiah couple must fulfill the role of the parents who guide the Abel-realm tribe of their relatives and their Cain-realm brothers and sisters with whom they have formed connections in their neighborhood and mobilization areas, bringing the two together to make one restored tribe. This requires finding ways to fulfill the needs of those in the tribe and help them overcome their deficiencies. If we can do this successfully, the members of our tribe will recognize us, saying, "Our heavenly tribal messiah family is truly a model family with Heavenly Parent as its center! They are the parents who truly love us." When we are recognized by our tribe in this way, it means we have been truly victorious in our mission as heavenly tribal messiahs. This recognition will mean we have come to stand in the same position as Heavenly Parent and True Parents, as parents who have loved and rescued humankind. Our position in the realm of restored parents also will be recognized by Heavenly Parent and True Parents. This means we will inherit the kingship of our tribe. We also will find the road to join the royal family by entering Heavenly Parent's recovered direct lineage.

In this book, *Heavenly Tribal Messiah Collection 3*, we have gathered and published the testimonies of heavenly tribal messiah families who have restored the Cain and Abel realms of their tribe, accomplished a tribal community of 430 blessed couples, and are now walking the way of restored true parents. In these stories we can see how they have shed blood, sweat and tears as they gathered their tribe, educated them, blessed them and worked to bring them to be dedicated Unificationists.

If we take the heavenly tribal messiah path by following the mission given to us by Heavenly Parent and True Parents with a heart of absolute faith, absolute love and absolute obedience, Heavenly Parent and True Parents will be there right by our side, and miracles will come. We will read about the John the Baptist figures who already were prepared to meet these brothers and sisters, and about the assistance they received from the local, regional and even national governments, which can only be called miracles. The path of the heavenly tribal messiah is nothing less than the way of the *hyojeong* filial heart leading directly toward Heavenly Parent and True Parents. We earnestly hope that the stories in this book will guide and inspire you and help you to be victorious as heavenly tribal messiahs.

February 1, 2018
Family Federation for World Peace and Unification
International Headquarters

CONTENTS

PREFACE 4

Chapter 1 Young Energy of the Second Generation

1. Realization of Cheon Il Guk through the Fulfillment of the Heavenly Tribal Messiah Mission 13
2. The Yes! *Ajumma* Called by God 33

Chapter 2 Connecting to Relatives and Building a Tribe

1. Please Make Me Stronger, Like a Flower That Takes Root in a Rough and Desolated Land 61
2. My Tribe Is the Heavenly Tribal Community That Is Attending God 77
3. Only the Practice of True Love Can Move the Hearts of Our Tribe 93
4. Knock with Sincerity, and I Will Surely Help You 107

Chapter 3 Working with Religious Groups

1. When I Reached the Place You Commanded Me to Go, There Were People Prepared for Me 125
2. True Parents Have Shown Me the Way 145

Chapter 4 One-on-One Divine Principle Education

1. My name Is Elias and My Legacy Is Love 161
2. A Life of Faith Lived in Oneness With the Will of Heaven 179

Chapter 5 Restoring a Neighborhood

1. The Heavenly Tribal Messiah Mission Is the March to the Blessing 199
2. Heavenly Tribal Messiah Work Is the Way to Become True Parents 217
3. A Fruitful Life Sharing Heaven's Blessings with the World 229
4. I Will Make You a Great Nation and Make Your Name Great 245
5. When We See the World Through Parents' Eyes,
   Love Is the Only Way 261
6. May Your Sorrow and Pain Become a Glorious Medal of
   Happiness and Joy 277

Chapter 6 Collaborating with the National Government and Public Agencies

1. Blessed Are the Poor in Spirit, for Theirs Is the Kingdom of Heaven 297
2. Cheon Il Guk Can Be Realized by Accomplishing the
   Heavenly Tribal Messiah Mission 317
3. Find and Establish God's Nation in the Very Place Where
   You Are Standing 341
4. Change of Lineage in Jerusalem, and in All Judea and Samaria,
   and to the Ends of the Earth 357
5. True Parents Have Come and the Gates to Salvation Have
   Begun to Open 377

Chapter 7 Interreligious Peace Activities

1. The Moment I Met You Was a Miracle in My Life 393
2. he Heavenly Tribal Messiah and Eternal Life 409
3. Making True Parents' Wish My Own, by Becoming a Tribal Messiah 429
4. I Will Be There, Where Your Will Needs Me 447

A GLOSSARY OF KEY TERMS 464

Chapter 1

Young Energy of the Second Generation

Dr. Lek Thaveetermsakul

Person giving Testimony	Wife's Name	Region	Nation
Dr. Lek Thaveetermsakul	Vipa Thaveetermsakul	Asia	Thailand
Blessing Information	Number of Children	Spiritual Children (couples)	Number of Families Attending Church
6,000 Couples	1 son, 2 daughters	430 couples	430 couples

Realization of Cheon Il Guk through the Fulfillment of the Heavenly Tribal Messiah Mission

> We have great hope that we are establishing the foundation to build Cheon Il Guk substantially in the near future. We have the conviction that we can realize God's nation by 2020, which is True Parents' vision. We gained a lot of strength and encouragement from True Father's words in which he says that when 12 tribal messiahs unite in one nation, they surely will fulfill their mission.
>
> We hope to launch a movement of pure love, filial piety and patriotic spirit, so that young people will love and serve their families, hometowns and nation. With the True Family Movement, we are seeking to launch a new model family and a movement to realize new village communities throughout the nation. We pray every day that through this vision and strategy we can realize Heavenly Parent's and True Parents' dream of Vision 2020.

A Couple Must Work with Passion to Open the Gate of Heaven

I would like to offer my deepest gratitude to True Mother for the special grace and blessing that she has given to our family and all of our heavenly tribal messiah blessed families. It is such an incredible grace and blessing that we could not even imagine. It is only because of Heavenly Parent's guidance and protection and because of True Parents' victorious foundation that we could successfully accomplish the mission of tribal messiahs. I believe that the heavenly tribal messiah mission is one of amazing grace to establish the substantial Cheon Il Guk.

As I retired from my public position as the national leader of Thailand after nearly 20 years, our family decided in 2006 to begin our mission as tribal messiahs. However, when we began our activities to complete this mission, we didn't know how to do so. We only knew that we needed preparation on all internal and external

Heavenly tribal messiah Dr. Lek Thaveetermsakul's tribe celebrates the victory of completing the Blessing of 430 couples

foundations. The first thing that came to minds was that there has to be unity between the husband and wife. Together with my wife we talked about this issue and prayed about it. Then we determined to begin heavenly tribal messiah activities. Thinking back on it now, everything was possible because my wife played a key role in leading these activities.

Educating Cain-Realm Children and Abel-Realm Children at the Same Time

We began to reach out to young university students at the Ramkhamhaeng University. The first thing I needed was a few dedicated active members. I sent the university students I met to attend three-day, five-day, and 21-day Divine Principle workshops. Then I raised them up with our children in our own home, just like adopted children.

The university students attended early-morning hoondokhae together with our family and then went to study at the university. When they had free time, they joined in student witnessing and fundraising activities, as well as community service projects. Our home slowly became like a small hoondok family church.

We started to reach out to young university students one by one. After two years we had more than 20 members, and we had to find a new house nearby where these members could stay.

Even though we were able to increase the number of members gradually, it was not easy to maintain or increase the growth of student membership. This is because by the time we met the university students, many of them already had many problems. It was not easy to find pure and self-motivated young university students on campus. Therefore, we went to the northeastern region of Thailand with our student members. That is where the high school they graduated from is located. We started doing purity campaigns and service projects within the school, and this allowed us to reach out to high school students and develop relationships with them. Through this trust and support that we built with the high school students, we were able to find many good and pure students.

Model Youth Programs as a Plan for Realizing the Heavenly Tribal Messiah Mission

Gradually we developed our pilot project and opened our homestay Model Youth Program. With the agreement and consent of the school and the parents, this program is designed to help students to enter Ramkhamhaeng University in Bangkok. We looked for students who wanted to enter this distinguished university and study there and brought them up to the city from the countryside. We also gave them scholarships. We accepted only students who had passed through a series of our pure love education workshops, service activities and interviews. The parents felt reassured that their child would get help from people they could trust and be guided to become exemplary and wholesome young people. They were also very happy that their children would be protected from smoking, drinking, drugs and exposure to sexual problems.

Once the students graduated from high school, we had them enter our programs in Bangkok. For the first five months, they went through orientation and a series of education programs and Divine Principle workshops. We guided the students through step-by-step training. After six months, almost all of them became faithful and dedicated student members. These students who became members then went to their hometown high schools to guide and witness to new, younger high school students. They met and guided these younger students so that they could participate in the Model Youth Program next year. Every year the number of students recruited increased, going from 20 to 30 to 40 to 50. We continued to maintain trust and develop good relationships with the high schools and the parents.

Through this program we were able to systematically find pure and self-motivated university students. We educated and trained them, and we were able to successfully raise these students up and set them on the path to become the future leaders that we want. By the year 2012, we had six student centers accommodating more than 100 student members. The students who graduated gradually became Blessing candidates and core members. However, we were still far from achieving the goal of blessing 430 couples. It was not enough to nurture these students from their high school days.

We established an even more systematic plan. We thought that if we continued to increase new members until we had 100 each year, and everything went according to plan, we could reach 400 to 500 members in the next few years. We thought that the number of people who would receive the Blessing also would increase in the same way, since these students would be blessed about a year after graduating from university. Using this method, it would take us four or five years to reach the goal.

Overcoming Suffering and Welcoming Heavenly Fortune

The reason and motive for me doing the heavenly tribal messiah mission centering on young people is because of a history of suffering in Thailand. After 1991, the Thailand church went through severe national persecution and criticism. After prosecution for severe charges under the national security act of the military government of the time, my wife and I, along with six other young leaders, had to undergo 21 months of imprisonment. The core members of our church were put on trial, and it was a fight for the survival of the Unification Church in Thailand. I still feel sorry today when I think of how worried True Parents must have been and how much pain it must have brought them when they heard the news from Thailand during that time.

We finally were released on bail in 1993, after the democratic government replaced the military government following a bloody demonstration against the military government in May 1992. Starting from that time, I, as the national leader, along with my wife, battled a court case that lasted 21 years to defend the name and dignity of our True Parents and our movement. We made it our mission to revive and rebuild the Unification movement in Thailand and began to offer jeongseong. After 12 years, we were found not guilty and won the case. However, the government appealed the case and it went to the Court of Appeals. After two more years, we gained victory again at the Court of Appeals. There were absolutely no grounds for the charges, and we already had won the first two courts, so we knew what the end result would be. Despite this, the government used its maximum power and authority to continue to push the case up to the Supreme Court. Legally this was an extremely unjustified and unusual measure against us. We knew that surely we would win in the end; it was just a matter of time. But our case became mired and delayed in the Supreme Court without any clear time frame.

Finally, after another seven years, on September 1, 2011, this 21-year indemnity period came to an end. Even Satan no longer could accuse us and finally had to surrender. It was like Jacob's course, and we concluded the case with an absolute victory. Only then were we able to cleanse away all the pain before Heaven and truly feel that the time had come when our path would shine forth with glory.

Even today, I cannot forget how happy True Parents were when we reported this final victory and liberation of the legal case to them. It became a day of liberation and joy for us and a day in history that we never will forget.

Following this, on September 21, 2011, Thailand became the first country in the world to launch a UN Interreligious Council. Centering on True Father's vision, with support from UNESCO, top religious leaders and the government, the Interreligious Council for Peace was inaugurated on the national level. We reported this victory in Thailand to True Parents. We felt that just as this nation had caused much pain, now it could bring about amazing miracles and works.

The First Gift in Realizing True Father's Final Prayer

When we were halfway through the year 2012, we heard the news of

True Father's passing while we were working on the hometown providence. We were so shocked and felt so sad that True Father had left us before Foundation Day. I felt so sorry. I felt ashamed that we had not accomplished enough of our responsibilities and had not brought more joy and glory to True Father while he was still with us. We began to think about what we could do to comfort True Parents' hearts.

With the great support of Dr. Yong Chung-sik in October 2012, after True Father's Seonghwa, we held our first Asia Regional UPF International Leadership Seminar in Songkhla Province. This event become the model for the Southern Thailand Peace Movement and the Interfaith Peace Blessing Ceremony. It was a great challenge for us, because we were determined to hold an Interfaith Peace Blessing that could stand as the model and the foundation to launch ongoing heavenly tribal messiah Interfaith Peace Blessings with the support and cooperation of UPF and FFWPU Thailand.

We began to hold campaigns and mobilizations to gather people for the Marriage Blessing ceremony. One of the staff members who was working with us said that she had a dream about True Father. In her dream True Father had a big smile on his face and came to find her in the hall. There were many elders in that big hall, and they were all listening attentively to a Divine Principle lecture. True Father was seated in the very front row and told the participants, "Thank you. Thank you." When I heard about this dream, I gained even more conviction that True Father is always with us. I truly believed that we would be victorious in mobilizing people for the

Dr. Lek Thaveetermsakul's family receives an award from True Parents as the first family to complete the heavenly tribal messiah mission

upcoming seminar and Blessing ceremony.

When I heard about this dream, I thought of the video in which True Father spoke about the tribal messiah mission in the final prayer he offered before he went to the spirit world. I determined to find a way to give the Blessing to 430 couples before Foundation Day, as an offering to Heavenly Parent and True Parents. I had a strong conviction that if even one couple out of all the blessed families could achieve this legacy that True Father had left us, then the words that he left on this earth would not go to waste.

To do that, we had to develop a special strategy to complete the education and the blessing of 430 couples before December 2012. Therefore, in the beginning of November 2012, with the goal of 500 couples, we called on all the student members. All the students who were spiritual children were also determined to help in achieving this goal. We encouraged all our student members to go back to their hometown to invite their parents and relatives to attend two-day UPF-FFWPU family education programs, followed by an Interfaith Peace Blessing on December 1 and 2, 2012.

On the day of the event, more than a thousand people filled the hotel grand ballroom in Khonkaen in the northeast region of Thailand. This was the first breakthrough event for Thailand. There were 650 couples, more than we had expected, who had come to participate in the Blessing Ceremony. This was the first victory that we brought in the name of the heavenly tribal messiah mission. We achieved this victory just one month before Foundation Day. This became an offering and the first step toward the realization of True Father's final prayer.

The Honor of Being First in the World to Fulfill the Heavenly Tribal Messiah Mission

Finally, on Foundation Day, our couple was recognized as the first in the world to fulfill the mission of heavenly tribal messiah. At the Foundation Day event, we had the honor of offering flowers of gratitude to True Parents on behalf of all the blessed families in the world.

After the Blessing ceremony, I returned to Thailand and began to educate all the couples that had participated in the Blessing ceremony. We carried out the indemnity stick ceremony, 40-day separation, and three-day ceremony. We educated them about the traditions of blessed families and established a standard for them to become true blessed families. Many of them started to voluntarily follow True Parents' tradition to become dedicated blessed families.

To our surprise, many of the couples who had completed the three-day ceremony started to have deep spiritual experiences. Many of them had dreams and revelations about True Parents. They also experienced good financial fortune, protection from life-threatening accidents, and life-changing experiences in their families, finding the inspiration and strength to end such life habits as smoking, drinking and domestic violence.

These phenomena testified clearly to the fact that good spirit world and good ancestors are ready to come down to support and protect blessed families after the three-day ceremony, just as True Father told us would happen if we did tribal messiah activities.

The good spirits and ancestors were able to come down to the earth and liberate the blessed families and their hometown from Satan's realm of dominion. They will protect those families and establish their hometown on the heavenly side. The public institutions in the region as well as the clans also actively helped. If this was the general trend we could look forward to, I gained the conviction that we could start from our hometown and, based on the foundation of tribal messiah activities, expand the heavenly sovereignty, people and territory to establish the foundation for Cheon Il Guk.

An Interfaith Peace Blessing officiated by Dr. Lek Thaveetermsakul's family

Therefore, we are convinced that the substantial change of blood lineage to heavenly lineage through the three-day ceremony is the crucial key to spiritual and physical rebirth for all the newly blessed couples and previously married couples. Those who receive the Blessing can be reborn as sons and daughters of Heavenly Parent and True Parents and be connected to become Cheon Il Guk citizens. Ultimately, the heavenly tribal messiah mission sows the seeds of Cheon Il Guk, which are the starting points where Cheon Il Guk can bloom in our hometown, our nation and throughout the world.

After this seminar, we encouraged all other blessed families to start heavenly tribal messiah activities in their hometown. In the first 21 months after beginning tribal messiah activities, from

November 2012 until July 2014, twenty families joined us in doing tribal messiah activities. During that time we held 13 Blessings in 12 provinces including Bangkok. This foundation opened the gate to expanding tribal messiah activities to a national level in Thailand.

However, not all the couples who participated in the Blessing Ceremony completed the three-day ceremony. We are working harder to achieve the goal of 430 couples who have completed the three-day ceremony. We held two more Blessings, of 600 couples and 100 couples, in Buriram on May 4, 2014, and in Bangkok on Sept. 14, 2014, resulting in a total of 1,318 couples who have been blessed so far.

We continued by setting up follow-up education programs for these 1,318 couples, and in October 2014 we finally had 454 couples who had completed the three-day ceremony. The participants included 162 full-time student tribal members.

Bless This Nation and Realize Your Nation

On September 8, 2014, in order to expand this tribal messiah providence to the national level, we also launched the UPF-FFWPU National Peace Tour as a family seminar in 77 provinces. We were able to get the cooperation and support of the provincial governments for this family campaign. The provincial governors agreed to provide provincial government meeting halls for the seminars and invited all the concerned government officers, community leaders,

A gathering of heavenly tribal messiah Dr. Lek Thaveetermsakul's tribe

NGO leaders and other participants to attend the seminars.

In these seminars we announced that the basis for the happiness of the community and the nation is a healthy family. We suggested expanding the Interfaith Peace Blessing that transcends ideology and thought. We emphasized absolute sex and purity and gave them the core teachings of True Parents and the Divine Principle.

Through this Peace Tour, we expand the FFWPU Blessed Family Network and started the True Family Movement for National Unity and Peace. This movement has been receiving a lot of support from citizens and active support from the government. The Peace Tour is becoming the hope of the people and this nation. Some provinces already have signed MOUs (Memoranda of Understanding) with

UPF-FFWPU to support education and activities, including financial support. This process has been completed in 45 of the 77 provinces. Our blessed families have been receiving the cooperation of the government and community everywhere they go and have opened wide the way for tribal messiah activities. We are planning to complete all 77 provinces like this by Foundation Day of 2015. I believe that this is a good strategy to bring about the settlement of the mission of tribal messiahship on the national level.

We continue to encourage all blessed families to join heavenly tribal messiah activities and education and to participate in Blessing activities nationwide. At this time in Thailand, with the cooperation and hard work of our blessed families, we have held 31 tribal messiah Blessings in which more than 12,000 couples have been blessed. Through follow-up education, more than 1,500 couples have completed the three-day ceremony.

Our Hope Is to Become the First Heavenly Nation through Heavenly Tribal Messiah Activities

In March 2015 my wife and I began to hold special one-day Preliminary Education Workshops for all the newly blessed couples who had completed the three-day ceremony in our tribe. From March 18 to 24, we completed four more workshops, with a total of 250 couples participating. The purpose of the workshop is to educate the participants to become true blessed families who can practice

The families of Dr. Lek Thaveetermsakul's tribe during a heavenly tribal messiah workshop at Cheon Jeong Gung in October, 2014

the tradition of blessed families. We want them to take responsibility and ownership as Cheon Il Guk citizens. It is also to help them to become heavenly tribal messiahs for their own community and village. After this workshop, we continued our follow-up by visiting them and guiding them to practice the tradition of hoondokhae in their family. Later we began to choose blessed couples who had completed the three-day ceremony but were not attending church yet, so that they could become family hoondok group leaders, organizing hoondok groups in their village. In this way we gradually could establish the family hoondok tradition and the hoondok group tradition in which the family gathers and forms the four-position foundation in the community and village.

Through the settlement of the tradition of hoondokhae in the family, the newly blessed families could continue to grow spiritually and understand the Divine Principle more deeply. If we continue to increase the numbers of blessed families in the communities and villages, a new village movement can start and, in the near future, expand to change the society and nation.

We have great hope that we are establishing the foundation to build Cheon Il Guk substantially in the near future. We have the conviction that we can realize God's nation by 2020, which is True Parents' vision.

We gained a lot of strength and encouragement from True Father's words in which he says that when 12 tribal messiahs unite in one nation, they will surely fulfill their mission.

We hope to launch a movement of pure love, filial piety and patriotic spirit so that young people will love and serve their family, hometown and nation. With the True Family Movement we are seeking to launch a new model family and a movement to realize new village communities throughout the nation. We pray every day that through this vision and strategy we can realize Heavenly Parent's and True Parents' dream of Vision 2020.

Kang Deok-rye

Person giving Testimony	Husband's Name	Region	Nation
Kang Deok-rye	Lee Gye-hyeong	Korea	Korea
Blessing Information	Number of Children	Spiritual Children (couples)	Number of Families Attending Church
1800 Couples	3 children	550 couples	400 couples

The Yes! *Ajumma* Called by God

2

> When I practice witnessing, I always invite my guests to my home after meeting them three times outside. I have them meet my family, so they can see how a blessed family lives. Then I would help my spiritual children and physical children unite and build relationships like real siblings. I have tried to give them true love that is more active than love in the satanic world. My spiritual children who were moved by my family's lifestyle would witness to their friends, and their friends would witness to their friends and, later, witness to their siblings and parents. Like a sweet-potato vine sending out new branch vines, one spiritual child led to another spiritual child. The secret was to create an environment in which my spiritual children could experience a new world and a new culture of love through sharing their hearts and connecting with each other.

Introduction

On August 20, 2006, at the Korea International Exhibition Center (KINTEX) in Gyeonggi Province, when True Parents were conducting the Blessing ceremony at the Rally for the Victorious Liberation of Homeland Restoration for Cosmic Peace Based on the Return of Heaven and Earth to God, they saw my husband and me standing in front of the podium as one of the representative blessed families and nicknamed me the "Yes! *Ajumma* (Lady)!" This was an unimaginably tremendous blessing for me. True Parents have given me direct instructions and guidance through various spiritual phenomena. Moreover, whenever they gave me directions or advice, they also prepared an environment in which I could handle that mission.

I am always confident that True Parents' instructions and counsel will come true, no matter how impossible they may seem. Therefore,

I have lived my life with absolute faith, absolute love and absolute obedience toward any mission given by them. I think True Parents gave us the nickname, "Yes! *Ajumma*" because I have lived my life by an established standard that my life is not my life alone but represents True Parents and the blessed families. I would like to give a brief introduction about how my husband and I joined the Unification Church, how we fulfilled our mission as heavenly tribal messiahs, and how we have carried out our life since then.

Establishing the Model of a True Family

Ever since we received the Blessing, my husband and I have promised to live for the providence in complete harmony. As True Parents said, "Before seeking to dominate the universe, first achieve dominion over the self!" I have always lived with the realization that I must always look for the source of any problem not in the other person but within myself. Since there is still fallen nature within me, the existence of "me" is exposed when I become angry. Therefore, I have persuaded myself that if I spit out anger, I must surrender to Satan, because I cannot achieve dominion over myself. I must die to win over Satan. This has become a promise for my husband and me and a motto of our life of faith. As a result of defending this principle, my husband and I have never fought in 42 years. We have controlled ourselves with the perception that "My partner's shortcomings are my shortcomings."

I think my three physical children, along with my spiritual children, were able to take part in the Blessing with such a heart because they have seen how my husband and I have lived as a couple. Our two sons and one daughter received the Blessing when they were young, so we already have ten third-generation grandchildren. Thanks to our family life principle, on our 30th Blessing anniversary my husband presented me with a plaque in recognition

The family after the Cheon Il Guk Foundation Day Registration Blessing (February 22, 2013)

of my 30 years of keeping the heart of a parent. I also gave my husband a plaque of appreciation to express my gratitude to him. Furthermore, our spiritual and physical children gave us a plaque in appreciation for showing them an example of how to live diligently based on True Parents' instructions as their mom and dad. In practicing True Parents' words, I think the key to our family life was the truth that an absolute object arises from an absolute subject.

Becoming the Bridge to Restore Cain

Another mission True Parents gave us when we received the 1,800 Couples Blessing was to "become the bridge to restore Cain!"—which is witnessing. The first mission True Parents gave me was to witness to young people. My first spiritual son was 22 years old when he joined the church. Interestingly, all the spiritual children I witnessed to back then were 22 years old. Most of my mission in witnessing was to witness to young people and to lead them to the Blessing. As a result, the second-generation children born to my spiritual children have reached considerable numbers by now. There are not many already married blessed couples or spiritually blessed couples among my spiritual children.

When I practice witnessing, I always invite my guests to my home after meeting them three times outside. I have them meet my family, so they can see how a blessed family lives. Then I help my spiritual children and physical children unite and build relationships like real siblings. I have tried to give them true love that is stimulating than love in the satanic world. My spiritual children who were moved by my family's lifestyle would witness to their friends, and their friends would witness to their friends and later to their siblings and parents. Like a sweet-potato vine sending out new branch vines, one spiritual child led to another spiritual child. The secret was to create an environment in which my spiritual children could experience a new world and a new culture of love through sharing their hearts and connecting with each other.

Difficulties I Experienced in Witnessing

It was never easy to lead my spiritual children to the Blessing. When I went out for witnessing at Inha University, I met a student who strongly opposed the Unification Church. Soon after, he went to the army. After that, I wrote a letter outlining the Divine Principle. When I visited his house one day, his mother came out and said, "Why did you take my son to the Unification Church?" and splashed a bucket of water on me. For a moment, I was disconcerted and upset. However, I thought Satan would love it if I just left. I endured by telling myself, "Why should I do what Satan likes? I will not make True Parents cry!"

After that, I visited his house many times. As a result, although his family opposed the Unification Church, he joined the church and received the Blessing. Today he has four children, and his eldest daughter who received the Blessing has given birth to a beautiful third-generation child. This was not an easy path.

True Parents loved us while burdened with suffering. I think we should take responsibility to pay back at least some of the love we have received from them. I was led by a simple desire to return at least a small part, if not everything, of what we received, and the results came by themselves.

Expanding through Spiritual Children

When I raise my spiritual children, I emphasize internal family education rather than external witnessing. I think I should be able to frequently invite my guests to my home and show them an example of a principled life. Of course, witnessing can be done through theoretical Principle education. But they will surely face difficulties at some point, if there is no role model to show them an example of how to deal with life's changes.

I started witnessing in earnest in Gochang County in Jeonbuk Province. My first spiritual son, Elder Kim I-jung, still lives there. When Kim I-jung was 22 years old, he was staying in Jeongeup, where his sister lived, and I met him during my 40-day witnessing period in Jeongeup and led him to the church.

In 1991, True Parents told all blessed families to return to our hometown and become tribal messiahs. I strongly pushed my first spiritual son, Kim I-jung, who then was working at the Ilshin Stone

Co., to leave everything behind and return to his hometown, according to True Parents' instruction. I told him, "If you stay at your company, you will become comfortable there. You will have no foundation in your hometown, if you return later." I sent him back home saying, "We must become True Parents' filial sons and daughters by following their instructions with absolute faith, absolute love and absolute obedience." As a result, he has created a foundation in his hometown and is doing well in his path of faith.

Fulfillment of 430 Couples Is the Victory of Our Tribe

One day, I had an experience in which God's heart suddenly revealed itself to me. I went into the closet and prayed with tears all day. It was already evening when I came out of the wardrobe. There I promised God I would never cry again. Forty-two years have passed since then. At the Cheon Il Guk Foundation Day Registration Blessing Ceremony, eight members of my family attended the Blessing to represent the eight lost family members of Adam and Noah [Sermons 354-181]. My husband and I, my three children and their spouses attended the ceremony and realized True Parents' wish. True Mother said, "The blessed families should have created the environment that Heavenly Parent wished for." Based on these words, we held an inauguration ceremony for our heavenly tribe at the former headquarters church in Cheongpa-dong on 6.20 by the heavenly calendar in the first year of Cheon Il Guk (July 27, 2013).

Heavenly tribal messiah Blessing ceremony for 430 couples in Gochang, Jeonbuk Province (January 13, 2015)

When I visited the BonHyang Won (True Father's resting place) on December 1, 2014, I asked True Father, "Father! How can I help you?" Then True Father planted a message in my heart, "Go out and witness on the front line!" Also, during hoondokhae True Mother said in tears, "You must become heavenly tribal messiahs!" Furthermore, the president of FFWPU-Korea said, "Witness to 12 new members per family!" On that very day, I went to Gochang County and held a meeting with my spiritual children. Through this meeting, we decided to bless 12 couples per family. The fact that my spiritual children were going out witnessing made me very happy and delighted.

Back then, True Mother appeared in my dream and encouraged

me, "You can fulfill 430 couples if you keep up your work in a calm and orderly way!" My eldest spiritual son, Kim I-jung, formed a witnessing group with his spiritual siblings. Ten of my spiritual children gathered and promised to fulfill 430 couples by blessing 120 couples, which is 12 couples per family. The fulfillment of 430 couples was a splendid achievement realized through the teamwork of my spiritual children. I encouraged them and told them, "You can do it, if you go for it!" Up until that time my husband and I had blessed 118 couples and our spiritual children had been able to bless 217 couples, so we could see that fulfilling 430 couples would be possible if we just added 120 more couples.

There was a time when I worked very hard in witnessing, along with my first spiritual son, Kim I-jung, and his wife. When Mr. Kim and his wife brought in guests, I would go down to Gochang County and give Divine Principle lectures on a small table. I did everything I could to encourage and support them. There was even a time when I made two round trips in a day to Gochang County from Seoul. We made a regular repeated pattern of witnessing, raising and leading people to the Blessing. Not only my spiritual children but also spiritual grandchildren called me, and each time I would rush to the scene and give a passionate lecture on the Divine Principle. This was how we made our heavenly tribe. The base of our sustained activity was Gochang. I was able to fulfill the blessing of 430 couples as a result of working hard with my first spiritual son, who returned to his hometown in Gochang to fulfill his responsibility as tribal messiah.

My Spiritual Children Call Me *Mapo Omma*

I am very thankful to my spiritual children because they are the driving force to establish my family and tribe. My spiritual children call me by the nickname *Mapo Omma* ("my mom from Mapo," a district of Seoul). It helps us feel closer and more familiar with each other. Every morning, I find nice verses from the *Cheon Seong Gyeong* as I read it and send those verses to my spiritual children and my tribe by KakaoTalk (the leading instant messaging application in South Korea) so they can read them at the same time at 5:00 in the morning. When I input a lot of text to send out, my shoulders ache as if they are going to fall off. But I feel a sense of satisfaction every time I combine my jeongseong with True Parents' love and send out the text with the heart to start our day with True Parents' words. This way, I have created an environment in which my spiritual children can read True Parents' words every morning. This became a good chance for my tribe to create a strong hoondokhae tradition. The reason I send them True Parents' words every day is to provide them with spiritual food. As we read in the Bible, "Man shall not live by bread alone, but by every word that comes from the mouth of God." [Matt 4:4] We must eat not only physical food but also spiritual food, so that we will not be tested by Satan.

I frequently make phone calls to the ten central families among my spiritual children. I collect a variety of items together to help me share True Parents' words and other information from the church with them. Then they contact their spiritual siblings around them to share the grace. When we have a path of love and heart through this kind of communication system, our lives are bound together. I strongly believe that spiritual children cannot help but follow their spiritual parent's effort.

I have a way to manage my spiritual children. There are two spiritual children who received the Blessing as one of the 6,000 couples. All my spiritual children who received the Blessing after that are Korean–Japanese couples. So, most of my spiritual daughters-in-law are Japanese members. When they first moved to Korea, my house was a training center for them to prepare for their family life. Holding on to True Parents' words in their hearts, my Japanese daughters-in-law were people who came to Korea with the belief in True Parents alone. They received the Blessing when they barely knew their husband's face, and they came to Korea without knowing anything. How anxious would they feel? Because I thought of them as my real daughters, I decided to send all of them to a Korean language institute to learn Korean so they could adapt well in Korea. Living together at my house, I taught them how to make kimchi stew, doenjang stew, and other Korean food so they could adapt to the Korean lifestyle. It made me feel sorry when I imagined how embarrassed they would feel if they went to their husband's house without any preparation. Therefore, I took care of them for seven months so they could get used to Korean cultural and behavioral nuances to a certain degree.

Since my husband and I had to raise not only our spiritual children but also our physical children, we were like ministers guiding them in faith. We tried to spend as much time together as possible. For example, we went to Yeouido to ride bicycles on Children's Day. Our whole family gathered together to visit the Paju Weonjeon. We also held summer and winter camps for the second-generation children. We always encouraged the children to join our activities. We held Christmas parties and graduation parties at our home. When they entered puberty, we held seminars to teach them about growing into womanhood. Every time we held an event, such as a 103-day dedication ceremony for a new baby, a first-birthday party, a Blessing anniversary, an engagement ceremony, a Holy Wedding pledge service, a third-generation baby shower, etc., we had the second-generation children take part in it so they naturally could come to think, "I hope I can receive the Blessing and live like that soon. I wish I could have babies, too."

I have educated second-generation children for a long time. It was like a routine for us to hold second-generation tribal workshops during vacation periods. My spiritual children and I have been holding workshops and education for our second-generation children for more than 15 years so they can unite as a heavenly tribe. After True Father's Seonghwa in 2012, we made firm resolutions to educate our children well according to True Parents' teaching.

On the first anniversary of True Father's Seonghwa, we held an eight-day workshop in Gochang with 80 second- and third-generation children. On the second Seonghwa anniversary, we made a pilgrimage tour to the holy grounds in Korea to trace the course of True Parents' heart. On the third Seonghwa anniversary, 33 of our

Visiting a family during heavenly tribal messiah activities

second- and third-generation children made a pilgrimage to the western United States and visited Twin Peaks, Shim Jeong Garden, Lake Tahoe, Young-jin nim's temporary *weonjeon* in Reno, Las Vegas, Cheon Hwa Gung, Grand Canyon, Sedona, and other places for 14 days. This trip required a budget of more than 100 million won. I was able to overcome this financial issue because True Parents directly appeared in my dreams and gave me instructions. On the fourth Seonghwa anniversary, we inherited True Parents' heart by making a pilgrimage to various places True Parents had visited in Korea.

We were able to conclude the pilgrimage tours in Korea and the United States safely due to the contributions of our spiritual children.

As a result, we were able to inherit True Parents' heart and connect it to the members of our tribe who could not take part in it. By uniting our second- and third-generation children through workshops and pilgrimages, they can rely on each other as they grow up and they can be prepared to receive the Blessing when they reach maturity. Furthermore, when second-generation families have babies, we all can celebrate with each other. I hope my tribe can keep such a tradition alive through this kind of education.

My Motivation Was True Parents' Direction

On November 25, 1993, True Mother was on a world tour and True Father was in Jeju Island to educate 50,000 women from Japan. I went to Jeju with three elder members to inherit True Parents' heart. True Father told the three of us to give testimonies in front of 2,980 members. When True Father heard my testimony, he told Rev. Lim Du-sun, who was then vice president of the Korean church, "This girl is smart! Let's give her family a True Family award and send her to Japan for witnessing!" To follow this command, I traveled back and forth between Korea and Japan as True Father's secret emissary for 21 years.

On September 26, 1997, I attended the Jardim 40-day workshop held in Pantanal, Brazil. On the next day, which was Chuseok, True Mother took me on a boat ride and gave me a lot of love. I gave True Mother a hug and said, "Mother! I will live a good life for you!" That evening, True Mother sent me a dress through Mrs. Wonju Jeong McDevitt with a message, "You should wear this when you give lectures in Japan!" After concluding my 21 years work in Japan in 2014, I have focused on activities in Korea. During those 21 years when I traveled back and forth from Korea to Japan, whenever there were providential events such as True Mother's tours in Japan, I rushed to the site and offered jeongseong. Since I have five spiritual children who are in the ministry in Japan, they often invited me to give guidance to their members.

Educating Your Children in the Mission Field

I think the best way to educate people is to let them see and experience for themselves. I always used my house as a training center of living faith. This was before True Parents built or even bought the land for Ocean Cheon Jeong Gung on Geomundo Island. True Parents gave me an internal direction to go to Geomundo Island. Therefore, I unconditionally headed for Geomundo Island with five spiritual children. Since it was our first visit, we unconditionally focused on the large acres of land and prayed. Then suddenly True Parents' helicopter came flying by. When I spiritually asked, "Father, what should I do now?," he said, "Just offer a prayer and go." Back then, nobody knew that True Father was planning to build Ocean Cheon Jeong Gung on Geomundo Island.

During a hoondokhae session that took place right after my trip to Geomundo Island, True Father asked the participants, "Do you know what I am planning to do on Geomundo Island?" True Father made me visit the site three times, and each time, Father appeared in the helicopter. I realized later that True Father was setting up a condition to have someone explore and pray there before starting the construction work of Ocean Cheon Jeong Gung in Geomundo Island. Sometime after True Parents completed the book *Pyeong Hwa Shin Gyeong* and soon after they held a rally in Seoul, they visited the *Hayan* (white) *Jip* (house) Inn on Geomundo Island. At that moment and in that same inn, I was reading *Pyeong Hwa Shin Gyeong* with my spiritual children and Japanese in-laws, in the same room where True Father held hoondokhae. Then suddenly Ms. Yang Yeon-shil entered the room and, in astonishment, told us that True Father had come. In this way, True Parents let me experience their true love in in the mission field.

I think what True Parents emphasize the most to blessed families is the four great milestones. True Parents said, "Each blessed family must establish a Parents' Day, a Children's Day, a Day of All Things and a God's Day of their own. You must achieve tribal or racial victory and pull it up to the level of a nation." [*Blessed Family and the Ideal Kingdom II*, 177] Therefore, our tribe has declared our four great milestones on behalf of all blessed families, and on each holy day we gather together and offer pledge service. Furthermore, it is a must to visit the Paju Weonjeon. When I hold such events, True Parents occasionally appear during my meditation or in my dreams to give me some message. I put effort in offering substantial achieve-

Heavenly tribal messiah gathering in Gochang, Jeonbuk Province

ments before God and True Parents by following these missions and messages.

I would like to share some of my experiences. My tribe has followed a tradition of education through attendance for 33 years. We do this at the Paju Weonjeon. We visit there on holy days and honor the members of the True Family and blessed families who lived a noble life on the providential path. One time, I had an amazing experience. True Father had been using the Chinese character *weon* (元), which means "the best," in writing *weonjeon*. One day, however, on a banner I made I inadvertently wrote the Chinese character as *weon* (原), which means "cause." That same day, True Father proclaimed that the Chinese character for *weon* in *weonjeon* would be changed to *weon* (原), or "cause." I believe that substantial communion between the spiritual world and the physical world drove me to do that.

On the Day of Victory of Love on January 2, 2014, I made a banner that said, "Inauguration Ceremony for the Cheon Il Guk Providence of the Union of the Spiritual and Physical Worlds" and brought it to the Paju Weonjeon. On that very day, Hoon-sook nim and Shin-whul nim also came, and our tribe had the opportunity to pray together with Heung-jin nim's family at the weonjeon. My spiritual children were inspired to have such a special opportunity and felt the spiritual world was working directly with us. At the same time, they realized, "Ah … so this is the providence of the union of the spiritual and physical worlds," and were able to strengthen their conviction and faith.

I also had an experience in which True Parents appeared in my dream and said, "Build a resting place for True Parents that resembles Cheonseong Wanglim Palace." When I built a resting place for True Parents on some land belonging to one of my spiritual children and dedicated it on January 13, 1998, True Parents told my family to proclaim our own True Parents' Day. Three years later, on January 13, 2001, True Parents conducted the Coronation Ceremony for God's Kingship at the Cheonseong Wanglim Palace. At another time, I received spiritual "mail" to build an education center for our children. So I constructed a building and on April 14, 2002, dedicated it as the Children's Education Center, where we also proclaimed our family's True Children's Day. On the same day, True

Parents held the dedication ceremony for the main building of Sun Moon University.

One year later, in 2002, I received God's command to "bring the eldest sons or eldest daughters to the elder-son nation of America and restore the number 1 ten times!!" Following this command, I took more than 50 people who were the eldest sons and daughters to the United States. On November (the 11th month) 11, 2002, at 11 hours, 11 minutes, and 11 seconds I restored the number 1 ten times. While doing so I also restored the number 10, which is a number of unity, and was directed to proclaim our Day of All True Things. Then, on January 13, 2005, I suddenly received God's command to build an official residence for the True Children. At first, the words "official residence" seemed so onerous and weighty. However, although the difficulty was beyond expression, because it was God's command, I worked hand in hand with my spiritual children and built an official residence for the True Children and dedicated it on May 5, 2005. Then God told me to proclaim this day as my family's True God's Day. By the way, the dedication ceremony of today's FFWPU Korean headquarters was held on the very same day. This is why I had no choice but to answer, "Yes!" to the commands given to me by God.

Through such unbelievable and amazing experiences, our tribe has been able to feel a real depth of faith and heart. I believe True Parents gave me the nickname "Yes! *Ajumma*" because they knew I have acted on all the revelations they gave me. They were spiritual communions between True Parents and me. If something is True

Parents' command, I must do it. There were inexpressible hardships that arose through that process. However, True Parents trained me to strengthen my faith, whatever the experience.

My Positive Lifestyle

I do not worry about tomorrow. When I do something, I complete it within that day. I marked my plans on the calendar every single day and made a promise with True Parents in my heart that I would fulfill all plans within that year. It was not easy for me to get into such a habit. I communicated with True Parents every day, in my heart, "Father, didn't I do a good job today? Didn't I give you happiness?" This way, I pushed myself and encouraged myself, so I would not get tired, and told myself that True Parents were with me.

I think the most daunting enemy is a bad habit. I can improve my life by improving my habits. When I developed positive habits, I became a positive thinker and positive results came about. This taught me the lesson that maintaining absolute faith, absolute love and absolute obedience was the best and only way of life. According to True Parents, when God created human beings and all things, He created them with absolute faith, absolute love and absolute obedience. I live my life of faith with the conviction that True Parents have led the providence in the same manner. I believe the life of absolute obedience is the only path for us to live.

Overcoming Financial Issues

My husband was an office worker when I was witnessing to young people, so most of his salary went to support witnessing. I never sent my physical children to after-school academies or other private lessons; but I now know by experience that it has benefited our family to use the money for witnessing.

When I witnessed to college students, most of their parents were against the church and the Blessing. Because they were still students, it was not easy for them to stand on their own feet without any financial help from their parents. My spiritual children in college had to pay the Blessing fee if they were to receive the Blessing, and they needed pocket money if they were to take part in church activities. Each time, I had to provide financial support for them. Therefore, witnessing has become my occupation, while my daily life has become a sideline.

True Parents often would help me when I needed money for the providence. It happened in 2003, when True Parents were speaking on stage at the CheongPyeong training center and I was sitting at the very back of the hall with one of my spiritual children. True Father was talking about the peace rally that was to be held in Israel and explaining that more than 3,000 people had to take part in it. Hearing this, I whispered to my spiritual son, "I guess every blessed family must take two persons with them." At that moment, True Father said, "Every blessed family must take two persons with them." I said to my spiritual son sitting next to me, "We must do this," and, centering on him, we made contact with my spiritual children in Korea and Japan. As a result, we gathered the money for the necessary expenses for three people to visit Israel and I was able to take part in the rally with a district delegate and a representative of a women's organization.

In this way, every time there was a special providence, my spiritual children helped me out financially with the heart of coming along, even if they could not actually take part directly. All of this is True Parents' work for letting my children believe and follow their instructions. Of course, even today there is no end to financial issues. However, I am working on solutions as I talk and consult with my mature spiritual children.

The words "heavenly tribal messiah" remind me that since God is with me, today I should not worry about the future. Each time I made up my mind to follow True Parent's direction and began offering jeongseong, God moved people by sending them spiritual mail and we were able to solve our financial issues. It may be hard to believe, but this was how I overcame financial limitations.

Conclusion

What does witnessing mean for me? First, witnessing is True Parents' love and heart. I could not have made it without True Parents. Second, my motivation has been based on God's tears and agonized search to find His lost children. I became who I am today when, through my own struggle and my own blood, sweat and tears, I started to feel True Parents' agony, blood, sweat and tears to search for and recover each blessed family.

Therefore, when God connected me to someone, I had no choice but to treasure that relationship. Furthermore, when I was blessed, True Father directly gave me a mission to "become the bridge to restore Cain." Those words alone have been a very strong motivation for me, up to this day, to endure difficulties. When I go out witnessing, I do not think that I am giving my love to people but that I am conveying God's love to them. This way, people will receive God's absolute love instead of my love and will come to feel the world of God's love.

My motivation to carry out heavenly tribal messiah work was the first love given to me by True Parents. If I let go of that thread of first love, I will lose my value. I am grateful to Heavenly Parent and True Parents for letting me walk this path with unchangeable absolute faith, absolute love and absolute obedience for 42 years since that day when True Parents gave me their first love, and for their giving me the nickname, "Yes! *Ajumma*." Aju!

Chapter 2

Connecting to Relatives and Building a Tribe

Motou Furuta

Person giving Testimony	Wife's Name	Region	Nation
Motou Furuta	Kyoko Furuta	Japan	Japan
Blessing Information	Number of Children	Spiritual Children (couples)	Number of Families Attending Church
777 Couples	3 sons, 1 daughter	467 couples	427 couples

1

Please Make Me Stronger, Like a Flower That Takes Root in a Rough and Desolated Land

> 1. The members of the Furuta Tribe shall believe in and attend the Messiah of all humanity, the True Parents of Heaven, Earth and Humankind, inheriting the traditions of their lives and studying their victorious words that have investigated and revealed all the problems on earth and in heaven that no others have solved throughout history, as expressed in the *Divine Principle, Cheon Seong Gyeong, Pyeong Hwa Gyeong* and *Chambumo Gyeong* as the instructions for life, and living diligent lives of absolute faith.
> 2. We shall humbly practice the lifestyle of "living for the sake of others," which True Parents have suggested throughout their lives, and make it our goal to become persons possessing a character of love.
> 3. We shall ceaselessly seek to harmonize with others and put unwavering effort into serving not only the members of our tribe but also the other people with whom we are acquainted, our neighbors, those in need and, furthermore, the society and the nation, with the spirit of mutual support.
> 4. We shall cooperate in maintaining and supporting the environment around us so that our descendants can properly inherit True Parents' teachings and way of life.

A Delightful and Joyous Path of Faith That Bloomed through a Life of Hardship and Suffering

I was born in 1942 in Hsinking (now called Changchun), in the Jilin province of Manchuria, where my parents used to live. My father was drafted into military service in May 1945 and later was held as a prisoner of war in Siberia. Therefore, my mother lived in anxiety while raising me during the Second World War. In May 1946 the government gave instructions for families with children to return to Japan as soon as possible. It was hard for my mother to leave, because she had lost contact with my father, but she had no other choice. She left Manchuria with her two young sons, carrying my younger brother, then two years old, on her back and holding me by the hand.

Since I was only four years old, I do not remember that time very well, but I have remembered bits of it when I heard my mother speak about it. During our desperate flight from Manchuria to

Japan, my younger brother died of starvation. I still remember when he drew his last breath as he cried in a whisper, "Mommy, Mommy." My mother hurriedly dug a hole in the ground and buried him before continuing her journey in tears. There was nothing else she could do, because the last ship to Japan was about to depart, and we barely managed to get aboard. It took us 20 days by ship to get from Jinzhou to Fukuoka. I do not remember how we managed to reach our home in Gifu after that. Even now, I cannot hold back the tears when I think of how my mother kept going while trying desperately to keep me alive.

My father returned to Japan in 1947. Although he had survived the cold and hunger of Siberia, he died of a brain hemorrhage on a cold winter day in December 1954 when I was in sixth grade in elementary school. Seeing her husband off and remembering in her heart the son she had buried, around this time my mother started to take an interest in the spirit world. She entered a small religious association with me, where they taught people that they could obtain Buddha's grace if they would give and share. She offered jeongseong, and, as time passed, many people acknowledged her for her sincerity and faithfulness. Our life had reached a certain degree of stability when my mother met the Unification Church. Although she had grown up in a polytheistic Shinto culture, she had always thought that there was only one God. So when she heard the Divine Principle, she recognized that it was the truth she had been looking for. As soon as she came home, she gathered the family and the people who trusted and followed her and proclaimed, "I heard a

Relatives who took part in Motou and Kyoko Furuta's Tribal Messiah Proclamation in February 1992

one-hour lecture at the Unification Church today and have decided to join them." Then she asked, "How about you? Will you go with me?" Everyone was taken by surprise, but all the family agreed to go with my mother, because she had demonstrated strong leadership up to that day, in spite of her suffering. That evening, ten people, including my whole family and the people who worked in our family store, all joined the church as a group. However, although it was my own mother's decision, I was the one who felt the most conflict and resisted joining the church. Back then, a man named Jin Ryu had counseled me to follow my parents, no matter what. Because I loved my mother, who had gone through such a long period of difficulty, I decided to follow her and learn the Divine Principle. When I finally met True Parents, I made up my mind to live for the True Parents of humanity. For me, the path of faith was the path of loving my mother and a path to happiness and a greater purpose.

Since then, for the last 52 years, my family and I have walked a life of faith to become true filial sons and daughters. In September 2005 in Kodiak, Alaska, True Parents acknowledged my mother, who paved the way for our tribe's faith, saying, "Furuta's mother took the lead in organizing Japan's eight million Shinto spirits, gods and deities and bringing all of them before God. This made it possible for Japan to start its role as the Eve nation."

My Mission as a Heavenly Tribal Messiah Began from True Parents' Grace and Blessing

On July 1, 1991, True Parents declared the tribal messiah providence and gave us the direction to return to our hometown. Back then, I was in charge of the marine fishery business in America. One day, True Parents called me and said, "Furuta, you must go back to your hometown, gather 120 relatives, and gain their approval to hold a ceremony proclaiming you as their tribal messiah." At that point my mother had been bedridden for ten years as a result of her age and the physical toll that her difficult life had taken on her health; however, she gathered all her strength and wrote letters to gather all of our relatives. On February 21, 1992, we succeeded in gathering 120 of our relatives at the Nagoya Church and held a

True Mother presents the Furuta family with a certificate honoring them for completing their heavenly tribal messiah mission (February, 2017)

Tribal Messiah Proclamation Ceremony. When I reported this to True Parents, they bestowed a calligraphic motto on our tribe that says, "The First Tribal Messiah Proclaimed in Japan."

In 1995, our eldest son, Tomimasa, received a second-generation Blessing in the 360,000 Couples Blessing. His wife is Ms. Hae-young Kwak, a second-generation Unificationist from Korea. My mother cherished the joy of the settlement of the realm of three generations as she saw her first grandson's marriage. In 1996, at the age of 77, she completed her life, which had been full of ups and downs, and entered the spirit world. It was my mother who built the foundation for our victory of blessing 430 couples by guiding 110 relatives with single-hearted devotion and faith. The feeling of gratitude and affection toward my mother grow larger and larger as time goes by. Throughout my life of faith, my mother has always been an unforgettable model of faith and a symbol of absolute faith toward True Parents.

When True Father's autobiography was published in 2009, my wife invested most of the money for our daily living expenses in securing 430 copies to distribute. She put special effort in distributing them to the Fukuyama tribe. Some of them refused, but 150 of them accepted the book. Among the members who joined the church after 2009, there were those who came to us to say, "I'm a relative of Mrs. Furuta." Many of our Unification Church members left their families behind when they joined the church. My wife is one of those members, and she had a hard time recovering the relationship with her parents and siblings. However, as time passed and she prayed for them and distributed the autobiography, the way opened to rebuild the relationship with her family. One day, one of my wife's relatives came to meet us after asking around and going through several people to find us, and asked, "I have been given the same book twice, and this time it was from a lady named Kyoko Furuta. Do you know her?" Every time she looks back on that day, my wife gets excited and says, "It was like winning the lottery!" (Although she has never won the lottery before, it was an unbelievable experience.)

We were grateful to God for guiding our families and relatives in various ways in addition to directly conveying True Parents' words. We were also very grateful for the fact that the number of my wife's relatives who are willing to walk the path of faith with us has increased from seven families to 21 families after distributing the autobiography.

Establishing a Foundation for Victory as a Heavenly Tribal Messiah

My wife always strives to work in response to the providence of the times. Especially after she received great blessing in the 30-day workshop held at the central training center at Sutaek-dong, in Guri, Gyeonggi Province, Korea, in July 2012, even I was inspired by the way she devoted herself to achieving True Father's will for us to complete our mission as heavenly tribal messiahs. Although there were times when she stayed home for three days in quiet prayer if she had been treated inconsiderately and irrationally in the process of witnessing, she soon composed herself and carried on her mission. After my mother passed away, my wife has become the center of our family and clan and has established today's foundation from the seeds planted by my mother in cooperation with my brothers, uncles and aunts as she worked hard as a heavenly tribal messiah.

As the providence moved on to the time of the family church in May 1995, we remodeled our house to start our family church. Since then, we have held events such as family workshops, Marriage Blessings and holy wine ceremonies, wedding receptions, lectures and get togethers for local members of parliament, and various kinds of study meetings. In June 2016, the Japanese church headquarters designated our family church as an "officially approved tribal messiah family church."

As the national messiah providence started in 1996, six couples among our tribe were appointed as national messiahs. My wife and I were appointed to Argentina in South America, my younger brother Katsuto's family to Botswana in Africa, my uncle Fukubo Goto's family to Equatorial Guinea in Africa, my cousin Akemi Hendricks' family to Mongolia, my spiritual son Eichiro Minami's family to Ethiopia, and Kenjiro Aoki's family to Russia. The Furuta family has also engaged in missionary or business activities in various places including Japan, North and South America, Germany, Britain, China, Hong Kong, Indonesia, Vietnam, North Korea, Russia and Africa. We are receiving great blessing internally and externally through these activities.

In July 2015, the International Headquarters at Cheon Jeong Gung sent Professor Yoon Do-yeong of the CheongShim Graduate School of Theology and his colleagues to research our activities. In commemoration of this opportunity, we held a celebration of "The 50th Anniversary of the Furuta Tribe Joining the Unification Church." We also prepared a Furuta Tribe Education Plan under the guidance of Professor Yoon to set up a system for our descendants to inherit our religious tradition.

The Furuta Tribe Education Plan for the Completion of the Heavenly Tribal Messiah Mission

1. The members of the Furuta Tribe shall believe in and attend the Messiah of all humanity, the True Parents of Heaven, Earth and Humankind, inheriting the traditions of their lives and studying their victorious words that have investigated and revealed all the problems on earth and in heaven that no others have solved throughout history, as expressed in the *Divine Principle, Cheon Seong Gyeong, Pyeong Hwa Gyeong and Chambumo Gyeong* as the instructions for life, and living diligent lives of absolute faith.
2. We shall humbly practice the lifestyle of "living for the sake of others," which True Parents have suggested throughout their lives and make it our goal to become persons possessing characters of love.
3. We shall ceaselessly seek to harmonize with others and put unwavering effort into serving not only the members of our tribe but also the other people with whom we are acquainted, our neighbors, those in need and, furthermore, the society and the nation, with the spirit of mutual support.
4. We shall cooperate in maintaining and supporting the environment around us so that our descendants can properly inherit True Parents' teachings and way of life.
5. We shall carry out all our activities in alignment with the realization of these purposes.

A meeting of Michinoku 369 group, part of the heavenly Furuta tribe

At the fifth Foundation Day in February 2017, my heart was full of eternal gratitude and honor on receiving a Heavenly Tribal Messiah Award from True Parents. Since the time when we held the Tribal Messiah Proclamation Ceremony in 1992, it took us 25 years to fulfill our responsibility of organizing our tribe by guiding 430 families of Abel and Cain children to the Blessing. In the process of visiting our relatives and spiritual children, we counseled them regarding solutions to their numerous burdens, comforted them in their suffering, shared their pain, and shed tears together in difficulties beyond our imagination. Although it was not an easy path, our heart of gratitude grew deeper as we grew to become the parents of our tribe.

True Parents are the ones to save and liberate the long history and all humanity in the spirit world and the physical world as the Messiah of heaven and earth and the True Parents of humanity. I have realized that True Parents are suggesting to us that we inherit their way of life at the tribal level and walk a parental path by becoming little messiahs. They taught us to meet our tribe and listen to their twists and turns in life and accept their difficulties as a microcosm of the patterns of all problems borne by humanity. True Parents have enveloped and embraced all these problems with indomitable faith and perseverance and with love that is grand, deep, high and wide. In the same way, we were able to experience their practice of love through the path of the tribal messiah. I now understand that the path of the heavenly tribal messiah was, after all, a path of blessing and gratitude. I finally have realized how grateful I should be that I am able to serve my family and tribe and the people around me and to live for their sake to my heart's content in my last stage of life.

Please Let Us Continue to Grow without Stopping (Tribal Education and Management)

The Furuta tribe currently holds second-generation gatherings in Tokyo, Nagoya and Osaka. These are primarily organized by myself and by my eldest son, who travels and interacts with second-generation families in each area when he has a chance to come back from the United States to visit Japan. The second-generation families in Nagoya have formed a club called the Miroku (3-6-9) Tree Branch Club, and they hold assemblies on a regular basis hosted by the association Fuji Sakura Gathering. Another group has been formed to research our members who are working in society. Another one is focused on establishing a strong financial foundation. There are currently nine families in our tribe who are working in ministry. My eldest son teaches extracurricular classes in local schools while managing a Japanese restaurant in the United States. He serves the community as he runs the business, and also sponsors arts activities for second- and third-generation children.

Since my spiritual children live in many places around Japan, we have made an organization called 3-6-9 (Miroku) Club in each of the local Family Churches. From our perspective, *Miroku*, or Maitreya, is a symbol of the Second Advent, in other words, True Parents as Second Coming of Christ, Buddha, Confucius and Mohammed. Moreover, the Japanese race tends to approach and understand all kinds of religion through the "faith for *Miroku*." Therefore, we made 3-6-9 Clubs as conduits for witnessing in each district in cooperation with the local blessed families. Currently we have the Michinoku 3-6-9 Club, the Nara Ginga 3-6-9 Club, the Amami Islands 3-6-9 Club and the Nansei Islands (Okinawa) 3-6-9 Club. We also gather and hold seminars once or twice a year for ambassadors for peace.

At the Tokyo branch, we have opened a Health Salon (health-care shop) hosted by the association Oasis Japan. We invite experts to lead seminars entitled "Mental and Physical Health" and "Family Counseling," centering on "wave therapy." Nowadays, more than 100 participants are taking part in these seminars every month and they have become a base for witnessing. At the Nagoya branch, they have started to interact with other organizations and religious groups while holding services, family gatherings, various research groups, lectures and liaison activities.

Our next task is to support families with many spiritual children to achieve their missions as heavenly tribal messiahs. Since each member must witness to three spiritual children and organize 36 families, 72 families and 120 families on the foundation of 12 families, it will take some time. However, if we can move forward without losing sight of our goal, we can achieve that goal more quickly. I am longing for the day when 12 families in Japan can inherit heavenly fortune and realize the settlement of Cheon Il Guk by restoring their tribes. The Furuta tribe will work diligently and play a central role in building this foundation.

Jintendra Shrestha

Person giving Testimony	Wife's Name	Region	Nation
Jintendra Shrestha	Nila Shrestha	Central Asia	Nepal
Blessing Information	**Number of Children**	**Spiritual Children (couples)**	**Number of Families Attending Church**
400 Million Couples 5th phase	1 son, 1 daughter	430 couples	20 couples

2

My Tribe Is the Heavenly Tribal Community That Is Attending God

> We had many difficulties working as heavenly tribal messiahs. We began tribal messiah work in 2011 and accomplished our mission in 2015. During those four years there were many times the persecution was difficult to overcome. We prayed many times with sweat and tears. Sometimes I wanted to quit, but my wife always offered positive thoughts and did not give up. She remembered True Father's suffering course, and her goal of meeting True Mother helped her to keep going. She would tell me that becoming heavenly tribal messiahs was the only path to meeting Heavenly Parent and True Parents and would never give up. I realized that experiencing the path of suffering of Heavenly Parent and True Parents in this way was helping us to truly become children of True Parents and true blessed families.

Even for the Prodigal Son, There Was a Way

My name is Jitendra Shrestha, and my wife is Nila Shrestha. We received the Blessing from True Parents, and we have a son named Pyeong-gil and a daughter named Jinho. I joined the Unification Church in 1995, when I was 16 years old. Before I joined the church, I was an aggressive person and did not believe in God.

One day a man named Rudra Bujel came to our store and talked to me about the Unification Church. He invited me to attend the seven-day workshop. I told my family that I had decided to go to a workshop and that I would be back in seven days, but I did not return for a long time. Ironically, my family did not even bother looking for me. That's how little connection of heart there was between me and my family.

Later, in 2005, after I got matched to my future wife I came home and introduced her to my family. Fortunately, from that point on I started to get closer to my family.

After I joined the church, I completed seven 40-day workshops that included fundraising on MFT and attended a seven-day Original Divine Principle workshop. After this I changed completely, and from that time until now I have been a full-time member of the Unification movement. Currently I am working at the headquarters in Nepal as the personal assistant to Special Envoy Ek Nath Dhakal.

During my 40-day conditions on MFT, I experienced the real heart of Heavenly Parent and came to understand how much True Parents suffered for the sake of humankind to establish the kingdom of heaven on earth. Despite being rejected by my family, I realized why I was alive and on the earth, and I decided to dedicate my life to following True Parents and establishing Cheon Il Guk.

After Meeting My Lovely Wife and Receiving the Blessing, I Began the Restoration of My Tribe

Our regional president, Dr. Yong Chung-sik, has visited Nepal several times, and he inspired and encouraged me and my wife to be the first couple in Nepal to restore their tribe as heavenly tribal messiahs. My wife was very inspired by the testimony of Dr. Lek Thaveetermsakul, who was the first to successfully complete the heavenly tribal messiah mission in Thailand. I was very busy in the field as the assistant to Ek Nath Dhakal, but I always supported my wife as she did the heavenly tribal messiah work.

A heavenly tribal messiah home meeting of the Jintendra Shrestha tribe (October, 2017)

At the time, only our relatives had been witnessed to. We offered jeongseong, such as reading the *Divine Principle* and offering bows. My wife insisted that we witness to our families and relatives first, and then expand to other people. She felt that it would be wrong to approach others if we could not even witness to our own families. Our first goal was to prepare 12 couples from our families and hold a Blessing. But God inspired them, and finally we had 17 couples. This gave us great confidence, and we set up an even more ambitious plan. We continued our activities, and then we had a tribal messiah Blessing for 40 couples and then 70 couples, and finally we had a Blessing for 500 couples. This was the largest heavenly tribal messiah Blessing ever held in Nepal. While we were preparing those

500 couples, we worked for a month, visiting each home to educate them and continued to meet them until the Blessing. During all the work for the tribal messiah Blessings my wife and I were very united, praying together, offering jeongseong and sharing our experiences and feelings. This was one of the most important things that contributed to making our work successful.

The One Who Interrupted Our Lives Brought New Life to Our Tribe

We were very lucky that we got to spend time with Dr. Robert Kittel's family and learn True Parents' traditions from them. Around the time we first started holding home group meetings with his wife, Theresia Kittel, my wife invited her sister-in-law's friend from her hometown to visit. Her name was Saraswati Shrestha. She was having a problem with her husband, and at the time she was considering getting a divorce. But unexpectedly, when she heard True Parents' words, she shed many tears. After listening to her painful story, my wife related everything with me, and we started thinking about how we could save her life through the Blessing. We decided to invite Saraswati and her husband to participate in a Blessing ceremony and to hold the Blessing on my wife's birthday. That would make it easy to invite her husband, since he is a friend of my wife's.

After they attended the Blessing, Saraswati called to say that her husband had. It was hard to persuade her husband to do the 40-day separation period, but finally he agreed to it. They also completed the three-day ceremony, and after that they had many spiritual experiences. She continued to attend hoondok meetings, and sometimes she held hoondok meetings at her home. She even has organized some heavenly tribal messiah Blessing activities. Now her daughter has joined the second-generation program and attended the Global Top Gun Youth (GTGY) workshop in Korea. This family is now one of our three core families, and they participate actively in all kinds of church programs. She is very grateful to God and True Parents for saving her marriage.

Saul, Saul, Why Are You Persecuting Me?
(The Secret of the One Who Comes Later)

My younger brother was a typical Abel type, and he actively supported me because he saw how much my life changed after I joined the church. After he received the Blessing, his business grew stronger, and he often said that it was because he had come to believe in God and True Parents. He has always supported me economically and of course in other ways as well. I am very proud of him, both as a brother and as a spiritual son. He is one of my most reliable spiritual children, and that could happen only because of Heavenly Parent, True Parents and the heavenly tribal messiah Blessing.

Among our other spiritual children, my wife's brother was the hardest one to witness to. When my wife talked to her brother and suggested that he participate in the heavenly tribal messiah Blessing, he got very angry with her and said he would never do that. But I felt that if he finally would receive the Blessing, one day he would become one of our most dedicated members. We never gave up and kept educating him about True Parents, and at some point a miraculous change began. At the time he was having many physical health problems. However, after the 40-day separation period and the three-day ceremony, he was healed spiritually and physically and his life changed dramatically for the better. After that, he was the person who provided us with the most support when we were doing tribal messiah Blessings. Even more amazing is that he also has completed his 430 couple tribal messiah Blessings. This was a great moment of joy for our family. It was like the way the apostle Paul, who had persecuted Jesus, changed his mind completely after he received Jesus. This is something we never would have believed possible, if God had not made it happen right before our eyes.

Because of his impressive transformation, we now have four couples in our tribe who have completed 430 couples. We are very grateful to Heavenly Parent and True Parents for this great blessing. We felt that this is the beginning of our victory. We started with a goal of restoring our family first and then restoring others. In reality, we still have a lot of work left to do. We have given them birth, but we still need to help them to grow spiritually according to God's Will.

The Principle of Our Family's Heavenly Tribal Messiah Activities

When we decided to become heavenly tribal messiahs, my wife said, "We must witness to our family first and then extend it to include others." We prepared our first Blessing ceremony in our home on my wife's birthday to make it easy for our family members to receive the Blessing while celebrating my wife's birthday. Our second Blessing we organized during a festival, so that people could come to celebrate the festival and receive the Blessing at the same time. And the third time, we had a big party for my wife's brother, who had just returned from Australia after being gone a long time. We invited everybody to come celebrate and receive the Blessing. After these successes we were inspired to work on the heavenly tribal messiah Blessing for 500 couples, which we held in my wife's birthplace, Sundarijal.

Blessings Come with Trials and Hardships, and You Must

Cross over the Peak I requested that the national headquarters help us in educating people about the Blessing. With their help, we gave educational programs, going from house to house and to schools and village community centers. My wife started to carry a small projector with her to each house. We got a lot of persecution while we were working in the field, but we did not give up and just kept moving forward. That was when my wife and I could really feel God's pain and our True Parents' hearts.

We experienced more difficulties after the Blessing than before it. Many couples had trouble with the 40-day separation period, which is very challenging, especially for the husbands. We got many phone calls from our relatives, saying they had problems and couldn't continue. My wife and I held hands and prayed for them and tried to persuade them to stick it out. During that time our national leader, and my friends Prakash Babu Thapa and Kasi Nath Khana, helped us a lot. Thanks to that teamwork, eventually we succeeded in helping the couples complete the 40-day separation period and three-day ceremony.

My wife and I have always focused on education, because just the Blessing alone is not enough. We educated the new families through home group meetings and encouraged them to send their children to attend workshops for second-generation members. There are many festivals in the Hindu tradition. We visited the families in the tribe during those festivals to develop our relationships with them. We also tried to tell inspiring stories about chastity and morality and strived to help them receive enlightenment from True Parents' teachings in their lives. Although this method takes some time, we will continue to try it as we think it is a good way that helps people understand.

Hoondokhae to Change People's Lives and

Build a Community of Small Groups

Even though we have given new life to our tribe, it is difficult to guide them according to Unification tradition. In Nepal most families are Hindu, and strange new traditions are hard for them to accept. We are always trying to find new ways to witness, and one thing we do is use Hindu traditions like the Teej festival to bring people together. We also have to find new ways of talking about Divine Principle and help them to receive enlightenment from True Parents' teachings.

We are working to establish traditions for our tribe. Every week we organize home group meetings in different places and invite them to FFWPU programs. Sometimes we get together for our son or daughter's birthday and celebrate according to our FFWPU traditions. We invite the key families to show them how we celebrate and encourage them to follow this tradition.

Sometimes after their children return from attending second-generation workshops, the children share with their parents what they have learned, and the parents can learn new things too—for example, how to bow to True Parents whenever you leave the house or return home. We teach them how to hold prayer meetings and holiday celebrations. We always have a goal to keep blessing new families. When we invite families to our home, we create a comfortable environment to make it a little easier for them to accept the teachings. And we pick the most moving sections of True Father's autobiography, so we can get more energy by reading about

A heavenly tribal messiah Blessing by the Jintendra Shrestha family (January, 2015)

his life. By sharing food, helping each other, and talking about positive things, we can develop relationships with them little by little, hear their stories and help them solve their problems.

It is a burden to have the hoondok meetings always at the same place, so every week we meet in a different home. This way we also can meet new families and get close to all the families. Sometimes we donate clothes for families who are having trouble or donate money for children from poor families. This helps us to find new guests.

Heavenly Tribal Messiah: A Name You Earn as You Become

the True Parent of Your Tribe

Usually we receive a participation fee from the participants when we organize a program. However, in some cases we cannot insist on a participation fee because they still do not understand the importance of the Blessing. In such cases we are using our personal funds, because it is our responsibility to bless them. But because our economic situation is not strong, we ask for support from the church or raise donations from the households. In this way we can offer participation in the Blessing ceremony free of charge to the family receiving the Blessing. But when they have been blessed and have experienced grace and spiritual assistance after finishing the three-day ceremony, people voluntarily offer a donation of gratitude.

We had many difficulties working as heavenly tribal messiahs. We began tribal messiah work in 2011 and completed our mission in 2015. During those four years there were many times the persecution was difficult to overcome. We prayed many times with sweat and tears. Sometimes I wanted to quit, but my wife always offered positive thoughts and did not give up. She remembered True Father's suffering course, and her goal of meeting True Mother helped her to keep going. And I realized that experiencing the path of suffering of Heavenly Parent and True Parents in this way was helping to truly become children of True Parents and true blessed families.

The heavenly tribal messiah mission has really allowed us to understand the path of pain of Heavenly Parent through thousands of years of waiting. Isn't that why True Parents started the heavenly tribal messiah mission—for us to feel one in heart with Heavenly Parent? I see so many problems every time I visit my community—problems like divorce, remarriage, immature relationships, and lack of moral education. I have been teaching True Parents' ideas, which can change people's lives and save them from Satan's attacks, thus contributing to building the substantial Cheon Il Guk in my nation of Nepal.

As heavenly tribal messiahs, my wife and I passed through many obstacles and were able to deeply realize the sufferings of our Heavenly Parent and True Parents. We learned about heavenly tribal messiah Marriage Blessings and other activities during the Original Divine Principle seminars and I wanted to share that education with my tribe I would like to hold seminars that the members of my tribe can come to experience True Parents' traditions, solve social problems, as well as seminars to train second generation members and young people how to become true sons and daughters. One other dream I hope to realize is to build a center for my tribe where we can do hoondokhae. This is the most difficult challenge for our family, but we will keep believing that, with the guidance of Heavenly Parent and True Parents, one day it could become a reality. I believe someday our dream will come true. I am deeply grateful to our loving Heavenly Parent and True Parents for choosing our family for this providence.

Hideo Oyamada

Person giving Testimony	Wife's Name	Region	Nation
Hideo Oyamada	Noriko Oyamada	Japan	Japan
Blessing Information	Japan	Spiritual Children (couples)	Number of Families Attending Church
43 Couples	4 sons, 1 daughter	440 couples	340 couples

3

Only the Practice of True Love Can Move the Hearts of Our Tribe

> When we meet our spiritual children, it is important not only to teach them True Parents' words and the Principle but also to guide them to solve the problems they are facing in their daily lives. When I was asked by my brothers and sisters to teach their children, I helped them to find practical solutions to the problems their children were facing, utilizing True Parents' words and the Divine Principle. As a result, they expressed deep gratitude for helping them solve those difficult issues.
>
> The practice of true love through all things has inspired the members of our tribe, and as a result, they have sent back seasonal fruits, rice and vegetables to our home in return. Every day I feel that the solidarity of our heavenly tribe has developed both spiritually and physically, due to the give-and-receive action of true love, not only through material gifts but also through offering jeongseong and prayer for the members.

From Joining until the Blessing I was born in 1941 in Yamagata Prefecture, Japan, and grew up in a Christian family, which is quite uncommon in Japan. Perhaps because of that influence, from the time I was a young man I had many questions about faith, passion, the Second Advent and the Last Days. In particular, there were three challenges in my life which I was determined to solve and which I prayed to find the answers to. The first challenge was to understand the fundamental principles of the universe; the second was to meet a teacher who could teach those principles; and the last was to meet a friend who could share my views or a spouse who would share my life until the end of my days. I thought that if I could not solve these problems, my life would have no meaning. Therefore, I thought that finding those answers was more important than my life itself, and I struggled to find them even when I was very young. I went to shrines and temples and prayed hard there. Once or twice a year I would take some time to pray and meditate deeply about these questions.

In the 1970s in Nagoya, I attended a three-day workshop for high school students and prayed in a field in the Chita Peninsula. I kept praying to try to find the meaning of life and the purpose of the existence of the universe. Then, like Moses receiving his revelation at Mount Sinai or Michelangelo's revelation at Mount Carrara in Italy, as a result of my earnest prayer and meditation I also had a revelation which was just like what is written in the Book of Genesis. When I was praying hard about God before He created heaven and earth, a vision of the creation began to appear.

When the universe was in a state of chaos without any form, there was the Word of God, "Let there be light." Then, everything in the universe began to be created. The moon and stars, heavenly bodies, fish in the ocean, birds in the sky, animals and plants on the ground, and finally human beings were created. The process of the creation of heaven and earth appeared vividly in front of me. In this way, I had the same experience as the saints and the prophets testified in the Bible.

After joining the Unification Church while I was a college student, I had another revelation when I met True Father for the first time. This time, I suddenly had a revelation from God, telling me, "Your wishes have been fulfilled." And at that moment, I realized that the three main tasks of my life, with which I had deeply struggled for many years, were completely solved by meeting True Father. The day when I met True Father was the beginning point of my understanding of the fundamental Principle of the universe, and the day I met the true teacher who would teach me that Principle. In addition, later I came to meet my wife, Noriko Kishimoto, who became my friend

Members of the Oyamada tribe on a pilgrimage to Korea (November 6–9, 2015)

and spouse with whom to walk the way of God's Will together for the rest of my life, and we were part of the 43 Couples Blessing in 1969.

My wife seems to have struggled deeply over the problems of life, just as I did. I was also frequently confronted with the "imitations" of life that existential philosophers have been troubled with. And I was deeply concerned about how I would die. Sendai, where I spent my college days, had many famous suicide sites. First, there was a 70-meter cliff on the west side of Otamaya, where the mausoleums of three generations of the Date family were located.

There was also another place, a suspension bridge over the "Evacuation Valley (Tachinoki-sawa)" on Mount Yagi. It was part of a secret escape route from the castle, which had been built in case the Date family were attacked and had to flee. A lot of people committed suicide there. In the past, Toson Shimazaki, a famous poet and novelist, lived in the area as a high school teacher because he could not bear the pain of his failure in love. Bansui Doi, who wrote the lyrics of the song *The Moon over the Ruined Castle* (*Kojo no Tsuki*), also established his base here. Matsushima was also a place where people who were distressed about their lives committed suicide by throwing themselves into the ocean. Because I had been exposed to such an environment since my childhood, as a young man I also was concerned deeply about death and began to think about it.

After seriously struggling over the issue of death, I became a member of the Unification Church and came to know and understand the Word. It was a very moving experience when, 10 years later, I came back to my hometown as a regional leader to deliver the word of life to people. It is amazing that a person like me, who always had been worrying, "What is death?" and "How should I die?," could be reborn after meeting True Parents as an evangelist who was thinking, "How can I save people?" In this manner, after I was newly reborn through True Parents, I started as an evangelist as well as a heavenly tribal messiah.

Establishing a Foundation to Complete the Heavenly Tribal Messiah Mission

True Father has always emphasized home church, return to hometown, and heavenly tribal messiah activities. I felt strongly that I was chosen to restore my wife's Kishimoto family, and my wife was chosen to restore my Oyamada family. When I was in the Jardim Training Center in Brazil in the 1990s, True Father told my wife and me, "You four Kishimoto sisters always have to be united and cooperate with one another!" Bearing his words in mind, my wife and her three sisters have always been united and worked together with me as a cornerstone of our work to restore our 430 families.

When True Father talks about the Blessing, his words are not aimed at the salvation of the individual, as are the teachings of other existing religions, including Christianity; rather, he is speaking of the route for restoring the family. When I visited my wife's Kishimoto family, her mother and all her family truly welcomed me with love. Even when my wife's father died, my mother-in-law trusted me so deeply that she asked me to be the chief mourner at the funeral rather than her own sons from the Kishimoto family. Every member of my wife's family welcomed me as a real brother.

When my wife visited my Oyamada family for the first time, they were all very interested in what kind of bride I was bringing to meet them and welcomed us warmly, saying, "You brought such a great and wonderful person!" My father often said, "I sometimes want to see my son's face, but I always want to see my daughter-in-law's face." Even my brother, who was against the Blessing, said, "You brought such a wonderful bride, I cannot win," and since then he has not opposed us.

After that, the three younger sisters of my wonderful wife were witnessed to and joined the church, which was a tremendous blessing. I had elder sisters, but I didn't have any younger sisters.

Therefore, I couldn't help thanking God because He gave me three wonderful younger sisters along with the Blessing. As True Father said, these four sisters, centering on my wife, have been united and fully cooperated with me. Thanks to that, we could dedicate the glory of the victory of 430 families before Heaven. I realized once again the greatness of the Blessing that our Heavenly Parent and True Parents gave to our tribe.

Attitude toward Spiritual Children and Utilizing CheongPyeong

When we meet our spiritual children, it is important not only to teach them True Parents' words and the Principle, but also to guide them to solve the problems they are facing in their daily lives. When I was asked by my brothers and sisters to teach their children, I helped them to find practical solutions to the problems their children were facing, utilizing True Parents' words and the Divine Principle. As a result, they expressed deep gratitude for helping them solve those difficult issues.

I and the four sisters have prayed earnestly every day while calling before God the name of each member of our tribe, along with keeping personal contact with all of them. Especially during the holy days, my wife has always sent gifts to the tribe. In addition, thanks to the love of fishing that I inherited from True Father, each time I spend time on the ocean, I also have fresh fish to send to the

A monthly "Oyamada Gathering" at the South Tokyo Church

members of our heavenly tribe. In this way, the practice of true love through all things has inspired the members of our tribe, and, as a result, they have sent to our home seasonal fruits, rice and vegetables in return. Every day I feel that the solidarity of our heavenly tribe has developed both spiritually and physically, due to the give-and-receive action of true love, not only through material gifts but also through jeongseong and prayer for the members.

When educating my nephews, I try to make good use of the various workshops and education at CheongPyeong, as well as the ancestor liberation and Blessing workshops and so on. Thanks to the providence and cooperation of CheongPyeong in both spiritual and physical aspects, many people of our tribe have been restored and naturally came to receive the marriage Blessing. My son and nephew also are working for public missions in CheongPyeong, directly attending True Parents. It is no exaggeration to say that without the providence of CheongPyeong, the heavenly tribal messiah activities we are doing today would not have been possible.

The Process from Witnessing to the Blessing to Settlement after the Blessing

I have many spiritual children from my early pioneer witnessing in Chiba, Kagoshima, on campus during university, and so on. As they matured in their faith and became involved in witnessing, it helped to expand the foundation for our heavenly tribal messiah activities.

Regarding witnessing, we have carried out witnessing activities through home visits, on-campus witnessing at universities, interreligious activities, hobby events, fishing jeongseong and many other ways. One of our focuses in witnessing is a style you could call "from elder siblings to younger siblings, from seniors to juniors." It is important to find a systematic way of expanding your witnessing results, rather than trying to restore all 430 families through heavenly tribal messiah activities alone.

We also hold monthly "Oyamada Gatherings," tribe meetings and worship services, to keep moving forward with witnessing, the Blessing and the settlement after the Blessing. In the past, we conducted these meetings in each family or local area, but now I have organized our heavenly tribal messiah activities by traveling the whole country and visiting each area (Tohoku, Tokyo, Nagoya,

Okayama, Kyoto, Oita, etc.) once a month.

Our spiritual children have held regular meetings and tried to keep communicating with those who were not restored yet through home visits. In our Oyamada Gatherings, we actively study inspirational educational materials, such as the Three Holy Scriptures of Cheon Il Guk, monthly magazines, activity reports from each member, testimonies; we also have Qigong treatments and other types of activities. We have continued these gatherings nationwide centering on my sisters, who are in their 80s, nephews who are in their 60s, and other relatives. Thanks to these steady relationships, we could build the foundation for successful heavenly tribal messiah activities.

Regarding the finances involved in our work, I have entrusted it to my wife's sister, who was a secretary of Mr. Furuta for a long time. My strengths are ministry, education and liaison work; therefore, in seeking for victorious work in heavenly tribal messiah activity, it is important to cooperate with talented people in each field in which I do not have professional skills. In other words, it is important for the heavenly tribal messiahs to cooperate organically with the members of their tribe by utilizing the various talents of each member, rather than the heavenly tribal messiah trying to do everything from beginning to end by himself.

Activities in the Greater China Region and the Northeast Continent Region

During the period from 2014 to 2017, when I was appointed to work in the Greater China Region, I first focused on special support for the construction of a new headquarters for the Greater China Region in Taiwan and support for the overall mission of the region. Secondly, I focused on my work as a special emissary for the Tohoku region of Japan, with monthly Oyamada Gatherings and pilgrimages to Korea. More recently True Mother has appointed me as the Japanese chair of the *Cheon Eui Won* (Cheon Il Guk Assembly) and given me a public mission in Japan.

In addition, we have a team of brothers who are making a special offering of jeongseong by walking a total of 36,000 kilometers (more than 22,369 miles), walking across Japan, South Korea, the United States, Taiwan and other countries, under the name of Hallelujah Great March. In October 2017, they passed through Taiwan, and the Taiwanese members came out to cheer them along. True Mother heard a report about the march and took a photo with them at the victory march after her Kanagawa (a prefecture of Japan) Hyojeong Peace-Loving Festival on October 15, 2017.

Challenges and Goals for Vision 2020

The are several challenges that we are facing in moving forward with our heavenly tribal messiah activities, such as the problem of the physical distance, with our tribe spread out in various locations, and the difficulties of finding good times to meet, due to everybody's busy schedules. Moreover, I have heard that among the members of our tribe, some have had difficulties guiding their husband and children and others have struggled to fulfill their goals in making donations. Despite these many difficulties, however, we are continuing our activities nationwide to ultimately build a community of true love and nurture our heavenly tribe with care and hope. Furthermore, when we see the number of new members growing every time, we feel deep gratitude.

There are two challenges and goals to solve in our heavenly tribal messiah activities as we work toward Vision 2020. First, about 30 core members of the monthly Oyamada Gathering will cooperate with one another to expand and strengthen their mission as heavenly tribal messiahs. (As of now, each is responsible only for their own region.) Second is the problem of ongoing Blessing activities and the inheritance issue of the second generation. Now the current core members have become elderly people, in their 60s and 70s. Therefore, it is our challenge to hand the current tribal foundation over to the second generation.

Finally, I offer my earnest prayer for all of our beloved blessed families to achieve the victory of the 430 family Blessing for the victory of Vision 2020, centering on Heavenly Parent and True Parents.

Floramie V. Comendador Paudel

Person giving Testimony	Husband's Name	Region	Nation
Floramie V. Comendador Paudel	Santosh Kumar Paudel	Central Asia	Nepal
Blessing Information	Number of Children	Spiritual Children (couples)	Number of Families Attending Church
400 Million Couples 2nd Phase	1 child	430 couples	18 couples

Knock with Sincerity, and I Will Surely Help You

> Once I met new witnessing candidates, I periodically contacted them and tried to stay in communication, and I offered prayers that they would be victorious in their lives. We invited them to humanitarian activities, peace rallies, leadership programs, service projects, and other events that would connect them to the Blessing.
>
> I would help my tribe with their preparations, such as clothes, rings, shoes, accessories, make-up, donations or filling out the registration forms. I also would try to make them comfortable by giving a simple gift as a small token of love.

Let Us Become People Who Can Impress Heaven and Earth

Before I joined the Unification Church, I was a Baptist who believed that Jesus was God. Now I have become a Unificationist who loves True Parents, the Messiah of humankind, and Heavenly Parent.

My life before joining the Unification Church was very ordinary. However, after I joined, I came to have a dream of making a positive, happy and healthy family. I have worked hard to achieve this dream, and the times when I have failed and felt it was impossible are very painful. But I have determined to keep starting over and overcome the hardships one by one.

To strengthen my life of faith and be closer to the heart of Heavenly Parent and True Parents, I offered many prayers and jeongseong. Now I have gained a strong belief that, no matter what happens, I can overcome any difficulty. I will do my best to move the heart of Heavenly Parent, True Parents and my family.

Inspire Your Tribe, and You Will Inspire Heaven

What I have felt as I walked this path of faith was that I could never reach any goal without sacrifice and responsibility. In my life of faith, I have prayed with tears. To raise the quality of my heart so that I truly could embrace everyone, I have earnestly prayed to Heaven to let me be a person who could care for, serve, and devote myself to my brothers and sisters.

Before visiting my tribe, I did hoondokhae, reading aloud with a strong voice, and recited the names of my tribe, one by one, as I prayed to Heavenly Parent and True Parents that they would be able to accept the Divine Principle and eventually be led to the path of the Blessing.

When I met members of my tribe, I tried to always have something to give them. I cooked delicious food for them, served tea and coffee, and sometimes made a special effort to bake a cake to share with them. We read True Father's autobiography together in the language of the tribe. I did whatever I could to unite with them in heart, though I could not do it perfectly. Sometimes, I even dressed in traditional costumes of their tribe. I greeted them with a bright smile, hugged them like they were family, held their hands and we enjoyed meals together. We also sang traditional songs and danced to create a relaxed atmosphere.

Whenever I heard that someone was sick or had any difficulties, I went to them first, even if they lived far away, and prayed together with their family. In the end, those who had been impressed by my sincerity came to attend seminars and workshops whenever I asked.

Children of Heaven Who Are the Fruit of My Tears and Sweat

I have experienced great suffering in finding my spiritual children. When I first approached candidates for witnessing, I was welcomed with friendship and warmth. However, after I sent several messages through Facebook or other online SNS services, they sometimes cut me off completely.

Whenever I told them, "I will make you a better leader than me," they treated me as a madwoman. They looked at me and said, "What kind of person are you? How can you make me like that?" as they shook their heads. Then I grabbed them and asked them earnestly if they would listen to what I had to say. When I told them the story about my cross-cultural Blessing, people were unbelievably amazed, saying, "How is it possible for people from two different religions to marry each other?"

As people became interested little by little, I did an Internet search and showed them that Rev. Sun Myung Moon is recognized by the *Guinness Book of World Records* as the world's best matchmaker. Of course, there were some who were a bit surprised and doubtful about this practice, saying that it was the work of a cult, but most of them started listening to me. Basically, after I found a solution for their concerns and built a friendly relationship, I invited them to a cafe or a restaurant. While we drank tea and ate food together, I asked them about their family, education, everyday life, and whether they wanted to marry a foreigner. Then, I told them, "We have an organization that promotes marriage, so if you want to marry a good person, please let me know."

In this manner, I tried to be friends with them and to tune in to their situation, no matter what kind of social position they came from. I respected them and lived for their sake, as if they were my own brothers and sisters. Eventually, they asked me for my business card and phone number, and we became good friends.

You Are My God

As I was raising up my first three couples, I prayed for them sincerely with tears. Though we were far away from one another, I kept calling out their names in prayer until they longed to see me.

When one of my spiritual children said, "You and your husband are our God," I felt a happiness deep inside. However, I told them that it was True Parents who were sent as the embodiments of Heavenly Parent, and that my husband and I only love and take care of people as representatives of Heavenly Parent and True Parents.

Sometimes one of my spiritual children contacted me and served me delicious food, or we went out for lunch together. We talked about the many things that have happened in our daily lives. We have shared our feelings, family stories, beliefs, insecurities, and secrets as sisters. Through these situations, we learned how to

A home group meeting as part of the Paudel family's heavenly tribal messiah activity

overcome the challenges that face us.

On the other hand, there are some spiritual children who have not had much contact with me or whom I could not meet for a long time. First, I sent a message to them. I prepared a special meal to serve them. Then I apologized to them for not being a good friend and a good spiritual parent, and I told them that I would try my best to take care of and serve them better in the future. I continued to give, give, and give anything I have, to find ways to become closer to them. This is how I maintained my relationships with the spiritual children with whom I have had distant or difficult relationships.

Sometimes they didn't answer my calls. Then I invited them to the center and prepared a simple meal. I tried to help them remember how much I cared for and loved them. Although they sometimes refused or ignored me, I still treated them as close contacts or friends.

I always prayed for the health, safety and comfort of my spiritual children. I have never given up my connections with them. I maintained those connections by doing something for them on their birthday, anniversary and festivals. A little interest and endless efforts were the first step to fulfilling my mission as a heavenly tribal messiah.

Heavenly Children Who Came through Sincerity and Effort

Once I met new witnessing candidates, I periodically contacted them and tried to stay in communication, and I offered prayers that they would be victorious in their lives. We invited them to humanitarian activities, peace rallies, leadership programs, service projects, and other events that would connect them to the Blessing.

I would help my tribe with their preparations, such as clothes, rings, shoes, accessories, make-up, donations or filling out the registration forms. I also would try to make them comfortable by giving a simple gift as a small token of love.

At the event, I made sure they had good seats for the Blessing ceremony and let them know what they would be expected to do during the ceremony. I also had them attend an orientation beforehand. In addition, during the ceremony I instilled in them a sense of responsibility, so that they could take ownership and feel the value of the Blessing.

What I did, right after the Blessing ceremony, was make time for them to tell me what they felt and experienced during the event. It would be a bit awkward if I asked questions directly, so I started out by congratulating them and thanking them for their participation in the Blessing ceremony, so that they could feel appreciated. After that, often they would open their hearts and talk about their experiences.

Then I organized a small meeting for the wives. I asked them for their help in persuading their husbands to attend follow-up programs. I did everything I could to gather them regularly. We held family meetings, such as picnics and potlucks, and talked about our experiences as couples and as parents on raising children. These gatherings became good opportunities for us to educate them naturally.

For people who had not yet attended any educational gatherings, we invited them to our home for lunch or dinner. It was a small meal, but we enjoyed it just as much as a meal at a nice restaurant. After the meal, I asked my husband to give some positive reports about our FFWPU activities, and then we invited them to attend our educational programs.

If they still were unconvinced, my husband and I asked them if we could visit their home. Perhaps they were too busy to come to our office and attend our educational programs and lectures. After a while, one of the two finally changed his or her mind, began to trust us and attended our educational programs. During the program I always sat next to them to interpret or help them feel at home. When I did this, they usually attended from the beginning to the end. We also provided transportation expenses, and sometimes my husband took them home himself.

Finally, we became very close friends and then brothers and sisters of faith.

Keeping Faith amidst Difficulties, and Blessings

Mr. Krishna and Mrs. Rabina Shrestha, who are members of our tribe, had financial difficulties before joining the church, so they started a small business near the school where many students stopped.

One day I was able to persuade Mrs. Shrestha and her husband to attend the Blessing ceremony as an already married couple. I prepared their holy robes and took care of them, and during the Blessing program they were chosen to go to the stage as a representative couple. After the Blessing ceremony, they lost their home in the earthquake, and they were living in a tent with their daughter for three months. When I went to visit them in their shabby tent, I realized that I didn't see the photo of True Parents that I had given them, and when I asked about it she said that it was too small. So the next day I brought a big photo of True Parents. When I visited them again the following week, True Parents' photo was on the wall.

Whenever people asked them who was in that photo, the husband told them that they were True Parents of all humanity, and he gave them a lecture.

A few months later, we gave this family some responsibilities. Because the wife was a local resident of Bhaktapur and had connections with people there, she could help us with arrangements for the Blessing ceremony. Even though there still were aftershocks from the earthquake, she helped us organize the local Newari people to attend the Blessing.

With her help, we finally had 1,200 families who attended the Blessing, and the hall was overflowing. After that their business became more and more successful, and they moved into a new shop three times larger than the one they had before.

Now their business is going well, and they have brought many of their customers to the Blessing and are regularly involved in our church activities. In particular, they have been working on liberating their ancestors.

They have regular customers and their small business is growing. If I had more money, I would have invested it in helping them to develop their business. At the moment, I am encouraging them to give tithes to the church.

Sometimes I invite the wife to have a meal or simple refreshment together. Recently she sometimes gives vegetables or some special yogurt to my close friends or prepares snacks for them. I feel that True Father in the spirit world is helping them understand the value and joy giving.

The Mission of the Tribal Messiah, the Growth of the Children

The tribal messiah's mission is not only to witness and bring their contacts to the Blessing; it is also to help them to grow and become tribal messiahs themselves. Therefore, we did not stop with witnessing and Blessing but kept wondering how we could help the members of our tribe grow and become true children of God.

My husband and I made a plan to encourage the members of our tribe to attend Sunday services. Initially we set a goal with each of them to organize a youth or Blessing program in the local area where they live. We encouraged them to attend the fellowship services on Saturdays or watch videos about ideal families.

For follow-up, we will create two-day, five-day, seven-day and 21-day workshops teaching the Original Divine Principle. If they have to work or are busy, we will schedule programs on Saturdays, so they will have no excuse not to attend.

We want to create lively and interesting workshops so that those families who attend our programs will feel special. For example, we could televise or broadcast interviews with the best families who have accomplished the mission as heavenly tribal messiahs so that they can explain their family's traditions. Sometimes we will gather at our house and read True Father's words in Nepali.

For hoondokhae, we use Father's autobiography. After studying True Father's life, they begin to understand how great our founder was. His achievements for world peace and his great life of devotion

A Marriage Rededication and Peace Blessing Ceremony in the Paudel tribe

make a strong impression on them. They come to realize that True Parents are the true Messiah, the *Kalki avatar*, who made the greatest sacrifice and offered their accomplishments for the sake of their society, nation, world and the entire planet. After we read, we take time to discuss what they understood from the reading.

In our home group meetings, we celebrate birthdays and anniversaries, and talk about what happened in the past week. We write down goals for the next week about what we want to improve in our husband–wife and brother–sister relationships to help us grow closer and happier.

We believe it is our responsibility not only to give them an opportunity to understand the teachings of True Parents and the Divine

Principle with their heads. It is also so we can transform those teachings into action in our lives, so we can grow together. We will do our best for this in the future.

The Hope and Desire for Future Tribal Messiahs

The most difficult thing for me as a heavenly tribal messiah has been to help people understand the important teachings of the Divine Principle, so that they can have life-changing experiences. It makes me sad when I see them facing difficulties and suffering, so I have a strong desire for them to elevate their spiritual level and their lifestyle to protect them from these difficulties. I pray every day that we can build a heavenly tribal messiah center, so that we can provide better support to our tribes. In addition, I would like the members of my tribe to attend Saturday worship services regularly and even start giving tithes. It is very difficult to explain the idea of tithing to them.

Unlike Christians, who understand giving ten percent as a tithe, it is very difficult for people from other religions to understand it, because there is no similar idea in other religions. I try to explain it to them any way I can and encourage them to make a donation, even though it might be a small amount at first.

We will pray and work hard to make it possible in the future to have a heavenly tribal messiah center where the tribes and home group members can visit freely, not only for worship but also as a place where they can feel at home and feel love. I also hope we can establish a livelihood to help provide a small income for heavenly tribal messiah members who are active in the church. Here is a summary of our vision for our tribe:

1. Joint Saturday services, gathering in nearby places and inviting a good speaker
2. Active home group meetings
3. A trinity system to connect the families, while they gradually increase their involvement to become blessed central family members who attend Saturday services and offer tithes
4. A livelihood program to provide a small income for mothers with skills and abilities, such as cooking (international cuisine), sewing, needlework, empowering women, etc.
5. Community service projects (such as cleaning) and creativity training programs
6. Cultivating the spirit to make new guests feel welcome at the center
7. Having a heavenly tribal messiah center in my mission area, Bhaktapur

Today I have dreams for my tribe. I hope that these dreams do become reality, one after the other. I am confident that the heavenly tribal messiah activity I am carrying out will be completed, because this is what Heavenly Parent and True Parents desire and what humanity has long wished for through each religion. Thank you.

Chapter 3

Working with Religious Groups

Masika Mutokambali Evelyn Chimfwembe

Person giving Testimony	Husband's Name	Region	Nation
Masika Mutokambali Evelyn Chimfwembe	William Chimfwembe	Africa	Zambia
Blessing Information	**Number of Children**	**Spiritual Children (couples)**	**Number of Families Attending Church**
30,000 Couples	2 sons, 2 daughters	862 Couples	12 Couples

When I Reached the Place You Commanded Me to Go, There Were People Prepared for Me

> Today I am taking a walk in a rural village, holding hands with my husband. I have no idea how I came to walk this path of God's Will. Sometimes this path is rocky and difficult. However, if it had been an easy path, I might not have followed it at all. There is nothing to be learned on an easy path. You cannot be enlightened about anything, and you will see no growth in your life. Moreover, you cannot meet God. The route by which I can meet God is through hardships. On that path of hardships, however, there are people who have not yet met God and True Parents. They are orphans who have lost their parents. It is our duty to teach them who their True Parents are.

Since Joining the Church, I Have Walked the Path of Public Work Together with My Husband

I am deeply grateful to True Father because, in the last prayer of his life, he bestowed to blessed families the mission of heavenly tribal messiah, which is the greatest blessed gift. I also would like to express my infinite gratitude to True Mother for her grace in providing financial support and encouragement for us to start heavenly tribal messiah activities in Zambia.

My name is Masika Mutokambali Evelyn Chimfwembe. I was born on November 26, 1970, at Mbujimayi of Kasai Province, Democratic Republic of the Congo. My husband is William Chimfwembe (born on October 22, 1966) from Zambia, who currently is working as a pastor. We participated in the 30,000 Couples Blessing. My husband and I both fulfilled the heavenly tribal messiah mission in 2017.

I joined the church on October 27, 1986, so that is my spiritual birthday. On the very first day I learned about the Divine Principle,

I realized right away that True Father is the Lord of the Second Advent. In fact, the lecturer who was delivering the introduction was quite amazed at my matter-of-fact attitude about it.

In December 1988, when I was a freshman in Kinshasa University majoring in pharmacology, I began to take part in CARP activities. After that, from 1990 to 1993 I worked as a full-time member on the Brazzaville team of CARP MFT. I thank Heavenly Parent for giving me the blessing of being the best fundraiser on the team, which is a precious memory from my younger days.

I received the Blessing in December of 1995, and since then I have been helping my husband, Rev. Chimfwembe, in his pastoral duties. We have four children, two girls and two boys. From 1996 to 1999 we pioneered a church in Kafue, Zambia, and we also witnessed to Bishop Banda, who is a John the Baptist figure in the southern region of Zambia.

From 1999 to 2002, I worked in the education department at the Zambian headquarters under the guidance of Albert and Vera Shandalala, and from 2002 to 2006 I worked in Zimbabwe.

While working for the church in my younger days, I witnessed to eighteen students. Of them, one is currently a professor at Zimbabwe University, and another is working at the intelligence bureau of Zimbabwe. Two already have passed away.

From 2007 to present day (2017), my husband and I have been working in Botswana where my husband is the national leader. I fundraise in Zambia to support the providence in Botswana and three centers in Zambia in Mpika, Choma, and Monze.

A Chimfwembe family photo

The Life Philosophy I Adopted after True Parents' Visit to Congo

When True Parents visited the Democratic Republic of Congo, I was unable to see them, for I had been entrusted again with the mission of taking care of the blessed children, since I had done it before in Gabon. Though everyone else went to the airport to welcome True Parents, I had to remain at the center with the children. I am sure you can more than imagine what I must have felt in this situation, when I had come all the way to Congo to meet True Parents and yet was unable to go to the airport to welcome them. However, I thought about God's love for these little children, and I expressed gratitude to God for choosing me to take care of them. I told myself, "It's okay, I'll get to meet True Parents next time." I had emptied my heart of all expectations with these words, when that very evening I received a call from my Abel figure, Mr. Josaka, who said, "Masika, you are truly in luck! I heard that True Parents are coming here tomorrow!" I became indescribably happy hearing this. I was so very grateful to God for reading my mind and bestowing this grace upon me. I repented for the fact that my heart had wavered for a little while, and I came to realize a lot of things: "God does not forget our good deeds. Let us never regret our sacrifices. Let us not complain when we are making a sacrifice for others." Ever since then, I have continued to practice a life of faith by constantly reminding myself of the meaning of absolute faith, absolute love and absolute obedience.

When I Went to the Place He Had Prepared for Me, Miracles Occurred

What motivated me to dedicate myself to the tribal messiah mission was True Father's last prayer. He mentioned the tribal messiahs even while he was gasping for breath. True Mother also spoke of the tribal messiahs in her prayer offered at the Foundation Day event. In 2015, Dr. Yong Chung-sik, the regional president for Asia, was invited to Zambia, where he gave a lecture on the heavenly tribal messiah mission. His words helped me make up my mind to become a heavenly tribal messiah, for I realized that it is the best way to restore a nation.

After that, I carried out heavenly tribal messiah activities most diligently and came to have seven spiritual children who were single. They were blessed in September 2017. No words can describe the joy I felt as I watched them receive the Blessing. I have a spiritual son (30,000 blessed couple) who lives in Japan. When I held his two daughters in my arms, I experienced the great joy of being a grandmother. I was reminded of True Parents' words, that we can become the citizens of the kingdom of heaven only when three generations live together, and I came to realize the meaning of those words. Whenever I face difficulties, I think of my spiritual children. Then the sorrow melts away and the joy I receive from carrying out heavenly tribal messiah activities fills its place instead. I worked hard to create even more spiritual children; just as Jesus had his 12 disciples, I too finally came to establish 12 spiritual children whom I can trust and depend on.

Centering on the foundation of the 12 children, in 2015 I began in earnest to work full time as a heavenly tribal messiah. As later results showed, the chemical reactions I had learned about in chemistry class in school also took place in my tribal messiah activities, which was truly amazing. One person who received the Blessing in the village of Monze contacted me to say that he wanted to hold a Blessing ceremony in Choma, his village of residence. What is incredible is that, in just one week, many other couples came forward, saying they wanted to receive the Blessing. Parents who had been moved when they heard about the true family movement requested us to open a workshop for their children. A week later, we created a program together with our second generation and held a workshop, which was attended by no less than 79 young people. After attending the workshop, they became determined to attend a seven-day workshop, and 22 youths from among them participated in a workshop held in the city. The youths who had attended the workshop invited their friends to attend it as well, and even persuaded their parents to take part in the Blessing ceremony.

In the end, the couples who were blessed came to the church along with their children and friends as well as their relatives, who then attended two- and seven-day workshops with sincere hearts. In this way, the chain of witnessing spread out and multiplied exponentially. Truly unbelievable events took place in accordance with God's plans, at full speed. The people who thus were witnessed to also became the starting point for the establishment of the Youth and Students for Peace (YSP). Afterward, the blessed couples started organizing their own meetings to learn more about the Blessing and FFWPU. As a result of such meetings, the Women's Federation for World Peace (WFWP) was established in Choma region on December 10, 2016. The inauguration was attended by 163 married women, who all joined WFWP as members and submitted signed applications.

Before WFWP was inaugurated, the women also had begun a business to raise money. The blessed wives and youths of the region became connected to a fishery expert, and they dug three ponds and put in bricks to begin a fish nursery project. The Samaritans especially have shown active interest in this project because it provides funds to educate women and children and helps maintain their livelihood. For the next stage of the project, they have begun plans to build a school where young people can learn aquatic science and receive basic training on running a fish farm. This is to teach them how to master the farming technology to scientifically mass produce livestock such as cows, pigs, chickens and fish.

In a word, through heavenly tribal messiah activities, the third great blessing of restoring all things is being realized. We hope to fulfill at least the three great blessings while carrying out the heavenly tribal messiah mission. This fish nursery project was begun thanks to the devoted efforts of Drs. Yasufumi and Colette Takigawa. Now, our local communities and citizens are taking a great interest in our activities. One of those citizens is the mayor of Choma, who attended the International Leadership Conference (ILC) held in Lusaka, Zambia, in November 2016. Another is the director of the local government office, who also received the Blessing. They are working together to inaugurate the Universal Peace Federation in the Choma region.

Oh, My Living God, Your Will Be Done

Our witnessing goal is to restore 12 tribes, and we have restored two tribes so far. As for the third tribe, we are working with the chief of the Chitoshi Chiefdom to restore his tribe. Another tribe to be restored is my husband's tribe of relatives, for whose restoration we are praying right now.

In the first seven-day workshop I attended, I had been praying for about 40 minutes when Jesus Christ suddenly appeared in front of me. Upon seeing him, tears welled up in my eyes and would not let up. I don't think I have ever cried so much in my life. After I sympathized with Jesus' sorrow and anguish deep within my heart, the emotion enveloped my whole body. The feeling at the bottom of my heart made me tremble so much that I could hardly bear it, and my body responded so violently that at each moment I felt almost as if I would die. After that, a strange energy started emanating from me. When I officiated at a Blessing ceremony, in particular, I went through even more spiritual experiences. Some people even screamed out when I sprinkled holy water on them. They said that when the holy water touched their heads, it was so hot that it felt almost as if their bodies were afire. One husband and wife were having difficulties, but after the Blessing the husband confessed his sins and knelt in front of his wife in tears and asked for her forgiveness.

When I experience such spiritual phenomena, I come to realize the value of the Blessing and the fact that God is alive. I also come to learn that therein lies the grace of consecration and rebirth bestowed on us by True Parents. I personally have experienced that spiritual miracles are not just things that occurred two thousand years ago in Jesus' time, but that they can occur to us at any time if we have pure hearts that are opened wide in the hopes of becoming one with Heaven. The difference between today and Jesus' time is that miracles only happen through people who are prepared. As I said earlier, though only one person from Monze village of Choma region had received the Blessing, he caused a chain reaction through which the Blessing was spread out wide, and this is a miracle that has taken place today. It means that the people prepared by Heaven for a long time can be found anywhere. I became convinced that it is our portion of responsibility as blessed families to find such people entrusted with the mission of John the Baptist.

The Time Has Come When Darkness Cannot Prevail against Light (Completion of 430 Couples)

As we continued to hold heavenly tribal messiah Blessing ceremonies, several miraculous changes took place. Couples who were on the verge of getting divorced came to be reconciled after passing through the five stages of the Blessing. Drinkers and smokers quit drinking or smoking, and cheaters became faithful.

When we first began our heavenly tribal messiah mission, we offered jeongseong with many tears to find and restore even one more couple. Now, however, there are so many people who wish to receive the Blessing that we have to worry about how we can bless 1,000 couples all together at one place. In fact, things reached the point at which we had to run away because we were unable to handle all the blessings bestowed on us.

This was in accord with the response I had received from God in December of 2015, when I prayed to Him to help me find couples who can receive the Blessing. He blessed me with the answer, "One day, so many people will come flocking to you that you will have to run away from all those who wish to receive the Blessing. You will be running away because you will not be able to handle so many people coming to you." At present, I still find it hard to believe that my husband and I have witnessed to thousands of spiritual children. My hopeful prayers have thus been realized.

I came to understand that, through such blessings, I had begun to rid myself of my fallen nature. I learned to love, to forgive, and to become one with the people who did terrible things to us in such places as Mpika, Lambwe Chomba and Lukwesa. One day while witnessing, I was almost stoned to death. Even encountering hostile environments like that did not stop us from giving the Blessing. The forces of evil led by Satan, however, did not back down easily. We faced frightful opposition from Satan, even during the Blessing ceremonies. In the Kilwa Island region, Rev. Mulenga, Rev. Chiboboka and I were almost drowned, but thankfully Heaven saved us. In Chisamba, we were charged with performing the Blessing ceremony without police permission and almost taken to prison.

Heaven gave us wisdom that amazed even Satan himself, preparing everything for us and working miracles. The conclusion I have reached from all of this is that darkness cannot prevail against the light of dawn and that, after a rainy night in the desert, there is no one who can stop life from growing in the morning sunlight. This situation perfectly describes the heavenly tribal messiah mission. True Parents said, "When you fulfill the responsibility of working for and testifying to True Parents, He will work miracles and appear in front of you," and I realize very clearly that such an age is now upon us.

My Method of Carrying Out Heavenly Tribal Messiah Activities

When I am doing heavenly tribal messiah work, I carry out many local activities. I establish local religious leaders as my co-workers in the position of John the Baptist. Through each of them, I become a part of their religious order and form a relationship with their congregation.

I do my best to get close to these religious leaders, close enough to share personal secrets and stories, and I work to maintain our connection. Then I try to form an even deeper relationship with them by lending a helping hand whenever they need my help. To achieve and maintain such a close rapport, you must approach them one on one. When I find a witnessing candidate from another religion, I try to manage it so that I can always keep an eye on them, no matter what, and if possible, I try to meet their spouse to form a connection with them both. This is because when you form a connection with only one person in a couple, that connection can have neither depth nor continuity. That is why I approach them one on one, but it is a one-on-one situation with the couple, not the individual.

When I bless couples, I urge them to take the lead in bringing their relatives, friends and neighbors to attend the Blessing ceremony as well. When I establish a couple who then bring others to the church, they watch their people develop and grow and ultimately share the joy of the Blessing; then they become central figures to these people. I also frequently visit the homes of blessed couples. I check on their domestic situation and explain to them that they also should carry out the 430 couples mission as heavenly tribal messiahs to become true families, enlightening them as to why that mission is so important.

The more we work for the Blessing, the more inspiration we receive from our Heavenly Parent. When I instruct the newly blessed couples about the five stages of the Blessing (one-day Divine Principle workshop, Blessing, indemnity stick ceremony, 40-day separation and three-day ceremony), I am amazed at how quickly they understand the words and providence of True Parents. At the same time, I too gain new wisdom and enlightenment every time I instruct them.

I have gained the wisdom by which I can persuade a witnessing candidate, after only ten minutes of talking to them, to go through the five-stage process and receive the Blessing. Talking about the introduction of the Divine Principle is enough to open the heart of any candidate. This comes from the spiritual confidence I gain and the concentrated information I accumulate every time I explain it to the candidates. My conclusion is that, if I am prepared, God speaks through me.

Next, I will explain how I manage the members of our tribe. In regions where many couples have received the Blessing, I select seven to 12 model couples in the position of Abel and appoint them as members of the FFWPU steering committee, so that they can manage the other couples. Surprisingly, they then begin to show confidence when they talk to others about the value of true families and urge them to make a new beginning; they manage the blessed couples in the region based on the ideal of the blessed family. They have a strong sense of responsibility, for they already have gone through the five stages. In short, they become solid members. The steering committee manages couples after they have received the Blessing, and it develops into an indispensable organization. It is the committee members' responsibility to keep track of the addresses of blessed couples, to guide them to observe the 40-day separation period, and perform the three-day ceremony, and to see that they actually carry them out. The couples who go amiss in the middle of the process are encouraged to begin the process again.

We invite them to participate in the two-day and seven-day workshops. In the case of the couples who can understand English, we invite their children to learn about the Divine Principle and urge them to join YSP. The wives are invited to join WFWP, and the VIPs are guided to form connections with UPF.

The Cain Realm Can Be Managed If Treated with Sincerity and Love

The best way to manage spiritual children is to make home visits. I visit their homes and take a lot of time to explain to them about the traditions of FFWPU. At the same time, I also explain about the value and meaning of the Blessing and make efforts to find methods by which I can help them financially in any way possible. Since there are centers in the three tribal regions (Choma, Mpika and Monze), when I send word that I am going to visit, most of them come to meet me at the center. For the couples who are unable to come to the center, I call them or visit them at home.

In the case of Mpika Center, its central staff members hold regular meetings while I am staying in the region. The subject of every meeting is anything related to the Blessing, and in our spare time we always study the words of the *Cheon Seong Gyeong*. They also have been teamed up in threes as trinities, so that they have teammates they can rely on when they carry out their work.

In the Mpika region, there are two trinities that are active. The first trinity has Rev. Chanda Joseph, Rev. Richard Mwalya, and Deacon Justin Mwila. The second trinity has Rev. Chiluba Amos, Rev. Carine Mubanga and Rev. Mary Chanda.

In the Choma region the first trinity has Matongo, Mushabati-Emmaunel, and Japhet Kamwendo. The second trinity has Kennedy Kalaluka, Rev. Frazer, and Mazuba.

In the Monze region, the first trinity has Bishop Banda Stephen, Mary Mapulanga, and Phiri.

Each town has a trinity that is in charge of a region and under their guidance are twenty groups. These twenty groups of trinities are responsible for smaller areas.

Thoughts about True Father's Intention in Saying That Food Is Love

Since financial problems are a serious consideration in our work, I am very interested in fundraising and I invest much time in it. Based on my long experience, I recognize its necessity, so I have organized the members into fundraising teams who carry out activities together. I am on the same team as Kiyomi Wakasaka, and we work together. After her day job ends, she joins the fundraising team and helps with various projects until the late hours.

Fundraising is not always easy. When you live in the city, you are not aware of the people who lead anguished lives in poverty. However, when you visit villages in rural areas to fundraise, you can see with your own eyes how ordinary people live in poverty and how difficult their lives are. Sometimes you come across scenes that you cannot watch without your eyes tearing up, because their lives are so sad. That being the case, many are the times when you become lost in thought because you feel a sense of duty to help them and you need to figure out how.

To raise money, we have asked for help from everyone who knows about our work in this providence. Some of them have helped us in their own way. With the aid of a philanthropist, we were able to begin a fish nursery project in Choma region. Though at present the project is being carried out in only one place, it is fast developing into a remarkably lucrative project. I think there is a need to expand projects like this to many other places. To that end, we have plans to recruit more people to join the fundraising teams. The plot chosen for the project was a piece of land in the village of Mochipapa in the Choma region, a city located in southern Zambia.

Of course, we encounter many difficulties in carrying out our work as tribal messiahs, because people expect too much of us. In particular, when they find out that FFWPU is an international organization, they think we can solve their financial problems. They want us to provide transportation or to help them send their children to school. Moreover, they also want us to support them financially so that they can start new businesses, but in a lot of cases we are unable to do so. Then some of those people grow distant from us. In such cases, we need to find new people who can establish the right motivation for joining us.

As can be seen, we need transportation to carry out the tribal messiah mission. Some regions are unreachable by public transportation, so we need to go there by car, which costs a lot of money.

What is more, we need small minibuses or four-wheel drive cars to carry out our work more effectively, because only then will we be able to handle the education of all the newly blessed couples. In particular, going anywhere in the rainy season without a car is almost impossible, because there is no public transportation for going from one region to another. To begin these activities, we need a laptop and a beam projector at least, and hopefully we soon will be able to acquire them.

Our community has the vision to eradicate drinking, smoking and the sex trade, because we have come to realize that such divine work can be carried out only by the FFWPU, and by doing so, we can make our community into a community filled with love where God and True Parents can come and dwell. To achieve this vision, FFWPU, WFWP and YSP are working actively in the Choma region. Our plan as heavenly tribal messiahs is to help all our tribe members to learn about the Divine Principle, to understand it, and to practice it. We also plan to train them so that each of them can also become a heavenly tribal messiah by 2020. If we can achieve this goal, we believe we can restore at least ten percent of the total population of Zambia. To that end, we are trying to find ways to raise the funds with which we can continue our activities related to the Blessing. Since this task is going to be a project that will help our tribes to earn a livelihood and become happy, we are doing our utmost to fulfill it. There is a proverb that says, "A hungry man is an angry man." Whenever we met True Mother, she served us a meal. As heavenly tribal messiahs, we should develop a community business model that can provide our tribes with food and the necessities of life.

Today I am taking a walk in a rural village, holding hands with my husband. I have no idea how I came to walk this path of God's Will. Sometimes this path is rocky and difficult. However, if it had been an easy path, I might not have followed it at all. There is nothing to be learned on an easy path. You cannot be enlightened about anything, and you will see no growth in your life. Moreover, you cannot meet God. The route by which I can meet God is through hardships. On that path of hardships, however, there are people who have not yet met God and True Parents. They are orphans who have lost their parents. It is our duty to teach them who their True Parents are.

Chrispin Mubiana Mwangana

Person giving Testimony	Wife's Name	Region	Nation
Chrispin Mubiana Mwangana	Violet Habwangi Mwangana	Africa	Zambia
Blessing Information	Number of Children	Spiritual Children (couples)	Number of Families Attending Church
400 Million Couples	3 sons, 3 daughters	18 couples (John the Baptist Religious Leaders)	200 couples

2

True Parents Have Shown Me the Way

> My vision as a tribal messiah is to see my tribe live a stable, healthy life centered on True Parents. Through the Blessing, True Parents have the vision of expanding the lineage of heaven to all the tribes in the world, creating one peaceful world of humanity under God. This is a vision that anybody can relate to. When we can successfully show the model of the ideal family, even people who have become full of doubt and no longer have trust in people will be able to share this vision.
>
> By working cooperatively with the local government and our church, we will be able to provide educational and spiritual guidance to the people of Africa. I hope that we also will be able to find international financial support to provide technical training in a variety of fields so that we can build the model of a healthy and stable community.

From Peace Ambassador to Family Federation Pastor

I became familiar with the Interreligious and International Federation for World Peace (IIFWP) in 2005, and later the Universal Peace Federation (UPF), when UPF Chair Gen. Malimba Masheke invited myself and some others to attend a workshop at the Peace Embassy. I was awarded the title of ambassador for peace, and when I saw True Father's signature on the peace ambassador certificate, I wondered, "Who is this person, the Rev. Dr. Sun Myung Moon?" It was an unusual name, and the activities that were introduced in the workshop were also new to me. I wanted to find out who this person was and learn more about what he was doing.

I started to learn about the organization, and I had the privileged opportunity to attend two-day and seven-day Divine Principle workshops. As I listened to the lectures, they revealed a truth to me that I had never heard before in any church teaching.

I came from a Christian background, as a member of the New Apostolic Church, where I was ordained as pastor in 2000. However, after I learned the Divine Principle, I decided to become a member of the Unification movement. My friend Joshua Ndhlovu and I were adopted as spiritual sons by Rev. Rudolf Faerber and his wife, and we were trained in the traditions of the church for three and a half years. Later we received further leadership training for youth ministry and were appointed by Rev. Park as leaders in the W-CARP/YFWP Zambia chapter.

True Parents Showed Us the Way to Go

Joshua and I worked there actively for several years, and our FFWPU national leader Rev. Faerber appointed me president of both CARP and YFWP. Working as a youth leader motivated me to learn a lot as I interacted with different people from different institutions pursuing the legacy of True Parents' work. I was inspired to become a model youth leader.

We used programs of character education as part of our youth activities. This laid a solid foundation to work with the young people and exposed them to Divine Principle workshops. Some of the young people became church members, but it was hard to get a large percentage of them to join. I felt there was a limit to the success we could bring with this kind of public service.

Then in October 2015, with the appointment of a new regional

Participants from an Interfaith Peace Blessing in the Mwangana Tribe (November, 2016)

president for East Africa, Rev. Bakary Camara, Zambia received new inspiration. As soon as he arrived, Rev. Camara encouraged us to begin heavenly tribal messiah activities. True Father had emphasized this with his last breath before he went to spirit world, because he had a burning desire to reach and restore all the seven billion people in the world.

Rev. Camara urged all the blessed couples to take ownership and responsibility to go to their hometown and work as heavenly tribal messiahs to restore our clans and tribes. He said we should work to bless at least 430 couples and bring special heavenly grace. From that time on, the members in the Zambian church began heavenly tribal messiah activities in earnest. We scheduled a three-day workshop and started looking for people to attend it.

Wind Blowing from Asia to a Workshop in Africa

The regional president organized a workshop for training tribal messiahs in Zambia. He invited the Asian regional president, Dr. Yong Chung-sik, and the national leader of the Philippines to give the lectures, and the workshop was held at the Barlastone Training Center. Hearing about the heavenly tribal messiah work in Asia gave us a lot of new hope to be victorious in Africa. After the workshop was finished, all the blessed couples gathered at a central place to offer jeongseong for 70 days to start the mission. Later, couples were paired up to go witnessing in different areas, introducing the Interfaith Peace Blessing ceremony with a focus on gathering 430 couples. Each evening we gathered in the prayer room with the leaders and other members to share testimonies about our spiritual experiences. This became a time for us to re-determine to be victorious in our heavenly tribal messiahship. Moreover, through each team's success stories and points for improvement we were able to set stronger strategies.

It was not an easy task to achieve on an everyday basis. As we witnessed to people, they had many questions which reached beyond receiving spiritual salvation to dealing with matters which could help them stabilize their livelihood. We had to teach them about blessed family life and the principles supporting it. My friend Joshua and I managed to organize a one-day clergy workshop at the Peace Embassy, where we also had to handle many difficult questions and religious issues. We gave Divine Principle lectures on Chapters One and Two and God's purpose for salvation to the 45 religious leaders who attended the seminar. However, only four couples went on to receive the Blessing. It was not easy for them to go through all the stages to get the Blessing (Divine Principle workshop, Blessing Ceremony, 40-day separation, blessed family education, three-day ceremony). Two of the four couples are not that active, but one of them, who is a member of the Zambian police, is my spiritual son, and the other, Pastor Chiboboka, is now working as a true tribal messiah.

Amazing Expansion through Religious Leaders

After this, Joshua and I were sent to a district about 265 kilometers (almost 165 miles) east of Lusaka, the Zambian capital, for a 40-day witnessing condition. We had a lot of support from the local district commission for our witnessing work. The district commissioner, Paul Kasongo, gave us the use of his car so that we could visit more than 40 religious leaders to invite them to a workshop. As a result, we gathered 18 religious leaders and their spouses, who listened to Divine Principle lectures given by Rev. Abdoulaye Wone, the head of the family department and leader for tribal messiah work in the area. They were very inspired to receive the Blessing and started to

Couples affirming their vows to each other during a heavenly tribal messiah Interfaith Peace Blessing held by the Mwangana family work in the Rufunsa District. The ministers attended special training and were mobilized as John the Baptist figures to prepare their congregations to receive the Blessing. Other religious leaders in the area also invited us to hold Interfaith Peace Blessing events for their congregations. We held Blessings for up to 457 couples a day, with an average of 124 couples a day. We continued to reach out and expand until the entire community had received the grace of the Blessing.

The Rufunsa District was the first district in Zambia that managed to hold the Blessing for 430 couples. Afterward we visited the various churches that had received the Blessing and shared with them True Parents' message and vision for humanity. The members of the congregation were organized into groups of 12 couples to discuss what they had experienced and the value of the Blessing. Many of them expressed their appreciation for the true family value activities we are leading to help build healthy stable families and communities.

The Rufunsa District is an extensive area with plenty of land, but it is isolated. We divided into three zones to manage our activities more effectively. Each of the zones has its own leader, with Pastor Timothy Zulu as the head of the east zone, Pastor Dennis Mupwaya, who is also a headman, leading the central zone, and Bishop Prince Chabala Musopelo managing the western zone. Bishop Musopelo is still an active member and has become a tribal messiah. After this, we decided to expand our heavenly tribal messiah activities into the far eastern part of Zambia, to the Chipata District.

A Righteous Person in the Region and Country

The expansion of heavenly tribal messiah activities into the central and eastern regions was led by Rev. Bakary Camara, Rev. Abdoulaye Wone and Rev. Rudolf Faerber. By the time we started working in these areas, Rev. Camara had been appointed as regional president for East Africa, and he agreed to provide financial support for the work. The bishop had a connection to one of the headmen under Senior Chief Nzamane of the Ngoni-speaking people. When we visited Senior Chief Nzamane at his palace to pay our respects, he was meeting some married couples who were resolving some adultery cases.

When the senior chief heard that we were from the Family Federation for World Peace and Unification, he ended the meeting so that he could introduce us to all the headmen who were there. He told them that he was familiar with the good work of our movement, that he had been appointed as an ambassador for peace, and that he had been invited by Maria Song (Mrs. Milingo) to visit Korea, where he received the Blessing and had the opportunity to meet True Father.

He instructed all the headmen to become John the Baptist figures and participate in our activities in his chiefdom for peace, love, unity, purity and fidelity. Later, he also assigned his most senior headman, Mr. Greyson Nkhuwa, to work closely with me and my team in all 326 villages in his chiefdom. So far, we have reached only 26 of the villages, so we still have a lot of work ahead of us.

Our work with this chiefdom made it possible for us to bless 1,600 couples in just over two weeks, and this is where I restored my tribe, as well as tribes for others through special heavenly grace. This is a unified tribe of couples who work together to do true family work and to support the other families in the tribe when they need help with farming or other activities.

The tribe has special venues where we hold hoondokhae, Divine Principle lectures, study of True Father's autobiography, Bible study, and other internal and external educational programs. Sometimes several families also meet separately as home groups or under the shade of a big tree for study during the hot seasons.

New Projects for Financial Stability

For our financial stability our tribe has the following projects planned.

1. Fish farming system. This will provide more income, along with improved nutrition for good health. We are working with the Ministry of Agriculture, Livestock and Fisheries to arrange educational programs for farmers.
2. Improved chicken production. Many of the families in the village raise chickens. We are working to help them learn how to maximize production and grow healthy chickens. We are also working with the Ministry of Agriculture, Livestock and Fisheries to send extension officers to educate the chicken

farmers to increase their profits and their standard of living.
3. A village bank. The members of the tribe want to create a fund which would provide financial support and help for villagers when they need it. The blessed families are working to engage a responsible person to manage the fund.
4. Members of the village would like to grow a wider variety of crops. By developing fields and gardens, they can raise nutritious crops and create a secure source of income along with a source of healthy, nutritious food for the people of the tribe.
5. People hope to produce various crops. My caring for a field, they can obtain nutritious food and a stable income as well as good quality food supply

It was a difficult time at the beginning when the John the Baptist figures were mobilized. But we continued, and after a while small groups of people began to receive the Blessing. Then we started to get assistance from spirit world, and more and more people received the Blessing. The vision of our community of blessed couples is to have a united, peaceful, God-centered community. We hope that each family will take responsibility for their own family and help other families so that they will become a harmonized community in unity with God.

Vision and Dream as a Tribal Messiah

My vision as a tribal messiah is to see my tribe live a stable, healthy life centered on True Parents. Through the Blessing, True Parents have the vision of expanding the lineage of heaven to all the tribes in the world, creating one peaceful world of humanity under God. This is a vision that anybody can relate to. When we can successfully show the model of the ideal family, even people who have become full of doubt and no longer have trust in people will be able to share this vision.

By working cooperatively with the local government and our church, we will be able to provide educational and spiritual guidance to the people of Africa. I hope we will also be able to find international financial support to provide technical training in a variety of fields so that we can build the model of a healthy and stable community.

With deepest gratitude, humility to True Parents and True Mother, with a humble heart I will do my best and I hope that our challenges and victories will inspire others around us.

Chapter 4

One-on-One Divine Principle Education

Zenilda de Jesus Kraczinski Almeida

Person giving Testimony	Husband's Name	Region	Nation
Zenilda de Jesus Kraczinski Almeida	Jose Elias de Almeida	Central and South America	Brazil
Blessing Information	**Number of Children**	**Spiritual Children (couples)**	**Number of Families Attending Church**
2,075 Couples	3 children	500 couples	500 couples

1

My name Is Elias and My Legacy Is Love

My husband, Rev. Jose Elias, was known among the church members and the community at large as a man who is loved and missed by everyone. He always witnessed by loving each person one by one, and built a foundation of one disciple, three disciples, and 12 disciples. To this day there are many people who testify with tears in their eyes how Pastor Elias was more than a father to them.

Sadly, Pastor Elias passed away in 2008 due to cancer, leaving me and our three children. At the Seonghwa ceremony there were 4,000 VIPs and general people who came to pay their respects throughout the day. Once somebody asked him in an interview, "What is the secret to victory as a tribal messiah?" He answered promptly: "There is no secret. I just did it again and again."

Love and Love Again Until You Are Done

I am Zenilda de Jesus Kraczinski Almeida, the wife of José Elias de Almeida. We were blessed in 1982 as part of the 2,075 Couples Blessing and have three second-generation children. I began my public life in the Santo Amaro area of Sao Paulo and witnessed to many spiritual children in the first half of 1980 through the tribal messiah providence. True Father directly gave me a special word of blessing: "You have been victorious in the tribal messiah providence." From 2003 to 2006 I served as national leader, and since then I have continued working for the tribal messiah providence. My husband, Elias, has about 500 spiritual children as a result of witnessing, both in Brazil and abroad. Pastor Elias' method of witnessing was to visit every single person at their home and educate them.

At the time, True Father in his speeches was emphasizing home church, and so we visited 360 families in their homes, always bringing them vegetables or fruit and building a relationship. I brought medicine to those who could not afford it or volunteered to serve the local people by distributing milk every week. At the same time, every day I visited people in those 360 families in our home church area and witnessed to them by teaching the Principle. My husband has been involved in these activities and also my son, and altogether our family has been doing this for 35 years. We witnessed not only to spiritual children but also to our parents and to 23 other members of our families.

It is impressive how all the brothers and sisters in Santo Amaro Church really miss Pastor Elias as if he were their real father. He works to build a relationship of love with each one of them and guides them to meet God and fulfill the three blessings. Our work as heavenly tribal messiahs continues, and our tribe now has expanded to the third generation.

My husband, Rev. Elias, was known among the church members and the community at large as a man who is loved and missed by everyone. He always witnessed by loving each person one by one and built a foundation of one disciple, three disciples, and 12 disciples. To this day there are many people who testify with tears in their eyes how Pastor Elias is more than a father to them.

Sadly, Pastor Elias passed away in 2008 due to cancer, leaving me and our three children. At the Seonghwa ceremony there were 4,000 VIPs and others who came to pay their respects throughout the day. Once somebody asked him in an interview, "What is the secret to

Part of the Elias tribe gathered for tribal messiah true family education (April, 1988)

victory as a tribal messiah?" He answered promptly: "There is no secret. I just did it again and again."

Now there is a new church leader, the second-generation pastor Lee Ro-han, who inherited a sound foundation from my husband. I am working with him to care for the members in this area. Activities are still being carried out on the victorious foundation of witnessing that was established in the 1980s. We love and educate the people of our 360 families, who in the meantime became 500 families. Because spiritual children are, from the spiritual point of view, still babies, in order to keep them from returning to the world of Satan we need to take care of them on a daily basis, which is not easy. We have to nurture and raise up those families for a certain period of time;

many conditions are necessary as well as a lot of training until they can walk the path of faith.

We Need to Set Up Activities and Our Organization Based on the Teaching of True Parents

Elias based his tribal messiah activities on True Parents' words. Every day before going out to work he would do hoondokhae and would challenge himself. The core of the message he read would be something like this:

> "What is the meaning of home church? Providentially, it means a home centered on God. If Adam and Eve had not fallen, surely they would have made an ideal family, and their bodies would have become God's holy temples. If Adam's family had become an ideal family of God, His heavenly ideal would have been created. If human beings had not fallen, there would have been no church in this world, because Adam and Eve, as a church or as an individual, would each have been a temple of God. Then all their descendants automatically would have been born as original temples of God. We cannot go to Heaven without a home church, because home church is the final stage of the return of history."

Based on True Parents' words, Pastor Elias would make a daily schedule for both witnessing and fundraising. When he met people, he would preach the word with great determination and energy. He based all his work on the words of True Parents; our witnessing work was organized with the following guidelines:

First, after selecting a neighborhood of 360 families, he would visit every family in that selected area without missing even one house. He thought it would be unacceptable to visit some houses but skip others. He felt responsible to give the chance of salvation to everyone who was ready. That's how he would find 360 families in that area. As a condition he would tell everyone he visited that he was representing the Family Federation for World Peace and Unification. Then he would say that he had come to serve that neighborhood. The next step was to divide the homes he had visited into three categories, A, B, and C.

The A group were those for whom the Divine Principle was considered true and the people were open about it and wanted to know more. The B group was appreciative of our efforts to serve but had certain doubts. Finally, the C group was those who were mostly negative.

Then he would select the best 72 homes from the A group, and after that he would select 12 homes from those 72. Finally he would choose three central families out of the 12. These three families were the pillars of the home church. He would then move some families from group C to group B and later to group A, if there was progress, and he would give education based on the group level. He would give them responsibilities over other families, first to the main three families and later to the main 12 families.

He also had eight points that he felt were important to becoming a victorious person.

Eight Points for a Victorious Person

1. Start from the lowest point to develop my activities with my love for others.
2. Invest my heart completely to save those in my witnessing area who are spiritually ill.
3. By doing my best for home church, become a great champion for the central figures of God's providence.
4. No matter how hard I am persecuted in my witnessing area, I will never give up; I will become a great victor.
5. Let's take ownership of the witnessing area by working hard and applying wisdom and strategic vision.
6. Let us establish a higher standard of loyalty and faithfulness for God's providence of restoration.
7. Determine the priorities for visits.
8. I am determined to restore my hometown.

How Pastor Elias Joined and How He Witnessed

From now I will describe my husband's testimony and witnessing activities, based on the autobiography he left behind. My husband joined the Unification Church in 1978. He was a home member for three months, but his spiritual father always strongly encouraged

Members of the Elias tribe at worship service at the Santo Amaro church in Sao Paulo

him to become a devoted member. Then one day God appeared to him in a dream. In the dream he heard God's voice calling him. My husband desperately ran to find the place where God was calling him. He ran as crazy as 200 kilometers per hour, across the room and down the stairs, up and down, looking for God, but he could not see Him. He went into the last room left, and in it there was one man sitting in the center of the room, and he was smiling brightly. The man asked my husband, "Why are you running?" He said, "I am looking for God. God called me." The man answered, "I am God's representative. I am God." My husband was amazed and asked, "What do you want me to do?" and He said, "I want you to become a dedicated member within 15 days." For the previous three months Pastor Elias had been bringing many people to attend the lectures, and yet had not even thought about becoming a core member. After that dream, he made up his mind and told his family, "I'm going to study for 40 days." Thus, he started his church life.

Elias started practicing giving Divine Principle lectures and fundraised on the weekends. His academic background seemed insufficient, having graduated only from elementary school; so he got up early and practiced more than the others. One day, the national leader told him to become a Divine Principle lecturer. Elias said, "I am ashamed of being here. There must be someone more suitable." However, the national leader said, "Since God has called you here, this is a mission given to you by God."

He joined as a full-time member, and when he got to the seventh month, the church leader told him to take a break and go witness to his family, so he went to the state of Ceará, where they lived. He stayed in Ceará for 24 days and gave Principle lectures for 12 days in a row. Sometimes more than 100 people attended his Principle lectures, and he also lectured about the Divine Principle at a school for nuns. How was he able to teach such high-level people, although he had just started teaching? God inspired him and did amazing work through him. People would listen to his lectures and sometimes ask questions; Elias would answer without having to think about it. That's because God would answer the question through him.

He had a very interesting experience at the nuns' school. After the lecture, one person called him aside and asked, "Are you the

Messiah?"

He was caught by surprise. He answered, "No," but at that moment he experienced the greatness of the Principle.

The Birth of the First Home Church Family in Santo Amaro

After work Elias would go out and witness with a questionnaire. He visited homes to ask about difficulties in the village. Then he would invite them to a workshop, so that they could learn how to solve their problems. Thus, he conducted his first seminar at his house on February 16, 1980, with 11 people attending.

He started lecturing. People were listening with a lot of interest, except for one lady who began to laugh uncontrollably, disturbing the atmosphere. Elias thought at that moment, "I must not be defeated by Satan." There were many such phenomena throughout the four days of the workshop. It was difficult. In addition to this, there were many children crying and people would come and go frequently, making it difficult for others to concentrate on the lecture. Elias said that he prayed, however, to spiritually separate his mind from that environment so that he would not be defeated. As a result, there was a great blessing from God in the last lecture. The participants understood who the Lord of the Second Coming was, and people came to accept the Principle, except for one couple who attended together and a girl who had doubts about the Protestant Church.

One day, one of the people he had lectured to, named Chiaon, invited people to listen to a lecture at his brother Joaon's house. The brothers asked Elias to lecture. They made an appointment for the following week and got in Chiaon's car, but the car's accelerator was broken. He tried everything but could not fix it. My husband crouched down and held onto the accelerator with his hand so that we were able to get to the village.

We had a workshop for four days and three nights and on the last evening the attendees were very impressed; they even washed their hands of their drug habits. My husband and I felt that God was working through us. My husband held down the accelerator that first day, risking his life, and the families could be restored.

After that incident he decided to buy a car so that he could gather people every day. People were very inspired by the meetings. The number of attendees increased, and the room got very crowded. If there were a lot of people, sometimes they had to stand outside the classroom and listen to lectures with an umbrella in the rain. No one complained, though.

During this period, my husband was fired from the company he worked for, but he started to build a large lecture room for lectures and one more for the Sunday service. He told the members they did not have to contribute financially, because he knew they did not have money, but he asked them to come and help with the construction work. The lecture room was completed quickly, despite the difficult situation. However, the space soon became too small again. Joaon built a large adjacent room at his house, and Antonio continued to build another big room for his members. It was in August 1981 that we began our lectures in this way. After that, many amazing miracles happened.

By August 1981 we had more than 2,000 people who had attended lectures, and 400 of them had attended the seven-day workshop. The families that had heard the lectures first were already taking positions of responsibility. Elias and the three core families sent ten missionaries from our area to other villages with the goal for them to become like Elias. Chiaon visited his hometown in Bahia State and made a great base there with the help of his pastor.

Overcoming the Challenges Following the Revival

In August 1981, as the persecution of the church grew worse, and family members of the church were scattered. This period was the time when all over Brazil the communist-controlled media created full-scale persecution; church buildings throughout the country were in danger of being destroyed. There were many new members in the Santo Amaro church, but the church facilities were not well maintained and the members often left. Many students who thought that our church was antisocial tried to vandalize the church buildings one night. We managed to persuade them to listen to us for 40 minutes, and we introduced the Principle and gave them a lecture. They stopped trying to destroy the church building. I wanted to show them what the other rooms were like. I

The Elias tribe going out to do volunteer work in the community

opened the door and asked them to take a look. There were about 200 members inside, praying with tears. They were amazed when they saw that. Without a doubt, God worked on their consciences. After that they returned home and our church remained safe, thanks to God's protection.

Pastor Elias did not ask anyone to educate the members, but tried to do it himself, no matter how tired he was. He always lectured Monday to Thursday from 7:30 to 10 p.m., and once or twice a month he would do a special two-day workshop, counseling and caring for each guest with a parental heart.

One amazing thing about Pastor Elias was that, besides his schedule of ministry, he also fundraised to support the mission. This way of conducting his life inspired others to serve the people around them. He was lecturing and fundraising all the time. The church was crowded every day, and there were more and more members who wanted to be just like him. He held Divine Principle lectures for new guests every day.

In a church that was small but busy 24 hours a day, a member named Joseph would start to work at 6 in the morning, making food, cleaning and serving others until 10 in the evening. When people noticed this level of devotion, they also come to help out. At the celebration of the second anniversary of Santo Amaro Church, all the members donated money to Rev. Elias for a car. It was really gratifying and amazing.

The Economic Base of Santo Amaro Church

As Santo Amaro's home church grew, it became more necessary to invest in its economic base; we needed to maintain our activities and expand our buildings. So, we opened a fish shop with the cooperation of Joaon and Louis, who had experience selling fish. We called the shop Mansei Fish Shop. Seven months later, we opened our second fish shop; it was a big success. With this economic success, we launched the third shop five months after opening the second shop.

This third store broke all the previous records and made great progress in the economic sector of the Santo Amaro church. Within a short period of time, we opened seven fish stores.

Conclusion

The church of Santo Amaro had many difficult situations as it persevered through the home church providence. Sometimes it seemed that there was no solution, but God always showed us the way.

Today Santo Amaro Church is led by Pastor Lee Ro-han, who is following in the footsteps of his father Elias. The son is pastor of the church which was pioneered and established by his father; and most of the members are his father's spiritual children. The Church of Santo Amaro is naturally a tribal messiah church. Today it is developing organically in each field: home group activities and workshops, witnessing, activities done with foreign missionaries in UPF and NGOs, youth and second-generation education, and more. I would like to express my sincere gratitude to True Parents for all these things.

I will work harder for the victory of Vision 2020! Thank you.

Kim Myeong-dae

Person giving Testimony	Wife's Name	Region	Nation
Kim Myeong-dae	Cheon Ok-ja	Korea	Korea
Blessing Information	Number of Children	Spiritual Children (couples)	Number of Families Attending Church
124 Couples	6 children	515 couples	150+ couples

A Life of Faith Lived in Oneness With the Will of Heaven

This is my conclusion: There is nothing you cannot do if you are united with the center. If you have set the condition by which you will cast no shadow and are completely united with Heaven, you cannot but achieve your goals. Anything can be achieved if you follow the rules. The problem is that, if you go astray, you cannot realize the settlement of noon. If your mind is fickle and conflicted, you are bound to cast shadows and your work will become that much more difficult. The miracles of Heaven cannot be wrought in such an environment. [*Cheon Seong Gyeong*, p. 454–455]

One day, True Father asked me, "How were you able to do it?" I answered boldly, "I learned it from you. You taught us that if we have a clear purpose to achieve, there are ten thousand ways to achieve it. All I did was remember your words and translate them into action."

The Quickest Way to Live with God Is through a Life and Faith Based on the High-Noon Settlement

I came to know about the Unification Church in my hometown of Samcheok, Gangwon Province, after meeting Rev. Kim Young-hwi in March of 1957, and I officially joined the church on March 12, 1959. At that time, I adopted as my life motto "Life and Faith in Oneness with the Central Will," and that is how I have lived in faith until now.

I began working for the church in March of 1960 as a pioneering church leader. I began my 29 months of mandatory service in the Korean army on February 23, 1965. After I completed my military service, I dedicated my life to serving the church, successively holding the posts of Dangjin regional church leader, church pastor, church leader, regional director and the president of the church in Japan. When I reached retirement age, I was appointed as a revivalist and traveled across the nation, leading revival meetings in 153 churches. Most recently, in 2017 True Parents called me to work as a special international itinerant missionary for Cheon Il Guk. I am now well over 70 years of age, and my entire life has been a continuous struggle (to strive to achieve something no matter the emotional or physical pain with any means necessary) to do what little I can to contribute toward realizing the providential will of the True Parents of Heaven, Earth and Humankind.

I believe the reason I was able to achieve the Blessing of 430 couples as a heavenly tribal messiah is that I never forgot the motto I had adopted for my life of faith, the resolution I had made when I first became connected to our church and handed in my application to join (March 1959). When I first listened to the Divine Principle, there was a profound moment when I realized that failure or success in the history of the providence of restoration depended on whether unity was achieved with the central figure. My life motto came to have an even deeper meaning, based on what True Father talked about frequently from 2001 to the time of his Seonghwa, namely the "high-noon settlement," and his words became deeply rooted in my life. The gist of those words is that, when we establish God 100 percent at the very center of our life of faith, we stand in a position where shadows of darkness can never be cast around us, just as we cast no shadow when we stand in the sun at high noon.

That is why I believe that, before they can become a family of the high-noon settlement centered on the Heavenly Parent and True Parents of Heaven, Earth and Humankind, the husband and wife first must achieve high-noon settlement by uniting as a couple cen-

A special gathering of the Kim Myeong-dae, Cheon Ok-ja tribe at Cheon Bok Gung (January 31, 2014)

tering on Heaven. After that, they must become one with their children. When this horizontal foundation is connected vertically through True Parents, it then can be expanded on a wider scale.

To uphold this standard, for 40 years my family has kept a holy candle burning 24 hours a day and has offered jeongseong, from the time my sixth and youngest child was born in 1978 until now. It is my wife who usually sees to the altar and offers jeongseong. Sometimes, however, it is difficult for her to do it, because she and I both are traveling abroad or visiting other regions in Korea. At such times, my six children take turns coming to our home to keep the candle burning, competing to be the first to volunteer. We have established a family tradition in which all six children have been bestowed with holy candles, and they all offer jeongseong exactly at midnight. This practice of offering prayers and jeongseong at midnight every day has helped all of us to be connected as one spiritually, even at times when we are far away from each other.

Another important standard of jeongseong for me was to carry out the liberation and blessing of our ancestors, no matter how busy or ill I was. Our family already has completed the liberation of our ancestors up to 315 generations, and we also have completed ancestor Blessings for eight branches up to 308 generations. Our children helped us to accomplish this by attending in our place when we were unable to go ourselves, due to commitments with church work.

I have come to understand a lot more about my relationship to my ancestors by participating in CheongPyeong works. I realized that if I cannot become one with the ancestors who brought me here, I never can become a vessel that can wholly contain the heavenly fortune sent by God. I began to think so because I realized that, even though my ancestors do not have physical bodies and therefore can do things more easily than I, there is still a limit to what they can do if they do not have the foundation of good spirits. I believe that I must liberate and bless my ancestors before I can expect to have the cooperation of the spirit world when I witness to people. I also firmly believe that upholding this standard is crucial in creating the miracles that are needed to enable the 430 couples to become heavenly tribal messiahs.

It would have been impossible for me to fulfill my mission as a heavenly tribal messiah without such an internal foundation of jeongseong. Leading a life of faith is possible only when one has laid the foundation of being united as a family, with one's ancestors, and with Heaven. My family could fulfill the mission of heavenly tribal messiah and raise our children well only after we established that standard.

A Life of Absolute Faith, Absolute Love and Absolute Obedience

Although True Father with his last words gave us the mission of heavenly tribal messiah, at first I was at a loss as to how to do it. I was hesitant to commit to doing it. Until now, the number of spiritual children I personally have witnessed to, who are also regular church-goers, is 157 families. For seven years, I sent one person a month to attend the seven-day workshop as part of my efforts to witness to them, and I have received the witnessing award given by the president of the Korean church seven years in a row; and yet, witnessing is a task that never grows easier.

Reminding myself of what I felt as I witnessed to each and every one of them, I reconfirmed my resolve to offer jeongseong to achieve a life of high-noon settlement before Heaven. It was during that time that, at a meeting of elder church leaders and national messiahs held in Cheon Jeong Gung on November 12, 2014, True Mother called out my name and asked me to relate how I was leading my life of faith. After pondering what I should say, I related my experience of absolute faith, absolute love and absolute obedience to True Parents' words.

On March 31, 1991 (solar calendar), suddenly I was commanded by True Father to go to Japan as an emissary. Since I did not speak, understand, or read Japanese at all, I was completely inadequate to work there. However, True Father told me, "Go to Japan!" so as soon as he gave me that direction, I prepared and departed for Japan right away, even though I had no clear plan. I was afraid if I did not, I would fail in the mission and his words would turn out to have fallen to the ground, useless. I had learned through the Divine Principle that Heaven could send True Father to the chosen people of Korea based on the foundation established by the Mansei Independence Movement, starting on March 1, 1919 (lunar calendar), which was led by patriots such as Yu Gwan-sun. Therefore, the nation of Japan had to set an indemnity condition severe enough to make up for forcefully colonizing the chosen nation of Korea for 40 years. Moreover, for Japan to fulfill its mission as the mother nation, it had to establish the condition by which the messiah could visit the land of Japan, so I was at my wit's end about it.

I thought that if we held a memorial rally for Yu Gwan-sun in Japan, we could set the condition for True Parents to visit and bring fortune directly to Japan once again. In 1991, on the 1st day of the 3rd month by the heavenly calendar, we marched down the street in Tokyo, crying out, "Mansei," just as Yu Gwan-sun had done in 1919 in Korea, and thus the campaign to memorialize the spirit of Yu

Gwan-sun began. To set a condition, I slept on the ground with a newspaper as my blanket and ate roasted grain powder I had brought from Korea instead of regular meals. While setting these conditions, I was threatened numerous times by right-wing organizations opposed to the Unification Church and also was stabbed twice with knives, but still I persevered with the determination to offer my very life, and we succeeded in holding the rally. When I now look back on those days, a thousand emotions fill my heart. We marched on the street from Ginza to the Japanese Imperial Palace, waving a Korean flag and shouting, "Mansei," just as the members of the independence movement had done in Korea at the time of True Father's birth.

After that, I announced to the Japanese church members, "True Parents will visit Japan in ten months." The members around me were astounded by my sudden announcement. It was a time when the Japanese government was adamant in denying True Father a visa, because he had been imprisoned in the United States and also because he had entered Japan on a tourist visa to preside at an engagement ceremony of 6,000 couples in 1978. Some of those members said that I was rash to make such an announcement, but I was confident, firmly believing that it would come to pass.

If we set a foundation of conditions and then bring a victory, Satan cannot touch it, and this fact was proven by the miracle that followed. Ten months after the street march, I received a phone call confirming that True Father miraculously had been issued a visa by the Japanese Embassy in Korea. On March 26, 1992, True Parents finally came to Japan, and Japan could take on the important role of the Eve, Tamar, and mother nation in providential history.

After that, I offered further jeongseong based on the heavenly fortune bestowed by True Parents' visit. We expanded the activities of the Unification movement in Japan to enable Japan to fulfill its substantial responsibility for the providence. We established 91 churches for Koreans living in Japan, and we increased the number of people attending Tenchi Seikyo, a Buddhist-affiliated organization connected to our movement, from 5,000 to 75,000. I believe firmly that these "impossible" things were made possible through my 100 percent unity with True Parents and my continuous efforts at a life of faith based on high-noon settlement.

I said to True Parents determinedly, "As you can see, I was victorious in Japan despite my limitations of not knowing Japanese. There is nothing to hinder me in Korea, and so there is nothing I cannot do. I will do it without fail."

You Need Determination, Then People, and Money

My experiences were more than enough to awaken a desire that had hidden deep within me: to start heavenly tribal messiah activities. Though we encounter many challenges in carrying out the mission of heavenly tribal messiah, the one that most often makes members hesitant to step up concerns finances. I served as a pastor for 57 years, and during that time I went through countless hardships and

A heavenly tribal messiah Blessing of the Kim Myung-dae, Cheon Ok-ja tribe at Cheon Bok Gung (2015)

financial difficulties, but not once did I fail to achieve my goal because there was no money. True Parents have told us that if we set a clear goal and make a resolution, there will be 10,000 ways to reach that goal. I have had many experiences of money finding its way to me naturally, when I did what True Parents told us to do.

When I returned to my hometown, there were only 16 members in Samcheok Church and the monthly tithes totaled less than a million won (roughly 925 USD). I offered a prayer and set my goal first. I decided to hold a service three years later in the main hall of the Samcheok Culture and Arts Center to commemorate the third anniversary of my coming to Samcheok Church. My goal was to bring together the local leaders, who represent all the citizens of

Samcheok, to make a condition of spiritual unity for the whole city. For three years I offered jeongseong every day and dedicated my heart and soul to doing my best and accomplishing my goal. Three years later, something so incredible took place that amazed even me. Almost all the leaders of Samcheok attended the service, including the mayor and regional parliamentarians, and the 1,500-seat hall in the Culture and Arts Center was completely filled. Donations and flower arrangements arrived from more than 100 places across Korea. When I looked upon the people crowding the hall, all singing hymns together and taking part in the third anniversary service being held in my honor, I could not but express my heartfelt gratitude to Heavenly Parent and True Parents.

This is my conclusion. There is nothing you cannot do if you are united with your center. If you set the condition by which you will cast no shadow and are completely united with Heaven, you cannot but achieve your goals. Anything can be achieved if you follow the rules. The problem is that, if you go astray, you cannot realize the settlement of noon. If your mind is fickle and conflicted, you are bound to cast shadows and your work will become that much more difficult. The miracles of Heaven cannot be wrought in such an environment. [*Cheon Seong Gyeong*, p. 454–455]

One day, True Father asked me, "How were you able to do it?" I answered boldly, "I learned it from you. You taught us that if we have a clear purpose to achieve, there are 10,000 ways to achieve it. All I did was remember your words and translate them into action."

One of my life philosophies is that you should not try to make money. Once you have found heavenly work for which you need to spend money, money will come to you. The mission of heavenly tribal messiahs began in accordance with True Parents' will. Therefore, I believe that when we establish the standard in relation to that mission, the money we need will come to us. I cannot even understand not attempting to do something because of lack of money. That is why I think that setting a definite goal first and adopting the necessary attitude for it is important. This is because money is never the main character, but rather a supporting actor that assists in achieving the goal. In short, I established the right order of things, in which making a resolution comes first, the people come second, and the money comes last. After doing so, I felt as if I had already fulfilled half of my mission as a heavenly tribal messiah.

Witnessing Is Not the Goal, But a Part of Life

I began to witness every day to everyone I met, and I encouraged my spiritual children to do the same. For me, witnessing has now become a habit. With the belief that I can achieve my goal only when witnessing becomes part of my life, I have kept my eyes open and acted with that awareness within me whenever I left home to go somewhere. If you want to succeed in a certain field, you need to focus on that field at every waking moment. Similarly, I feel that Heaven will connect me to people to whom I can witness only when

I keep an active focus on witnessing. If I had forgotten that, I never could have fulfilled my mission as a heavenly tribal messiah. For example, when I witnessed to Kim Hyo-nam (Hoonmonim) in 1971 in Naju, South Jeolla Province, it was during a thirty-month period when I offered jeongseong such as three 40-day morning fasts, four 40-day late-night prayer vigils and a 100-day cold-shower condition (November 1, 1971 – February 8, 1972). It was on the final day of the jeongseong that she agreed to go to a seven-day workshop.

Another of my witnessing methods is the philosophy of caring about people. Wherever I go, even if I am only riding in an elevator, I always greet and talk to those around me. Once I witnessed to the person who worked at the front desk of the bathhouse I frequented, after holding a conversation with him. Another time, my car got stuck on a snowy road as I was driving to CheongPyeong, and I witnessed to the tow-truck driver who came to rescue my car. If I spend only ten minutes a day witnessing, Heaven shows me the way to do it. In the lounge for local work crews at the Seorak Library, there were several pamphlets advertising True Father's autobiography, but they had no contact information. I took all the pamphlets from the room, wrote my cell phone number on each, and put them back. Several days later, someone called me, and that led to an elder from a local Christian church, who was also the mayor of a nearby small community, joining our church.

I also follow another philosophy in witnessing, which is to look into someone's face when I talk to them, opening my heart to them so they can do so in turn, thus building trust between us. For instance, it took me 12 years to witness to a famous painter who had served as the chairman of the board of judges at the National Art Exhibition. It was not easy to open the hearts of the painter's family, because his wife was a deaconess of the Full Gospel Church, but in the end I not only witnessed to him and his wife but also to their son, who is now living happily as a Korean–Japanese blessed couple. When I was witnessing to him, I continuously offered jeongseong, met him face to face, opened my heart to him until he opened up to me, and built trust. I also showed him the way I lived and spoke to him about practicing the words of the Divine Principle in daily life, and finally I was able to send him to a workshop.

Fulfilling the Mission of 430 Couples as a Heavenly Tribal Messiah Is Not the End, Just the Beginning

Though I have accomplished the goal of witnessing to 430 couples, the number of families among them who actually come to church regularly and believe with their heart is 257. A large number of them are earnestly practicing their faith, but there are some families who are not. This is because firmly establishing them as flawless blessed families is so much more difficult than just having them attend workshops, fill in the application form and receive the Blessing.

After accomplishing my mission of 430 couples as a heavenly tribal messiah, I have set a new goal, which is to nurture those couples to become flawless blessed families. I will continue to guide them until all 430 couples become central members of the church. I constantly call and visit them so that I can bring at least 300 of those families to attend church regularly.

According to my calculations, I blessed a total of 515 couples in three rounds to complete the mission of 430 couples. Of those 515 couples, I have chosen 75 families who are not yet committed blessed families, and I continue to pay special attention to them. They are the families who have the highest probability of falling behind. The reason I am doing that is to make all 430 couples regular churchgoers, so that I can dedicate them to Heaven. I am of the mind that if any of them go astray, I should replace them. This is so that I can keep my standard solid and firm as I set the condition of having blessed 430 couples as a heavenly tribal messiah, as True Parents directed.

Now I have finally blessed 430 couples, as directed by True Parents, but this is only the beginning. I will do my best, as long as my health and other conditions allow me, to make sure that those 430 couples remain proud, perfect blessed families of our church and that the seed of witnessing is passed on continuously from generation to generation.

True Parents told all blessed families to become heavenly tribal messiahs. Today, as always, I try to live my life based on the settlement of noon, looking around me to check if any shadows have been cast in my life, so that my wife and I can be a blessed couple whom my tribe can be proud to follow.

Lastly, the most important thing in doing anything is offering jeongseong.

"Even God Himself bows down in front of jeongseong."
[*The Way of God's Will*]

Chapter 5

Restoring a Neighborhood

Etsuko Uda

Person giving Testimony	Husband's Name	Region	Nation
Etsuko Uda	Kim Sang-gyun	Korea	Korea
Blessing Information	Number of Children	Spiritual Children (couples)	Number of Families Attending Church
6,000 Couples	2 sons, 3 daughters	450 couples	200 couples

The Heavenly Tribal Messiah Mission Is the March to the Blessing

> I am telling you about all these awards not to brag about myself but to show how the process of the return of the birthright can be accomplished. Through the official recognition from the Cain realm, Abel's will be settled, as well as those of the heavenly tribal messiah. How could we ever compare our course with True Father's? In 1948, when True Father was in the North Korean death camp at Heungnam, he was chosen as an exemplary prisoner three times, gaining recognition from Satan's side. After that Satan no longer could test him. In a similar fashion I have been opposed by the local community, but by standing in a position of public recognition, I was able to experience restoration of the Cain realm that True Parents taught.

God, Who Leads Me and Shows Me His Love

I am Etsuko Uda, and my husband is Kim Sang-gyun. We are a Korean–Japanese couple blessed in the 6,000 Couples Blessing on October 14, 1982. We are raising two sons and three daughters. I came to Korea on November 20, 1984, and by the time the heavenly tribal messiah 430-couple providence started on September 24, 2016, I had lived here for 32 years. The grace that our family experiences today is due to guidance from Heavenly Parent and True Parents.

On December 24, 1971, in Kochi Prefecture, Japan, I met some members of the Unification Church who were witnessing on the street; later I joined the church. I was 16 at the time, and, due to my father's opposition to my joining the church, I gave up on my plan to start university and instead started to work at a bank in Kyoto. After moving to Kyoto, a Kyoto University graduate student who was doing a three-day fast gave a lecture about the Unification Principle on the last day of the fast. I was so moved and wondered how someone could be so passionate and speak with so much determination after three days of fasting. After listening to the speech, my heart went out to humankind. After that, realizing that God was guiding me, I started to visit the center regularly. The work at the bank was sometimes tiring, but nevertheless I had a burning desire to go witnessing after work and invite at least one person to the center to listen to a lecture. It was a time of intense dedication for all the members who were working full-time jobs while keeping up active mission lives in the center. This was a difficult thing to do. But I persisted and brought guests to the center and sat next to them, listening to the biblical and Divine Principle lectures again and again. I learned a lot and guided many people through their three- or seven-day workshops.

After one year I decided to completely dedicate myself to the church. I felt there was nothing to be gained by holding a job and living at the center at the same time. For the next eight years I witnessed and, whenever necessary, I sold Il Hwa ginseng, ceramics, miniature stone towers, stamps and other things. Most of our devotional lives were connected to the economic sector.

More than in other places in Japan, the young people of Kyoto had been deceived into becoming active in the communist party. The future of Japan depended on the minds of those young people. True Parents had foreseen this and thus developed the theories of Victory over Communism.

For 27 years we had to carry on a battle with the communist party members, using our Victory over Communism ideology. It was a time full of difficulty and hardship. The Kyoto governor, the Osaka governor, and the Tokyo governor were all leaders of the communist party, and the risk of Japan becoming communized was increasing by the day. So True Father directed Mr. Osami Kuboki, who was the national leader of the Unification Church of Japan, to mobilize our young people throughout the country to fully support the candidate of the Liberal Democratic Party, which was in the Abel position, for Kyoto governor. We obeyed the order and won the election. Finally, the communist party lost in a historic moment for us all. The communist party newspaper *Akahata* wrote, "We did not lose to the Liberal Democratic Party, we lost to the Association for Victory over Communism." Our influence had been recognized. The defeat of the communist party gradually spread all over the country, thanks to the victories in Kyoto, Osaka and Tokyo, and the communist party leaders of many cities became leaders of the Liberal Democratic Party. The true judgment and determination of True Father at difficult times in Japan led to the miracle that overcame the crisis.

This is how difficult our first providential steps in Kyoto were, not only spiritually but also in very real terms. Victory was brought with great effort, facing one barrier after another. Yet, if I reflect upon my life, that time in my youth was the best time. I feel this because our generation experienced the history of God and Satan confronting each other directly on the front line of the providence.

A heavenly tribal messiah Blessing of the Kim Sang-gyun, Etsuko Uda tribe (September 24, 2016)

Receiving My Mission through True Parents' Grace

In 1980, I was one of 12 Japanese representatives who went to the United States to attend the celebration of True Father's sixtieth birthday at Belvedere. True Parents encouraged me by saying in Japanese, "You have experienced a lot of hardship!" That is because those who were chosen to attend the birthday celebration were those who had been top in their missions in Japan. True Father told everybody there, "Take a look at these people who are the champions of the world and keep them in mind!" I still remember True Parents' faces from that day. In retrospect, that was one moment when I really felt our Parents' heart, as they wished to comfort and

offer everything to their children who had been weakened by confronting Satan on the frontline of the providence. True Parents are the source of true love, but we are the ones who must travel the train of indemnity until the last station, where we receive Heaven's forgiveness. Therefore, I was able to see the Messiah expressing love with a merciful expression as well as the True Parent who had resolute determination before the leaders.

Life in Korea and the Jeongseong of Three Women

After meeting True Parents, I was resolved to marry someone from the chosen nation and live there. So, in 1981 I was matched by photograph and received the 6,000 Couples Blessing in Korea on October 14, 1982. After three years of public life I came to Korea on November 20, 1984. At that time, I prayed to Heavenly Parent and True Parents to inherit Korea's faith and tradition. I prayed, "Please allow me to meet someone more faithful than I." I am grateful to say that that prayer was fulfilled. That person was none other than my mother-in-law, who joined the church in 1958 in Daegu. Despite the opposition of her husband, she witnessed to her two younger sisters and finally convinced her husband to participate in the 430 Couples Blessing. She received the Blessing as an already married couple, brought her own mother to the Blessing as an already married couple, and restored others in her family.

After the Blessing I invested my heart and soul in witnessing to my father-in-law, who had resisted other previous attempts to bring him to the church. My mother-in-law had always kept her faith, before and after I married her son. Together with my grandmother-in-law, we naturally formed a prayer group.

Whenever I was pregnant, my mother-in-law would pray for me continually; she would even make cotton diapers for our children. Amazingly, when I was pregnant, if True Parents showed me a girl in my dreams, I gave birth to a girl, and if they showed me a boy, I ended up having a boy. They have now gone to heaven, but the image of my mother-in-law and my grandmother-in-law taking care of the three grandchildren in a stroller still remains with me.

A John the Baptist Figure Appears When We Fulfill Our Portion of Responsibility

After the Blessing, I began witnessing in the Jeongneung neighborhood (*dong*) of the Seongbuk district (*gu*) of Seoul. In the beginning there were many Christians and others in that area who opposed the Unification Church; it was very hard. However, after True Father gave the direction to begin working on signature campaigns and education programs with the Citizens' Federation for the Unification of North and South Korea, there was an amazing change. I was able to invite many people to our activities, including local leaders, and through our cooperation, the opposition dissolved. While I was working on local breakthrough activities in the Jeongneung-2 neighborhood, there was good cooperation between neighborhoods. The local leaders from 33 neighborhood communities helped us to organize and hold programs on "Victory over Communism Theory and Citizens' Attitude in Preparing for Reunification" in local community centers, cafeterias, New Village (*Saemaul*) meeting rooms, and anywhere they could find to keep educating and preparing people. My mother-in-law and I prayed earnestly, holding each other's hands, that their homes and communities would receive heavenly fortune. As a Japanese, at first I didn't speak Korean, but my mother-in-law and I were united and the neighbors began to be interested, step by step, in our activities. Now they are good friends of ours.

After establishing this basic foundation, true family movement programs were held at neighborhood office on the 25th of each month. When local leaders had their meetings, I talked to them about the importance of the true family and purity movements. I received signatures from 160 leaders and their wives and took photos of them; then they agreed to receive the Blessing, so we held a Blessing of 160 couples.

These reunification activities in the Jeongneung-2 neighborhood influenced the local women's organizations, and we began to work more closely with them. I had the opportunity to meet the chair of the Seongbuk Saemaul Women's Association, through whom we had remarkable connections to the various Saemaul women's associations in the region. They invited all the Saemaul members to come to the Seongbuk church to listen to a Divine Principle lecture. After that they all participated in the Blessing at Sun Moon University.

We received help and support for our signature and true love campaigns from Seongbuk women's associations such as the Saemaul Women's Association, the Veterans Association, the National Unity Union, the Right Living Movement, and the Women's Union. Whenever we have the chance, we take their photos, guide them to fill out the Blessing form, and then send them to the Blessing.

Recognition for Achieving Mother–Daughter Unity and Restoring the Authority of the Elder Son

On April 10, 2004, Hwang Seon-jo, who at the time was the national church leader of Korea, visited the Jeongneung Church to establish the hoondok family church in the Jeongneung neighborhood. My mother-in-law was chosen to lead the hoondok family church, and my husband and I were also involved in starting it.

We have been working to find those who are prepared to meet our True Parents, and each year we have brought 12 or 21 couples to True Parents' Marriage Blessing Ceremonies. Thanks to our success in bringing people to the Blessing, I have received witnessing awards several times from FFWPU Korea.

At first the people who come from churches of other religions were opposed to us, but as they observed our steadfast and unchanging hearts they came to appreciate us. Looking back on it, I think their broken hearts were healed through attending Heavenly Parent and True Parents.

Luke 4:18–19 says, "He has anointed me to bring good news to the poor and sent me to preach freedom to those who were captives and recovery of sight for the blind, set the oppressed free, and proclaim God's grace." Similar to this description from the Bible, more and more people are starting to understand our church as they are educated through two-day workshops, our large and small rallies, and assemblies.

In December 2008, the chair of the Women's League, Seongbuk branch, gave me a plaque of appreciation on behalf of Seongbuk on the fourth floor of the Seongbuk District administrative office building, and the vice chair of the Korean Women's League was also there. The plaque honored me for coming to Korea as an international wife, attending my parents-in-law and serving the community with volunteer activities. There was a report about it in the local Seongbuk newspaper. In 2011, I received a National Assembly award prize, and in 2013 I was given an award certificate by the mayor of Seongbuk District.

I am telling you about all these awards not to brag about myself but to show how the process of the return of the birthright can be accomplished. Through the official recognition from the Cain realm, Abel's will be settled, as well as those of the heavenly tribal messiah. How could we ever compare our course with True Father's? In 1948, when True Father was in the North Korean death camp at Heungnam, he was chosen as an exemplary prisoner three times, gaining recognition from Satan's side. After that Satan no longer could test him.

In a similar fashion I have been opposed by the local community, but by standing in a position of public recognition, I was able to experience restoration of the Cain realm that True Parents taught.

From that moment on my campaign changed direction. At first I focused primarily on being accepted by the leaders of the local community who were in the role of John the Baptist. Next, God raised me up to the level that could lead and award our community.

As part of the true family movement, I was awarded the True Family Movement Award of Excellence, the Filial Daughter-in-Law Prize, True Family Award, Dasan Award—or Fecundity Award, created and given for having many children since Korea suffers from low birth rates, which are awarded to those recommended by the Seongbuk District Women's Association, for contributing to a healthy society through the true family movement. I continue to work in my community through the true family movement, gathering signatures, conducting educational programs, and awarding prizes annually to model families.

Spread the Heavenly Tribal Messiah Dream to All International Families

I was shocked by True Father's ascension on September 3, 2012 (7th day of the 7th month by the heavenly calendar), but hearing his last wish calling us to be heavenly tribal messiahs and establish 430 new blessed families, I determined to take on this mission. After True Mother completed her three-year period of memorial jeongseong, she also emphasized the heavenly tribal messiah mission as the way we must go to accomplish national restoration by 2020. I often have felt that I must support True Mother without fail, as she is now in the forefront of the providence, bearing a lot of responsibility.

In March 2013, I became the president of the Association of International Blessed Families in Korea. I decided that, in order to have a victorious Cheon Il Guk on Korean soil, each of the 10,000 international couples in Korea must fulfill the goal of 430 couples.

To prepare for this, the association selected 54 of the 700 international members who had received awards during their 20 or 30 years in Korea for dedication in attending their parents-in-law and serving their communities, and we put together an album to celebrate the accomplishments of all these international members. The members chosen had received presidential prizes, prizes from the mayor of Seoul, recognition as devoted daughters-in-law, public service awards, the Dasan (Fecundity) Award and other awards. On August 8, 2014, as we celebrated the second anniversary of True Father's Seonghwa, we dedicated the album to True Mother from our hearts, as filial sons and daughters.

The following year, on the third anniversary of True Father's Seonghwa in 2015, among 404 outstanding second-generation young people from multicultural families, we selected 38 from the region and all over the country age two and older, and made an album called *As an Olive Tree*. On September 11, 2015, we offered it to True Mother who said to the 20,000 second-generation members of the International Family Association, "Proud children of Blessed families be strong and grow like olive trees!"

Heavenly Tribal Messiah Activity Is the Completion of My Family and the Way of a Filial Heart

In 2016, on the anniversary of Foundation Day, I told my husband that we would be victorious in fulfilling the 430 couple Blessings as heavenly tribal messiahs. If my mother-in-law were still alive, we would have done it together, but sadly, in July 2004, while still the leader of the hoondok family church in Seongbuk, she ascended.

My husband gave me a lot of strength. He told me to go ahead and work on blessing the 430 couples, while he would support my work financially. Finally, we approached the Korean church president, Ryu Kyeong-seuk, asking him to preside over a heavenly tribal messiah Blessing on September 24, 2016.

First, we talked to the spiritual children of Korean–Japanese couples in Korea and confirmed the total number of spiritual children and spiritual grandchildren; we came up with 160 families. I decided to invite all of them including the 150 families who were registered at the family department at headquarters beginning in 2011, and the 100 people who received the Blessing before 2011. We also invited the 120 families we blessed with the cooperation of the Seongbuk church leader

The Seongbuk church leader, the elders and the Japanese missionaries in the Jeongneung church all helped us by inviting new guests for workshops at the church annex. We concentrated on visiting and inviting people from the Jeongneung-2, -3 and -4 neighborhoods, and many new people joined the church. Using a bus and the church van, we took these new members to the Pine Ridge Resort in Sokcho (a city in the northeast of South Korea) and held a two-day workshop for them. We held workshops at the Yongpyong Resort, and my spiritual children, especially the leaders of the Saemaul Women's Association, worked to bring people to them. Since we have done activities together for decades, especially with the Saemaul centers in the Jeongneung-2 and -4 neighborhoods, we have gained a lot of trust in each other and cooperate very well.

Sometimes when we did not have a venue, we conducted hoondok meetings in the house of the Saemaul Women's Association president.

Every day, we did hoondokhae and prayed and offered jeongseong for our witnessing, saying, "Please lead us to really good people." As a result, we witnessed to 120 new households and fulfilled the goal of 430 households of heavenly tribal messiah Blessings. On September 24, 2016, six buses were mobilized to take our spiritual children to Yu Cheon Gung (Korean FFWPU Headquarters) in Seoul's Dobong District, where 340 of my spiritual children were present for the Blessing ceremony that accomplished our goal of blessing 430 couples as tribal messiah.

On that day, the North Seoul regional leader came to the ceremony, as did the leaders of Seongbuk Church and their wives, elders, some 430 Couples elder sisters, my spiritual children and spiritual grandchildren from the Japanese and Korean–Japanese blessed couples. I was unable to control my tears of joy and happiness as I prayed to Heavenly Parent and True Parents offering them infinite glory.

At that time, my daughter dreamed that True Father came out of the full moon and gave us a wonderful gift, a treasure chest with a certificate of appointment inside. As soon as she had the dream, my daughter came to me smiling and said, "Mom, I really feel True Parents are happy."

Since that time, I feel that the spirit world has changed. My youngest son had wanted to receive the Blessing, but he could not find a match until then. After completing the declaration of our 430 families, I was introduced by a church leader to the granddaughter of the 36 Couple Jeong Su-won and Kim Kyung-nam, and my son was blessed to her.

Our family is truly grateful to be connected to the 36 Couples, who are the historical ancestors of the blessed families in our church. It is always necessary to pass on the traditions of the Unification Church to the first, second, and third generations, centering on True Parents. I was more grateful than anything for the fact that through the Blessings of the second and third generation members of our family, our faith could be rooted more deeply into the Korean soil.

On November 11, 2017, we took eight buses from Jeongneung to the World Peace and Unification Rally centered on True Mother. I will do my best to give strength to True Mother, along with my spiritual children from my mobilization area.

Thank you.

Lee Ker Shung

Person giving Testimony	Wife's Name	Region	Nation
Lee Ker Shung	Sui Chin Wu	Greater China	Taiwan
Blessing Information	**Number of Children**	**Spiritual Children (couples)**	**Number of Families Attending Church**
6,000 Couples	2 daughters	445 couples	41 couples

2

Heavenly Tribal Messiah Work Is the Way to Become True Parents

> These days I ask myself, "What does it mean to be a parent?" I have learned that it is a very valuable path to understand and practice Heavenly Parent's love through creating a harmony of unconditional love toward my children in the Cain realm, just as I love my physical children.
>
> I hope to set up an effective system to educate and organize all the families in my tribe and help them fulfill their own mission as heavenly tribal messiahs through blessing 430 couples. This is because I know that the path of a parent is to nurture and raise your children and help them to marry so they can have their own families.

Heavenly Parent and True Parents Gave Me New Life

I joined the church on June 1, 1974, when I was a sophomore at Taiwan University majoring in mathematics. It has been more than 40 years that I have followed True Parents and walked the path of faith, but I clearly remember this date because it was the day I was reborn through Heavenly Parent and True Parents with a life full of blessing.

I grew up in a Christian family. Every time I faced difficulties in my life of faith, my ancestors helped me, and they would appear in my dreams and encourage me to stay in the church. I was attracted by God's ideal of creation. I believed that God has guided human history throughout the history of restoration, and I simply believed that the heavenly kingdom would be built within three years.

A month after I joined the church, I did 40 days of pioneer witnessing with another brother. Six months later, I took time off from

A heavenly tribal messiah Blessing by the Lee Ker Shung, Sui Chin Wu family (2016)

school and became a full-time member to do fundraising and witnessing. The foundation of heart I learned during this period has become a great motivation for me to carry on my life of faith with the firm belief that I can fulfill my providential missions.

After three years of military service, I went back to school and continued my college studies. I became a CARP leader before graduating. Then I worked as a church leader to pioneer churches in the cities of Tainan and Kaohshiung.

My wife is Sui Chin Wu (Soo Gyeong-oh in Korean). She was born in Deuksan-myun, Seosan-gun, Chuncheongnam-do, Korea on the 13th day of the 4th month (May 25) by the lunar calendar, 1953. In 1972 she began her university studies in Taiwan and joined the church on April 17, 1974. We were matched in 1978 and was blessed in 1982 in the 6,000 Couples Blessing. We have two daughters. After the

Blessing, I was appointed national leader of Taiwan. Later I became the regional president of the Greater China Region, and currently I am the regional vice president of the Greater China Region.

True Father mentioned that if there were 12 heavenly tribal messiahs in a nation, that nation would be changed and restored. These words inspired me. I really wanted to restore Taiwan as God's nation, so I gave a lot of thought to the issues I must overcome in order to fulfill this mission. I was determined that the way to give back the great love and blessing given to me by Heavenly Parent and True Parents was to return happiness and glory by fulfilling my mission as a heavenly tribal messiah.

Hardships Lead to Blessings

When my wife was doing pioneer witnessing in the city of Kaohshiung, our church was banned by the government and we were prohibited from practicing any religious activities. Not only was it very difficult for us to go out witnessing, but the very existence of our church itself was in crisis. We were in a situation in which we could be questioned by the police or arrested anytime and anywhere. However, my wife did not give up and she carried on with witnessing.

One day, my wife entered a store while she was fundraising on the street. A young girl was looking after the store; this was very unusual for her, because she was not a full-time employee and she rarely looked after the store. It was only by chance that she was in the store that day. My wife asked the girl to buy some of the ballpoint pens she was selling. However, there was no reason for the girl to buy the pens because they sold many ballpoint pens at the store. My wife said, "If you cannot buy them, please come with me to study the Divine Principle." Later, my wife told me that even she herself did not know why she said that. Maybe it was because she felt the spirit world urging her to say so. The girl came to study the Divine Principle on a regular basis, but her parents were very upset and often would block her from coming to the church because they were strongly against Christians and Catholics. When she finished the Divine Principle study course, we encouraged her to quit her job and become a full-time member. At first, she hesitated because of her worries that her father could cause trouble or that he might become so angry that he could even die due to his high-blood pressure. But we told her that God would bless and protect him if she truly focused on God's providence. In the end, although her father got very angry and did everything to break up her relationship with the church, she made up her mind to join the church and become a full-time member. She left home and joined the church because she believed that God would protect her father and family.

There are some things I came to realize through this event. First, although witnessing may not be easy, around every corner there are people whom God has prepared and hidden for you to find. Second, Heaven can work when the conditions of jeongseong offered by the person witnessing match the situation of the person who is being witnessed to.

Find the Things You Can Do Around You to Meet Righteous People

I joined a reading club in my village. When I got the chance to lead the group's activities, I suggested that we read True Father's autobiography. At first, people were puzzled as to why I suggested this book, but after I introduced True Father's life course and we read the whole book, three persons came to me to join the church. I started giving them Divine Principle lectures after they signed the membership application form. I hope to raise them to be regular members and sub-leaders of our home group activities.

In this way, I started out by looking for the things I could do within my community, and such efforts have led to successful witnessing.

Lately, we have focused on an activity to carry out the Blessing ceremony through the local communities called *li*. On average, 2,000 families live in one *li*. Each *li* has its own activity center where people can gather together. I have been thinking for a long time that it would be great if we could gather people and hold Blessing ceremonies at these centers. I started offering jeongseong to put this idea into practice. Through the people I met there, I began to organize and teach Blessing seminars. When I introduced and explained the meaning and value of the Blessing, all the participants without exception reacted positively to our slogan, "Let's become true families!" To educate and guide our guests through the subsequent stages—the Blessing ceremony, the indemnity stick ceremony, the 40-day separation period, and the three-day ceremony—it was necessary for us to organize our home groups and staff. Therefore, we established the following guidelines:

1. Cooperate with the li leaders to hold the Blessing ceremony.
2. Create regular study courses for the Blessing participants.
3. Guide them to accomplish the three-day ceremony.
4. Set up a home group meeting in each *li* community, and hold ongoing seminars to educate guests.
5. Set up a leader in each home group to take care of the blessed couples.

I still am trying to organize my 430 families so that I can guide them effectively as their heavenly tribal messiah. Most of them live in different cities located in seven districts. Forty of them have become blessed families and attend the church as devout members. The rest of the families are those who need more Divine Principle education to become regular members.

In the beginning, I tried to educate all of them on my own, but it was very difficult because there were too many of them. It was hard for me to meet each of them face to face to teach them, and actually there so many that it was actually impossible to meet them all, even if I invested myself 24/7 to doing only that. Therefore, I decided to select seven couples among my spiritual children who have leadership skills and fundamental faith, who live in the seven cities where the families in my tribe are living. I trained them to become home group leaders, so they could play an intermediary role in developing

Lee Ker Shung and Sui Chin Wu officiating a heavenly tribal messiah Blessing

my tribe.

First, I appointed one of my spiritual children as my successor, to help take care of the 40 blessed families who are already church members. I then chose two of my spiritual children among the 40 blessed families to help me take care of the families in my tribe whom were not members yet. One of them is Rev. Yang Chang Shin, who takes care of 193 blessed families in the Y-lan area. He has a background in ministry, and we cooperate with each other in developing and managing educational programs.

The other one is Rev. Min Tai-si. He gives lectures to the blessed families in Y-lan County once or twice a month. I am planning to manage my heavenly tribal messiah activities as follows:

Myself and two other leaders set up as successors, working

together with seven more leaders who will directly manage my spiritual children, and at the next level outward, local blessed families of my heavenly tribe.

The Heavenly Tribe Is the Path of a Parent and the Path of the Messiah

Financial issues have always been difficult as I carry out my heavenly tribal messiah activities. I have to provide and manage all the expenses on my own. We usually hold gatherings, study meetings and services in my home. We also have a tradition in which every participating family brings one or two dishes to share with others.

Of course, it is not easy to move around here and there to hold all these home group gatherings, but I cannot let small difficulties like this block my work. I strongly believe that Heavenly Parent, True Parents and the good spirits are always with me to help me solve all my problems. Moreover, my irreplaceable, beloved spiritual children constantly give me the energy to move forward.

These days I ask myself, "What does it mean to be a parent?" I have learned that it is a very valuable path to understand and practice Heavenly Parent's love through creating a harmony of unconditional love toward my children in the Cain realm, just as I love my physical children.

I hope to set up an effective system to educate and organize all the families in my tribe and help them fulfill their own mission as heavenly tribal messiahs through blessing 430 couples. This is because I know that the path of a parent is to nurture and raise your children and help them to marry so they can have their own families.

I think I understand why True Parents have told us to become heavenly tribal messiahs. Heavenly tribal messiah activity creates an extended family community as a model to help perfect my own family. Raising my family to become a true family that represents God through nurturing and educating my family's spiritual children to become God's children brings amazing grace. After all, my family cannot reach perfection on its own. I have realized that I must enable the family of my spiritual children to reach perfection in order that my family can reach perfection. Furthermore, I have realized that heavenly tribal messiahship is a movement to extend the model of my family to my tribe, then help them make their own new heavenly tribe to perfect their family and eventually extend and engraft them to God's ideal family. In conclusion, the heavenly tribe community is the path of a parent and the path of the Messiah.

My remaining challenge as regional vice president of the Greater China Region is to complete the restoration mission of Taiwan by supporting 12 heavenly tribal messiahs to complete and fulfill their mission in Taiwan. My tribe has accomplished the blessing of 430 couples, so I will support my spiritual children to become heavenly tribal messiahs centering on this foundation. I will focus my utmost effort to guide my nation and my people to realize God's ideal, so we can sing a song of victory on that day of joy. Thank you.

Inariza Coco Lopez

Person giving Testimony	Husband's Name	Region	Nation
Inariza Coco Lopez	Francis Lopez	Asia	Philippines
Blessing Information	Number of Children	Spiritual Children (couples)	Number of Families Attending Church
360,000 Couples	2 daughters	430 couples	23 couples

3

A Fruitful Life Sharing Heaven's Blessings with the World

"
My longing heart to meet True Parents motivated me to do the work that would bring me closer to them. I realized that the way to be closer to Heavenly Parent is to unite with True Parents' words. We did hoondokhae every day, and every time we did hoondokhae, we felt that True Parents were with our family. As we read True Parents' words, we received the wisdom and power to accomplish what they have asked us to do.
"

It All Began with the Guidance and Love from True Parents

We are Francis Lopez and Inariza Coco Lopez. We live in the city of Antipolo in the Philippines. We received our Marriage Blessing in 1997, and we have two daughters aged 13 and 11. My husband, Francis Lopez, works as a lecturer at our workshop center, and I, Inariza Coco Lopez, organized a witnessing team in our area, so we could accomplish the heavenly tribal messiah mission and we were able to bless 475 families as our heavenly tribe.

We were motivated to do heavenly tribal messiah work after receiving spiritual guidance from True Parents. I used to dream of True Father, even before he went to the spirit world, and this motivated me to do heavenly tribal messiah work. True Father always hugged me warmly in my dreams. I felt he really wanted to tell me something, but I could not speak Korean, so he didn't say much; I just felt it with my heart. I think he was trying to encourage us to

Participants in an Interfaith Peace Family Blessing in the Lopez heavenly tribe

start our heavenly tribal messiah mission in the Philippines so that we could be a model to others of how to bring success, even though I was still lacking in many ways.

I told my husband about my dream and about my experience with True Father. It is True Parents' love for us that motivated us to do heavenly tribal messiah work.

We really love True Parents, and we have wanted to meet them for a long time. My longing heart to meet True Parents motivated me to do the work that would bring me closer to them. I realized that the way to be closer to Heavenly Parent is to unite with True Parents' words. We did hoondokhae every day, and every time we did hoondokhae, we felt that True Parents were with our family. As we read True Parents' words, we received the wisdom and power to accomplish what they have asked us to do.

As I was preparing to begin our heavenly tribal messiah activity, my biggest concern was our finances. My husband and I discussed it, and we realized that to do the tribal messiah work, we also would have to fundraise at the same time. We decided my husband would continue his mission as a lecturer. I had a teaching job, but I had a one-year leave. It paid a little, but not very much, so I had to find another job.

My witnessing area was rather poor. When we received the direction to restore 430 families, I thought we should find a place where nobody would want to go. My witnessing area always gets flooded when there are typhoons or storms. Two members, Bett and Joan, had a foundation in that area, so we made a trinity and went there for our witnessing activities.

Bett and Joan explained to me in detail the characteristics of the people in that area. They said there is a *barangai* (small township) where some members did holy wine ceremonies in 2005. So we went to that town and began visiting those couples who had received holy wine. First, we wanted to meet the church leader in the *barangai* and explain the purpose of our activities, but we were not able to meet him though we made several visits. We could not wait any longer, so we started our activities. A few days later, we bumped into him. He didn't seem to like what we were doing without any discussion or permission from him, but he did not reject or oppose it. A 13,000 Couples Blessing ceremony was being planned by the Philippines headquarters in Araneta a few months later, so we decided to bring our witnessing contacts to that Blessing ceremony.

Blessed Are the Poor, for Theirs Is the Kingdom of Heaven (Heavenly Tribal Messiah Activity)

With a clear goal of bringing people to the upcoming Blessing, and knowing how much time we had, we worked hard to focus on our witnessing activities. We reported daily to the national headquarters, and one week before the event, we confirmed that we had more than 1,200 candidates who were ready to come to the Blessing. People responded very positively to our invitations, and that encouraged us to work even harder. At the time, our national leader and regional director were checking our progress and praying for us, and when they saw a high probability for success, they sent more members to our area to support us. Twelve members who were attending a 120-day workshop at the International Peace Leadership College (the IPLC is an official school founded by True Parents) came to join us. We added three more *barangai* to our witnessing area. We divided the members into several teams and appointed one of the IPLC team members to lead each group.

In general, we visited people door to door, but we thought it would be more effective if we visited the leaders of each *barangai* and mobilized them to organize the activities. Therefore, when we visited the leaders, we tried to make good relationships with them

Member of the Lopez tribe attending True Father's Third Seonghwa Memorial (August, 2015)

first, instead of introducing the Divine Principle right away. While our members were working, I made good relationships with the leaders in the area, became like family to them and did volunteer work like cleaning the house and so on.

We had open meetings to explain what we were doing, and through those, we were able to bring many people to the Blessing ceremonies. We designated one place in the town, invited people and gave lectures on the five Peace Principles. Next, we introduced a part of the Divine Principle, had questions and answers, and finally we introduced True Parents as the founders of our Unification movement.

The pamphlet which we used to invite people had photos of True

A gathering of second generation children in the Lopez heavenly tribe

Parents and the *Divine Principle* book, and it was a very natural way to introduce True Parents. Most people in this area showed interest in true love, true parents and the vision of an ideal family. I invited my husband to give lectures to our guests. While my husband was giving lectures in one *barangai*, my family and the members who were responsible for inviting people to the lectures would move to the next *barangai* to prepare for the next meeting. Many people from each area and town showed interest. It was very important to mobilize wives from each town ahead of time. We made good relationships and became friends with them. While they were attending lectures, we looked after their children. We taught them many songs including our holy songs. People from really poor villages live in very humble houses, and their children don't have good toys to play with. So, when we visited those areas, we often provided food for them or at least some cookies and snacks to give to their children. We also gave them some toys and clothing we got as donations. In the Philippines, especially in the poor areas, people are happy if we give them something as a gift. The secret to our heavenly tribal messiah work was to find many opportunities like this to share with people.

God Works through Leaders Who Are in the Position of John the Baptist

We invited the *barangai* leaders to the Blessing ceremony. These people are usually very busy, as they have their own schedules and conduct many different projects. Therefore, we spent time meeting each leader in his own area. We sent True Parents' words by text message to those who were connected with us and had become blessed couples or made appointments with them to continue to share True Parents' words. After we had established some success with our Blessing activities in the *barangai*, surprising phenomena started to happen. One *barangai* leader in our area became a very close friend with us. I called him one day and said, "Sir, we educated and conducted the Blessing ceremony in your area last time, and so we would like to work in the neighboring area this time. What do you think?" and he said, "It would be difficult, as they have different commitments." "Then we should go to the next area to work," and he said again, "No. That place won't do." So I asked him where the best place would be, and he replied, "There are many people who haven't received the Blessing yet in our area. You should wait to go to other areas until after all our people receive the Blessing." As our Blessing movement spread throughout other areas, this particular town competed with them for the Blessing. We shared many stories with them about the grace of the Blessing, and as a result, they wanted people in their area to receive the Blessing first.

One day, they asked me to counsel and resolve an issue of a couple in their town who had had a big fight. We went to visit the couple, counseled them, and together resolved the issue. As our relationship with them grew stronger, they came to trust us more. On the day of the Blessing ceremony, we had to bring many people to the event location, and the leader in that area helped us with transportation using his own organization. We requested help from him when we visited again to follow up with the blessed couples who had received the Blessing education, and he always helped us and treated our activities as his priority. If he was too busy, he would call young leaders or people from his organization to give us a hand. We are making very good connections with the leaders. One day, this leader wanted to hear about the three-day ceremony. I said to him, "You are still single, so you cannot participate in the education for couples." He asked us to find him a bride, and he wants to receive the Blessing, so we are educating and witnessing to him.

As a Hen Gathers Her Brood under Her Wing (Resolve Organizational, Management or Economic Problems)

When we started, we never imagined how we could accomplish it. All I had was a truly loving heart toward True Parents and no desire to compete with anyone. Whenever I went witnessing with my husband, I thought to myself, "Even if we are so poor, let's love them, give them hope and help them. I will embrace and hug them earnestly." When our witnessing area was flooded, we cried in our hearts to save them; we didn't have much, but we tried to share food with them. Many people say people from these areas are very poor, but they are truly precious to us.

One time, Mr. Yong Jin-heon from the World Mission Department came to the Philippines and gave lectures on hoondok groups (home groups). I decided to make home groups because it was very difficult to follow up and take care of 430 couples. It is quite common to find witnessing contacts; however, it is not so easy to follow up and take care of them after that. Now I have appointed 12 team leaders in each area and plan to educate them more systematically. At least they can lead their own small groups. What we are hoping to do is educate a whole town to accept True Parents, then make a town for True Parents. Therefore, we organized small groups and appointed one hoondok leader for each group, so each leader can educate more than 12 couples. We want to educate them from the first chapter of the *Divine Principle* to the last chapter and prepare them to accept True Parents.

A heavenly tribal messiah gathering of the Lopez tribe

Some couples have different religions, but I don't hurry them to leave their belief and change their faith to ours. I would like to teach them to slowly change themselves. When we are having a hoondok meeting, we read from "True Family and I" and often share testimonies about True Parents and True Family. Most couples listen very attentively with deep interest. Some couples ask about the three-day ceremony, because they cannot understand its purpose. That is why we focus on educating wives first and then let the wives educate their husbands later. We formed groups so we could educate people in this way, and we expanded this model to other towns also.

There were many difficulties until we accomplished 430 couples, and one of the hardest was the financial burden. We prayed to

Heavenly Parent to send us someone who could help us. Stephen and Constance Gabb, who were also working on building their tribe, joined our team and took care of this problem. They helped to finance our activities tremendously. As we received help from them, we also prayed for their success in finding 430 couples. A heavenly tribal messiah partnership is very important.

Actually, when we accomplished the 430 couples Blessing, we didn't even know it. It happened in one moment, when we finally confirmed that we had accomplished blessing 475 couples. If no one fails in their 40-day separation or three-day ceremony, there will be more than 430 couples. Thus, we currently are educating 430 blessed couples. Among some of the blessed families, there are many children who are single and of marriageable age. We are interested in educating them as young leaders so that they can become Blessing candidates. We are in the process of educating the 430 couples and taking care of them, so they can multiply and take care of others.

You Must Experience Parental Love to Understand True Parents

We felt the most rewarding feeling after the blessing of 430 couples; those couples who finished the three-day ceremony were trying to truly love True Parents as my husband and I do. If I only wanted to fulfill the numbers of 430 couples to become a tribal messiah, I would have given up already. Actually, money didn't really matter when we did our activities. I experienced how God prepared and helped us when we needed it.

Through heavenly tribal messiah activity, I felt the earnest heart of True Parents, and every time I felt that, my love for True Parents grew stronger. Especially when I think of the pain True Parents went through, I want to lessen it. That is how I can keep moving on when I face challenges. When facing difficulties, I truly felt God and True Parents were with me and felt they loved us so much. What I felt in that position was something I could resonate with: parental love. When I look back on how we accomplished 430 couples, there were a lot of difficulties; however, I never complained to God even once. I only thought about following heaven's guidance with all my heart and dedication.

When I first visited God's homeland, Korea, I cried so much. I saw many people who were wealthy and had a lot of material things, but they could not understand True Parents' teachings or their directions. I always pray to God, "I will work hard, even offering my life."

When I heard how True Parents suffered all through their lives, I cried a lot at the Tree of Blessing while saying, "True Father, I am so sorry. I will accomplish True Parents' will with my family. I made up my mind. I don't have anything, but True Father continuously helps me. It's because God is alive and we are alive, too. I now understand the meaning of all the amazing blessings you have given me."

Marietes L. Sato

Person giving Testimony	Husband's Name	Region	Nation
Marietes L. Sato	Yoshihiro Yamaguchi	Asia	Philippines
Blessing Information	Number of Children	Spiritual Children (couples)	Number of Families Attending Church
6,500 Couples	2 sons	430 couples (162 couples finished three-day ceremony)	62 couples

4

I Will Make You a Great Nation and Make Your Name Great

> We have realized that doing tribal messiahship is not very easy. I have learned that although I have to sacrifice something Heaven always rewards that sacrifice. I was so busy carrying out the tribal messiah mission that there was hardly a day I could care for my own children. I could only see them once or twice a week and yet, thankfully, my children grew up well. I could only see my husband once a year and I could hardly spare the thought to care for him as well. Nevertheless, my husband did not hesitate to give me active support. My eldest son has grown up and already received the Blessing and my second has been matched despite his young age. My plan to focus on educating my tribe so that they can receive more blessings and to help other members become tribal messiahs.

The Family That Makes a Sincere Effort Is Following the Will of Heaven

I was born in the Philippines, and our family is very religious, especially on my mother's side. My mother gets up at 3:00 a.m. every day and starts the day with prayer.

I was influenced by my mother's devotion, and when I was in elementary school I had a desire to become a nun. When I was in college, this desire came back to me. At that time in the Philippines I was afraid of AIDS which was widespread and worried about how I could protect myself, so I would pray often.

The way I met the Unification Church is really a mystical story, but it is true. On June 24, 1984, I found a piece of paper with a message on it. The message was saying how I had to go to an organization. Otherwise someone would befall misfortune. I was very afraid to see this message. So I started praying conditionally. I did not rest during the day, but I prayed instead fifteen times a day. I gave this conditional prayer for a year. Meanwhile, on March 28, 1985, somebody invited me to the Unification Church, and I heard the Word. Then on June 12, I joined the church. It was just about a year since I had started being kind to everybody. I think now that God was guiding me to meet True Parents.

There is Good Fortune for Those Who are Poor

I am the first of six sons and two daughters. There were several temptations in situations where living conditions were difficult, but my mother was one with my father and kept my family until the end. My parents loved each other and us, the children had a very good feeling inside seeing this. We were living in poverty, but my mother was always very faithful to my father. In my memory, my mother has never upset my father.

It was really hard for them to keep all of my brothers in school due to our difficult circumstances. So my education was a problem I had to solve on my own. In order to make money to pay the tuition fee, I had to wash other people's clothes as a helper of a wealthy neighbor. I had a lot of brothers and I needed to be self-reliant. Nevertheless, I am always grateful and thankful that I was born, loved by, and was able to grow as a child of my parents. As a child I felt motivated to study hard in order to please my parents and I graduated from school with excellent grades.

A heavenly tribal messiah Blessing officiated by the Sato family

Leave your father's home in your homeland and go to the land that I point you to

Not long after I joined the church I had a spiritual experience right after the end of the 7 day Divine Principle workshop. Around that time my spiritual sister decided to devote herself as a full time member. I was still a college student and I could not be a full time member. At that time I was going to enroll in the school but I could not advance to my third year because I did not receive the report card from the previous school. So I decided to take advantage of the situation and become a full time member.

I went to the church center to report, and my spiritual sister was waiting for me. It was amazing how she and I knew I wanted to be a full time member. So when I asked what was going on, she told me about her spiritual experience. One day she was sleeping, and next to her in bed was someone who told her to quickly return to Butan. The sister was in a deep sleep state so the voices were dim but she heard the voice three times and so she came to pick me up in the city of Butan where I lived. So she said that she finally met me. She too could not believe her dream that day.

I went straight home to get permission from my parents. At the time my father was very sick. As the eldest of the eight brothers and sisters it was not so easy to leave as I had responsibilities. I was responsible for many things, but that same position did not stop me from dedicating myself to my Heavenly Parent. Because when I was a child, I wanted to devote myself to Heaven enough to make a decision to become a nun. My parents were shocked to hear this because they had not expected even in their dreams that I would become a missionary in my second year of university. I convinced my parents to let me go, and I told them the story of Abraham. Abraham had only one son, born when he was already 100 years old, but when God told him to offer his son as a sacrifice, Abraham listened to God. I told them I also wished to do everything in accordance with God's Will. My father did not say anything, but he gave me one last hug as he shed tears. I knew it would be a last hug, because I would not have any chance to return home to visit after I left. True Father went up to North Korea according to the Word of

God and preached the truth, and when he came to the south with his disciples after he came out of Heungnam prison, he was unable to visit his parents. I felt the heart of God as I did not meet my family for seven years. Five years after I left, my father passed away, but I did not know about it because I was completely involved in my mission.

My Commitment to Be Like True Parents

In 1990, I was selected to be a missionary in Korea, so I went fundraising to prepare for my mission. While I was fundraising, I met one of my relatives and he told me that my father had passed away. She said that since I wasn't there at the time of his passing, I should visit his grave as soon as possible, but I could not go because I had to leave for Korea. I shed many tears in my heart and asked forgiveness from my father in the spirit world. I told him that allowing me to serve Heavenly Parent, allowing me to become a missionary, was his best accomplishment in life, and I hoped he would feel happy about it. I am sure that I was right, because after my Blessing, my father came to me in a dream and told me that I was blessed well and that my husband was a good person.

Experiencing the Heart of Heavenly Parent through the Trials of Witnessing in the Early Days

Just after I joined the church in 1985, there was a 40-day workshop. At that time, I witnessed to a single sister, who became a full-time member. But she became pregnant three months later; the church leader encouraged her to have an abortion, but she disagreed. I was devastated when I heard about it. Because of that, I felt the heart of God for the first time. I realized the desperate feeling that the whole world had collapsed. She was deceived by her boyfriend, and had committed a fault that could not be cleansed in front of Heaven. She suffered from this experience. She gave birth to the baby and we decided to find someone to adopt. Fortunately, we became aware of members who had been wanting to adopt a child for a long time. The couple who adopted the child eventually received the Blessing, and the child was raised in a church environment.

I was quite lucky to be chosen as CARP coordinator as one of my earliest missions. I witnessed to a lot of students, but unfortunately, only one of them stayed. I witnessed to two sisters who attended the whole 21-day workshop. But unfortunately, right after the workshop finished, their boyfriends came to pick them up, and we never saw them again. I waited and believed they would come back, but they didn't. I realized how God must have felt when he lost Adam due to the Fall, and I understood how long God had begged him to return.

Once when I was very sick while I was attending my second

seven-day workshop, I had a dream. In my dream I went fishing, and all I could catch was snakes. I realized that the snake represented the sisters I tried to witness to and the dream implied that they were having Chapter Two problems. Yet I realized that the Heavenly Parent's was not worried. Therefore, I had a desperate need to reassure God, and without knowing my tears flowed in silence. It was so fortunate that I was able to find my Heavenly Parent's children again despite such pain and was comforted.

I had a spiritual daughter whose process towards the blessing was derailed. I hoped she would come back and go through conditions to receive forgiveness and receive the Blessing again but she did not. I'm still uncertain if I can be grateful before Heaven for what happened, but even with that result, I was able to realize that God does not break the broken reeds, nor does He turn off the flaming fire. Like God, we should keep trying to save our children until we succeed.

Tribal Messiahship is a Blessing Given by True Parents

I was a missionary to Korea on behalf of the Philippines. I worked at the International Training Center at the *Segye Times*, and True Father gave the message, "Tribal Messiahs" while educating many leaders. These words sounded miraculously accurate tome, and I am grateful that I was there at that time to hear it.

After being blessed with a Japanese husband in 1990, I remembered what Father had said, and I decided to become a tribal messiah. However, when I left the Philippines and went to Japan with my husband, I could not witness successfully, no matter how hard I tried.

Because of that, I became bitter and sick and eventually became seriously ill. I was always depressed and I did not know what to do with my life. So I decided to go back to the Philippines.

When I returned to my home country, I was miraculously healed and my health improved gradually. I decided to open a center in my hometown and start working for the providence again. I worked with a friend at the center until I was appointed as a leader. At that time, we Blessed a lot of single people. I started to do Blessings for already married couples, but only a few of them managed to do the three-day ceremony.

At that time, I had a strong connection with the mayor of my hometown and the congressman, so I had a good external environment for the tribal messiah movement. With the help of the congressman, we were given free use of city-owned facilities for our events. But suddenly I was called to Manila as the secretary general World Peace Youth League When I thought about the foundation in my hometown, I thought perhaps all the people we had witnessed to and blessed would drift away because I was not there to take care of them. However, in 2012 I was suddenly motivated to become a tribal messiah and to do tribal messiah work. Even though it was not in my hometown I felt relaxed.

In 2013, Yong Chung-sik, the regional director of Asia at the

A Heavenly Tribal Messiah Ambassadors for Peace Two-Day Seminar in the Sato tribe

time, encouraged tribal messiah activities and said that if we were to host a Blessing ceremony of 1,200 couples in a large-scale stadium in Manila, we would need to come up with 120,000 dollars. At once I sold the house that my father-in-law left us to donate the money. I purchased 430 copies of True Father's autobiography and distributed them. I then donated the remaining money to building a new church headquarters.

Some people laughed that I was crazy to sell the house, but I did not care much because I knew that True Father had already gave me the mission of the tribal messiah from his message in the 1990s. The idea of becoming a tribal Messiah was also the cause of being separated from the husband, as the tribal Messiah activity in Japan was not possible. At the time, I offered a lot of jeongseong and effort to witness for seven years, but no one was connected. We have realized that doing tribal messiahship is not very easy. I have learned that although I have to sacrifice something Heaven always rewards that sacrifice. I was so busy carrying out the tribal messiah mission that there was hardly a day I could care for my own children. I could only see them once or twice a week and yet, thankfully, my children grew up well. I could only see my husband once a year and I could hardly spare the thought to care for him as well. Nevertheless, my husband did not hesitate to give me active support. My eldest son has grown up and already received the Blessing and my second has been matched despite his young age. My plan to focus on educating my tribe so that they can receive more blessings and to help other members become tribal messiahs.

Blessing Events in Earnest

In this era of large-scale witnessing, we could no longer focus on just one person. One thing that is unique about my witnessing program is that I have a degree programs in 14 local villages in my hometown area. I am in direct contact with the leaders of the villages, and they can provide education to the families and young people in the village to which they belong. We work with the village leaders to organize seminars to strengthen the family bonds, and we will celebrate Blessings in the future. The leaders of the villages think that we are genuinely helping them, and they give us their cooperation for the Blessings we are preparing to conduct.

Based on their trust in us, they invite young people through the leaders of youth organizations. However, in order to focus properly on the villages, we have reduced the number of villages to five and currently we only work in four locations. Heaven has blessed us a lot and the process has been very educational. In particular, I was given various missions and responsibilities. These included education for the home group providence and trinities followed by establishing a tribal messiahship system. We can recruit members by holding two-day intermediate seminars each week. With the help of the Philippine headquarters, we have set up an education system for our tribe. Our education programs are about principles and traditions, the value of our ancestors and the tribal messiah movement. For teaching in the home groups, we use the *Divine Principle*, True Father's autobiography and messages from *Cheon Seong Gyeong*.

We also are still looking for ways to overcome financial problems and support our people. We have established plans for our tribe as follows:

1. Hold a general meeting of ethnic groups once a year
2. Appoint young people of our tribe as youth peace ambassadors
3. Register our Blessing Family Association in the community to get support from community leaders
4. Establish and operate a cooperative shop in each region

5. Organize and operate service projects to increase the influence of our tribe in the community

Organizing and Operating Service Projects to Raise Our Influence in the Local Community

At present, our tribe has 162 families who have completed the 40-day separation period and the three-day ceremony. We have blessed more than 430 families but within that number, there are still 270 families who need to complete the three-day ceremony. My challenge is how to educate them and guide them to complete the three-day ceremony and make them true children of True Parents. Fortunately, the home groups and trinity system give us a good system with which to manage and educate our tribe. This method plays an important role in establishing hoondokhae and one's identity as a Unificationist. We are creating good, cooperative relationships with the local communities and working on creating a center where our tribe can meet.

One of the things that we are doing is expanding cooperative shops with several local businesses or restaurants. While conducting a true family movement we are building a business alliance. It is a gathering of exemplary business owners who promise to maintain purity and unite with our spouses. These people then hang a certificate in their establishment and offer discounts to other members of the alliance. When these people become members, we hope that they can provide financial support toward the tribal messiah movement.

In conclusion, our plan for 2020 and our goal is to educate all of our people to become dedicated members and then help them to become tribal messiahs themselves and flourish. Thank you.

Mayuri Hoffman

Person giving Testimony	Husband's Name	Region	Nation
Mayuri Hoffman	Dennis Hoffman	North America	United States
Blessing Information	Number of Children	Spiritual Children (couples)	Number of Families Attending Church
2,075 Couples	1 child	1,358 couples	12 couples

5

When We See the World Through Parents' Eyes, Love Is the Only Way

> Every time I go out witnessing, I feel the heart of True Parents. I concentrate my whole mind on my guests, and I am anxious to know what they are doing all day. I cannot help but think of them with a parental heart, hoping that their faith will grow. I have thought to myself, "What makes True Parents true parents?" I get restless when I have even a few guests, but when I think about True Parents, who are reaching out to every one of us with a parental heart in order to save humanity, I realize, "Witnessing starts not from focusing on increasing the number of church members, but from facing each person with a parental heart. I am now in the process of being educated to become a true parent." This changed my perspective on witnessing. Witnessing is loving humanity and caring for the people around us with a parental heart.

God Who Came to Me and Loved Me

Before joining the Unification Church, I had been a Christian since I was five years old. Of course, I was merely following my parents' faith, but I still remember the feeling or atmosphere during Mass in the cathedral.

When I was ten years old, my aunt, who was paralyzed, was living with us. One day I heard my aunt crying. I did not understand why she was crying, but I remember her crying very bitterly. Having her living with us made my whole family very sensitive, and I too was very edgy. Since that time, I had mixed feelings toward my aunt. Knowing it was not her fault, part of me felt pity for her, but I also wanted to avoid her. I guess I was sensitive about it because I was in my teens.

During that difficult time Jesus came to me. He said, "I understand your suffering heart." His voice was so clear. Bewildered, I looked around to see if anyone was there, but nobody was around. Jesus came to me frequently, and I heard the same voice. I felt my whole body shiver.

Ever since, I have served him in my heart and approached him with love and respect. My love and admiration for him were much more than a simple external faith. Rather, they came from my inner heart. I started to give a lot of thought to religious faith. I was at a turning point and was re-examining my life and my faith. Up to that point I had simply gone to church to follow my parents. Searching for the truth, I read two books everyday related to religion and faith. Moreover, I prayed everyday with an earnest hope to communicate with God. By doing this, I developed a strong sense of mission in my heart.

That mission was none other than to "love the people." I have treasured this mission, given to me by God, deep within my heart, and it has been a driving force that has enabled me to work hard up to this day. Since then, I have put all my effort into loving the people around me with a sincere heart. Gradually I came to better understand my paralyzed aunt, and I started to love her from my heart with real sincerity. When I invest my heart in loving people, I find my relationship with God becoming closer, and I long to talk with Him.

I try to visit the Holy Ground every morning and pray to God, "I love you. I love you with tears."

Then God will say, "When you love your brothers and sisters, I will be with you."

Since my childhood, God has brightened my life by coming to me like this and resting within my heart.

Please Reveal Your Love within My Heart

Later I learned the Divine Principle and was called by God to join the Unification Church. My family in Japan has deep unity of heart centered on True Parents' words and teachings. This has prevented me from being lazy in church activities.

As I mentioned earlier, my family lived with and cared for my paralyzed aunt, and they had very good relationships with the relatives not only on my father's side but also on my mother's side. My family always cared for and cherished one another, and people envied us for being such a loving family. I believe that God's revelation to us about how to deal with difficulties through love has been the salvation of our family. Our family's happy atmosphere was the foundation that guided our relatives to join the Unification Church and lead them to the Blessing.

My parents were my first spiritual children. I witnessed to them when I was in Japan before getting Blessed. At first, they were very negative toward the church, but because they loved me, they opened their hearts in order to understand me. I was fortunate to have such goodhearted parents. After my father attended the three-day workshop, he began to understand what I was doing and to support me in church activities.

I Took the Path to Become a Parent According to His Practice of Love

Faith and trust helped me embrace God's deep love and maintain a devotional atmosphere even after I came to the United States to join my husband. My husband and I visited his family and friends and introduced them to the Divine Principle as we showed them True Parents' picture. Although it took some time, everyone in my husband's family attended workshops and received the Blessing. I am truly grateful to Heavenly Parent and True Parents for this.

When my husband and I came back to South Dakota, my husband took me to the holy ground. It was located at a Native American burial ground. I felt the suffering of the Native Americans. When I prayed in tears, I thought, "If even one Native American receives the Blessing, this suffering will be liberated." This is how I headed to the library to study the history of South Dakota's Native Americans.

As I studied, I learned about the Wounded Knee Massacre. About 125 years ago, at Wounded Knee, there was a spiritual movement that gathered to do the Ghost Dance, which was a dance to welcome the Indian messiah (the messiah of the Native American belief). While they were in the middle of the ceremony at Wounded Knee, the American soldiers killed over 300 people, including babies.

I am Japanese, and my husband is a white American. Suddenly I realized that we both had ancestors who had committed the historical mistake of torturing other races or peoples. Deeply repenting

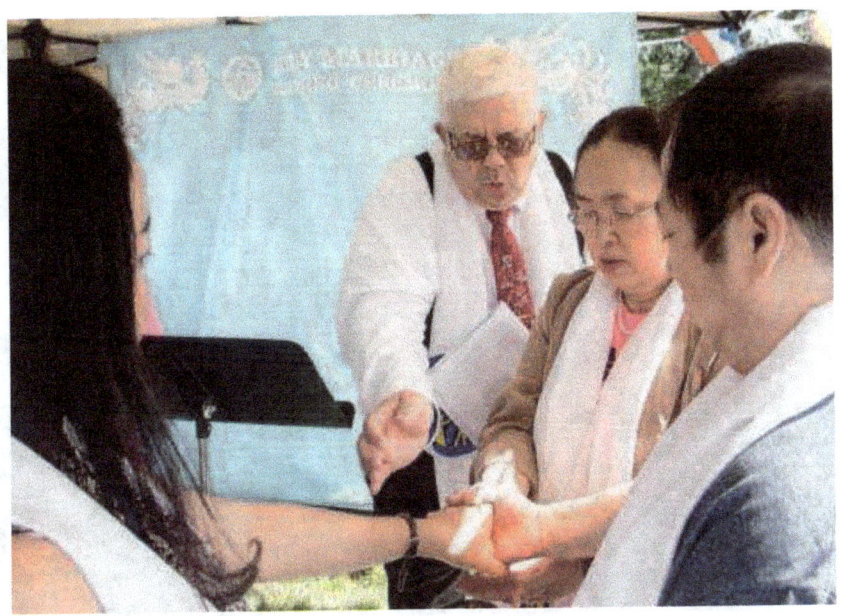

The Dennis and Mayuri Hoffman family officiating a heavenly tribal messiah Blessing

for our historical mistakes, we decided to make the eight-hour trip to Wounded Knee many times over the course of six months. We visited each family in Wounded Knee and spent at least two hours at each house, conveying True Parents' words through the Divine Principle, the value of true families and the Blessing, along with our apologies for the historical pain our lineages had caused them. We also prayed earnestly and strived to show them the heart of True Parents and God, who have loved us constantly as they carried out the providence of restoration.

God heard our sincere prayers. One by one, they began to join the Unification Church. We gave the Blessing to the principal head chief of Red Cloud; the bishop of the Native American Church of

True Parents with a Native American blanket presented by the members of the Hoffman tribe

Jesus Christ, Rev. Emerson Spider; the minister of the Native American Church, Rev. Rene Mills; and the community leaders, Mr. and Mrs. Charles and Elaine Quiver. All of them received the Blessing directly from True Parents in Korea.

At the same time, we gave the Blessing to Christian ministers. True Parents sent Japanese missionaries to each state, so we traveled with them as they visited each church in South Dakota, Nebraska and Iowa. As a result, more than 140 ministers received the Blessing. Seven ministers attended the three-day Divine Principle workshop, and one of them was blessed with a Japanese missionary by True Parents. They now have four beautiful second-generation children.

When I was carrying out the 360-family home church activities,

I had guests attending workshops every weekend. Two of them joined the church and received the Blessing. I remember offering a 40-hour fast for my guests every weekend. After they joined the church, I called them to pray and offer jeongseong together every day and support their spiritual growth.

Every time I go out witnessing, I feel the heart of True Parents. I concentrate my whole mind on my guests, and I am anxious to know what they are doing all day. I cannot help but think of them with a parental heart, hoping that their faith will grow. I have thought to myself, "What makes True Parents true parents?" I get restless when I have even a few guests, but when I think about True Parents, who are reaching out to every one of us with a parental heart in order to save humanity, I realize, "Witnessing starts not from focusing on increasing the number of church members, but from facing each person with a parental heart. I am now in the process of being educated to become a true parent." This changed my perspective on witnessing. Witnessing is loving humanity and caring for the people around us with a parental heart.

I listened carefully to my guests so that I could understand their happiness and their suffering. The more communication I had with them, the more I united with them in heart. As a result, they came to trust me very deeply. Whenever I asked for help, they would trust me and would help me out. For example, it took only one phone call for a Native American, Mrs. Elaine Quiver, to bring many leaders to our events in South Dakota.

She had her own radio station. Every time we visited that area, she announced, "Dennis and Mayuri will be visiting your home to give you the Blessing!" She also read True Parents' book *Gateway to Heaven* on the radio station. Everybody in the area heard True Parents' words and were educated through her. Moreover, she would read True Parents' words whenever there was a big meeting. When I called her and said, "Thank you a million times!" she said, "I am your angel!"

When the American Leadership Conference was held at Sioux Falls, I was wearing a blue dress. Mrs. Quiver told me that the dress was very beautiful, so I gave her the dress as a gift after the conference was over. She came to me and said, "I love you, and I will continue to help you!" Although it was a small gift, I learned that when you give unconditionally, people will give you their heart. I sometimes think about True Parents' love and how they taught us to continuously give and forget that you have given. I feel that practicing this kind of giving will grow my parental heart toward my children in the realm of Cain.

Usually, people stay home for a while after they lose their parents. However, when we held a meeting at Sioux Falls, Mr. Quiver said, "Mayuri is calling us. Let's go!" and attended throughout the meeting, even though it had not been long since his mother had passed away.

Parents Must Take Responsibility for Children in the Spirit World

My parents were my first spiritual children. I met my second spiritual son when I was witnessing on the street. My third spiritual son joined the church through a video center. Unfortunately, he died of cancer before receiving the Blessing. He received a single spirit Blessing on June 17, 2017. My husband went to the CheongPyeong Training Center in Korea from May 3 to June 19 to attend the single spirit Blessing. We also gave the single spirit Blessing to my aunt on my father's side who was paralyzed. Our spiritual children also received the Blessing. My husband and I love CheongPyeong and visit there often. My family and I think that ancestral liberation and ancestral blessing are parts of our activities as heavenly tribal messiahs. We are working on blessing our ancestors up to the 420th generation. So far we have completed blessing our ancestors up to the 267–273 generation group.

The Way I Guide and Establish Spiritual Children

We continued our home church activities to give the Blessing. For my husband and me, the core of witnessing is house-to-house visits. We carry out Blessing activities and connect our guests to the church through our visits. We also visit Christian churches. As a result, we have had seven ministers attend the three-day Divine Principle workshop. I visit not only the ministers' homes but also my spiritual children's homes with my husband on a regular basis to study the *Divine Principle* with them. To strengthen their foundation as blessed families, we study the Divine Principle DVD and read *Gateway to Heaven* and *Cheon Seong Gyeong* and discuss what we have read together so that they can understand and be inspired by True Parents' teachings.

I take the ministers' wives shopping and buy each of them a nice dress. Around Christmas, I buy gifts for all their children. I do not do this because I am rich but because my conscience tells me to love my children in the realm of Cain just like I love my children in the realm of Abel. When I behave like a generous parent to them, they treat me like a real parent without reserve. The amount of love you invest in others will be revealed in how they recognize you. This determines whether you are an acquaintance, a sibling or a parent to them.

I also take the time to share special events or historical materials with them. We watch DVDs of the Madison Square Garden event, the Fifth Anniversary of True Father's Seonghwa or the Holy Marriage Blessing to develop their understanding regarding True Parents' providence, and I listen to their feedback. We sometimes invite them to Rev. Hakim's house. He is an influential figure in this area. We read *Chambumo Gyeong* and discuss our questions and inspirations, so the guests can realize who True Parents are. Then we enjoy dinner together.

A Hoffman family portrait

Conducting and Managing Hoondok Family Meetings (Tribal Meetings)

Nowadays, at our hoondok family meetings, we show the videos of the Fifth Anniversary of True Father's Seonghwa, the Madison Square Garden event and the Holy Marriage Blessing. We also study *Cheon Seong Gyeong*, *Chambumo Gyeong* and the *Divine Principle* and have discussions based on our guests' feedback.

My husband and I both work full time to support our work. We usually hold meetings at our home or Rev. Hakim's home. For bigger events, we use conference rooms in local hotels or country inns.

Although we have a certain number of active members in our tribe, we still do not have a church building. This is our main difficulty in carrying out activities to accomplish our mission as tribal messiahs and to realize Vision 2020. We will continue to bless more people and give them Divine Principle education. We also will strive to practice what we have learned from True Parents' words. In *Chambumo Gyeong*, it says that "Tribal messiahs must go beyond the family messiahs. A tribe includes two family names—the wife and mother's name and the husband and father's name. The tribal messiah is the messiah for two names. Next, you must organize a people (in order to obtain the names of your mother and father). A people consists of 12 tribes. If these tribes unite they will be able to form a nation." [CBG 12:2:7:2]

We are striving to make this happen according to True Parents' words. Furthermore, according to *Chambumo Gyeong*, "As a tribal messiah you have three important missions: First, you must restore your ancestors; second, you must restore your hometown; third… you must live with God in your family." [CBG 12:2:2:26]

Although my husband and I have developed a foundation in this community to some degree, it is still not enough. We must look after our spiritual tribe and continue to give them systematic education. We must build a community center, too. We still have not done enough to be called the mother and father of this local community. I do believe we finally have gotten past the beginning stage and have entered the stage of extending and establishing the tradition of our tribe. Looking back, I realize that all this was possible only as a result of living in accordance with the practice of love we have learned from Heavenly Parent and True Parents. Thank you very much.

Ahn Dong-heon

Person giving Testimony	Husband's Name	Region	Nation
Ahn Dong-heon	Yoon Won-il	Korea	Korea
Blessing Information	Number of Children	Spiritual Children (couples)	Number of Families Attending Church
430 Couples	1 son, 1 daughter	500 couples (Thailand) 180 couples (Korea)	150 couples (Thailand) 40 couples (Korea)

6

May Your Sorrow and Pain Become a Glorious Medal of Happiness and Joy

"

Actually, I think there is no need for us to search for witnessing guests when we go out witnessing. There is a saying in Buddhism, "Even a chance acquaintance is decreed by destiny." True Parents told us to love even the crawling ants in our mission area. Having heard these words directly from True Father, I have them in mind whenever I go out witnessing. Therefore, every person I meet on the street seems like the person God has prepared for me to witness to.

Whenever and wherever I met someone and had the time and opportunity, I would prepare and convey something from True Parents' words that might apply to that person. One day, when I was making home visits, there was a person who stubbornly opposed True Parents. As I left, I gently said, "Let's meet again sometime," promising to meet in the future and shedding tears alone. Later, I started sending him a monthly magazine published by FFWPU every month without fail. At the end of 15 years, he was able to receive the Blessing.

"

While Longing for My Father's Love I Encounter God

I was born as the youngest of four children in the head household of my clan during a time when people strictly believed in Confucianism. My father died when I was five years old, so my mother had to raise four children alone as a single mother. Seeing my mother's loneliness, I often longed for my father and thought, "What would a father's love be like?"

One day, my married sister came back home divorced because of infertility. My mother and sister cried in bed every night. Curiously, many daughters of our clan lived in misery. Many of them were divorced due to infertility or else their husband or they themselves met an early death. Such situations made me decide to live a single life.

Giving up on marriage, I got a job raising funds to run a farm. I also started taking classes at a Chinese academic institute, thinking that since "knowledge is power," it would enable me to support myself as a single woman. The director of the institute, Rev. Lee Wol-seong, gave a lecture on ethics every Wednesday, which later turned out to be lectures on the human Fall. During one lecture, a question arose within me. When I asked, "What is Satan, to torture human beings like that?" the director said, "You will get the answer to your question in a lecture we have scheduled in a few days." A few days later, on the specified date, a visiting lecturer, Rev. Ahn Chang-seong, a 36 blessed couple, came to give a lecture on the Principle of Creation. Hearing his lecture, I decided to join the church.

I Must Fulfill the Heavenly Tribal Messiah Mission at the Risk of My Life

Since I joined the church, I have never been able to read through the Divine Principle or the volumes of True Parents' collected speeches all at once. It may seem like an excuse, but it is true. As soon as I read one page in the Divine Principle, I want to convey the contents I have just read to somebody else. When the face of the person I want to witness to pops into my head, I have to move my feet right away. I can feel at ease only after doing this. That habit has never changed up to this day.

I have always felt uncomfortable when I was not meeting people. The heavenly tribal messiah mission is an extension of my life of witnessing. I grew impatient as I reached the age of 70, and every

A yearend gathering by the Yoon Won-il, Ahn Dong-heon heavenly tribe (2015)

time I prayed I said, "I shall complete the blessing of 430 couples before I go to the spirit world."

I would pray, "Heavenly Parent, I cannot die without blessing 430 couples" and "You cannot take me to the spirit world before I accomplish my mission." Whenever a church leader was newly appointed to our church, I told him, "Please help me. I must not die before I fulfill my mission as a heavenly tribal messiah!"

When I was in this state of such dreadful anxiety, my son, Yoon Do-young, asked me, "Mother, do you want to fulfill the mission that much?" Since then, I have worked with him. Our family already had a foundation of more than 160 couples in Korea. My son took me to Thailand, and, with his help, I was able to accomplish 430 couples. I am fortunate to be writing this testimony today, because God worked through my spiritual children in Korea to provide the Blessing fees (Yoo Geun-ok cooperated while going through cancer treatment) and because of the hard work and jeongseong of the members in Thailand.

In Witnessing, You Must be Grateful Even for a Chance Acquaintance

Actually, I think there is no need for us to search for witnessing guests when we go out witnessing. There is a saying in Buddhism, "Even a chance acquaintance is decreed by destiny." True Parents told us to love even the crawling ants in our mission area. Having heard these words directly from True Father, I have them in mind whenever I go out witnessing. Therefore, every person I meet on the street seems like the person God has prepared for me to witness to.

Whenever and wherever I met someone and had the time and opportunity, I would prepare and convey something from True Parents' words that might apply to that person. One day, when I was making home visits, there was a person who stubbornly opposed True Parents. As I left, I gently said, "Let's meet again sometime," promising to meet in the future and shedding tears alone. Later, I started sending him a monthly magazine published by FFWPU every month without fail. At the end of 15 years, he was able to receive the Blessing.

Even if we join the church, it is not easy to continuously maintain a life of faith. There have been many cases when someone leading a life of faith suddenly abandoned his or her beliefs and drifted apart from the church as if they had never received the Blessing.

Each time this happened to one of my witnessing contacts, all I could do was simply believe that they had gotten caught up in some unavoidable circumstances and try to offer them some comfort. If I could have solved the problems they faced, witnessing definitely would have been easy. However, since the tests they face are part of their portion of responsibility to solve, all I can do is pray to God and treat them as if we have just met each other.

The part I like the most in the Divine Principle is the part on the "individual embodiments of truth." This is the part of which I remind myself the most whenever I try to understand people. I will tell myself, "That's right. God has created human beings as individual truth bodies." I avoid looking at people's' shortcomings and try to create a habit of liking people instead. Thanks to this habit, people around me who used to reject me stopped doing so. Through 16 years of social volunteer activities, I have mobilized thousands of people to True Parents' assemblies and still am mobilizing people without rest. I am very thankful for being able to do this.

Members of the Yoon Won-il, Ahn Dong-heon heavenly tribe visiting Yeosu holy ground (2016)

Spiritual Children Are Unexpected Good Fortune Given to Me by God

There are many outstanding spiritual children I cannot forget. I would like to introduce some of them here. My first spiritual child is my friend Pak Gil-ja. I introduced her to the church as soon as I decided to join. She is like a fellow traveler on the way to the kingdom of heaven, rather than a spiritual child.

There are also spiritual children who do not hesitate to offer their heart and soul to support me. I went church pioneering in Inchang-ri, Guri, in 1980 as part of the three-year mobilization of elder church families. The Hwang Jae-chan and Choi Myeong-im family was the first to whom my husband and I witnessed during the 360-family witnessing activity in Inchang-ri. This family joined the church and received the Blessing as an already married couple. They made their home into a church, dedicating themselves and treating us as ministers. Almost 90 percent of their village was witnessed to, centering on this family.

Our family moved to the city of Cheongju in Chungbuk province, which we set up as our witnessing post for the 360-family witnessing activity. Another spiritual child is Kim Yeon-soon, whom my daughter (Soon-shin) met at a local elementary school mothers' association here in Cheongju. She has a gentle character, and she does not change her mind easily, once she has decided something. She received the Blessing with her husband, Pak Bok-gyu, as an already married couple. She is one of the most active members among our heavenly tribal messiah group and has brought seven couples among her family and relatives to the Blessing. Her son has received an international Blessing with a Japanese wife.

There are also spiritual children who joined the church through unexpected good fortune from God. For ten years, from 1987 to 1997, thanks to God's grace, I was able to volunteer for the community as a New Village (*Saemaul*) leader in Cheongju while dedicating myself as an evangelist and assistant church leader at the South Cheongju Church. I would go to the church every day and visit the blessed families affiliated with the church. On Saturdays, I guided and taught the student members.

One day when I was teaching our student members at the church, a young man (Hong Seong-dal) came in, saying he had been drawn toward the building by the sound of holy songs, which he heard while passing. Right after I gave him a short lecture on the Principle of Creation, he filled in the membership application form and joined the church. He later was blessed as a Korean–Japanese couple and now has three second-generation children.

Only a Firm Vow, Action and Prayer Can Guide You to Victory

I always look for new people to witness to. Once True Father looked at me and said, "Why are you so greedy?" He was alluding to my constant desire to witness, which has been the motivation for me to tirelessly carry on my life of faith.

When I look back on my path of faith, I always have been delighted, happy and cheerful. Other members say that they are moved by testimonies of hardship. However, because I was always happy in my life of witnessing, I do not think I had a hard time. When I was witnessing in my appointed post, I lived on flour and salt soup, because there was no rice, and I could not warm myself in freezing cold weather. Life was tough when I ran short on food, clothing and shelter. However, all of these did not matter so much to me. It is the same now as it was in the past.

My motto in witnessing is intention, action and prayer. Whenever and wherever I met people, my first concern was how to guide them to the church. Moreover, I never gave up on people once I became acquainted with them.

In the 1960s when I joined the church, I visited my close friends and acquaintances to give them Divine Principle lectures. In the 1970s, I moved to the mission posts to which True Parents dispatched me and witnessed to my relatives and the local residents by handing out flyers and conveying the word to them. I would visit homes, and once a connection was made, I attended and served them, conveying the Divine Principle at the same time.

In the 1980s, during the 360-family witnessing activity, True Parents told us to love not only the people in our mission posts but also the cows, horses, pigs, dogs, chickens and even the ants. I searched for spiritual children by visiting homes with Victory over Communism newspapers and by inviting the people I met while I was doing social service work to events held by True Parents.

In the 2000s, I distributed the ambassador for peace newspaper to the people I met through community services and sent it by post to people who lived farther away. I also handed it out directly to people living in my neighborhood. In the 2010s, I distributed more than 500 copies of True Father's autobiography to my spiritual children and relatives and mobilized guests to ambassador for peace educational programs and events held by headquarters. I think I can sum up my method of witnessing as "home visiting and mobilization of guests to church events."

Since 2013, my tribe and I have formed groups for full-scale heavenly tribal messiah activities. First, we formed a special prayer

Members of the Yoon Won-il, Ahn Dong-heon heavenly tribe attending a workshop in Korea

team and offered 40 bows and 40-day special prayer for three years. I divided my spiritual children into groups—Divine Principle education, Korean traditional music, choir, etc.—and had them perform or lecture at church events. I made pilgrimages to holy grounds with my spiritual children. If there were events, such as a Korean traditional game tournament or a year-end party, I gave Divine Principle lectures in the middle of the event. I also guided new members to the Blessing. I still am supporting them, so they can fully establish their faith. Moreover, with the cooperation of the members in Thailand, I was able to fulfill the heavenly tribal messiah 430-couples Blessing in 2016. I am truly grateful to the members in Thailand.

Create a Tribal Culture and Establish a Tradition

The mission of the heavenly tribal messiah doesn't end with the Blessing. We must raise each member of the tribe, so they also can become heavenly tribal messiahs. Hence, guidance and education must be provided starting from the stage prior to the Blessing.

For members who are not yet blessed, I usually put priority on giving them Divine Principle lectures and mobilizing them to church events. I then embrace them with love and guide them to the Blessing. Second, I tell them to read the one-hour manual of the Divine Principle and encourage them to become lecturers in order to develop their faith. Third, I encourage them to offer 40 bows and prayer every day. Fourth, I urge them to report every matter to their tribal messiah. Lastly, I believe it is very important to keep track of my spiritual family's major life events families joys and sorrows. I develop my relationships with them through home visits and phone calls and take part in commemorating their births as well as deaths.

I think it is also important to establish a tribal tradition. We practice the following among my tribe.

First of all, we emphasize church traditions. Therefore, on the eight major holy days, we celebrate the holy day at the house of a heavenly tribal messiah, or at the home of a family in the tribe that wants to host the event, before attending the event held at the church. All members of the tribe take part in preparing the offering table, participating in the pledge service, and enjoying a hyojeong (filial heart) concert.

Second, we hold Korean traditional cultural events. On lunar New Year's Day and *Chuseok*, we set up an offering table for True Parents at our heavenly tribal messiah's house. The family of the heavenly tribal messiah and other members of the tribe prepare the offering table.

Third, we make pilgrimages to the holy grounds together for the unity of our tribe. Since a pilgrimage tour is a combination of sightseeing and faith education, not only does it have a high educational effect but also it is something tribe members like to do.

Furthermore, we hold gatherings in which members of the tribe can spend their leisure time together pursuing true family happiness through hobby activities. To make this happen, it is important to support small group activities. We organize small group activities according to groups based on age, hobbies, and talent and encourage them to hold monthly meetings. During the meetings we encourage the group members to hold hoondok sessions, read True Parents' words, discuss tribal events, and attend church events. One of the most attended activities these days is the tribal hyojeong concert.

Operation and Management of a Hoondok Family Church (Tribal Gatherings)

(1) Textbooks

- One-hour manual of the Divine Principle, True Father's Autobiography, *Cheon Seong Gyeong*, *Pyeong Hwa Gyeong*, and

Chambumo Gyeong

(2) Organization (Korea)
- (Korea) Home groups in Cheongju: establish a general affairs department, education department, culture department, and second-generation department
- (Thailand) Seven home groups (Sam Chai and Kham Muang District in Kalasin Province)

(3) Hoondok Sessions
- Read the one-hour manual of the Divine Principle 100 times; read True Father's autobiography in full; read *Cheon Seong Gyeong, Pyeong Hwa Gyeong, Chambumo Gyeong* during prayer sessions

(4) Our Way of Operating the Four-Position Foundations (Small Teams) and Home Groups
- Organize a special prayer team, offer 40 bows and conduct a daily reading session

(5) Topics of Prayer
- For the successful accomplishment of Heavenly Parent's providence
- For True Parents' long life
- For the purpose of our tribe (to serve Heavenly Parent and live a principled life)

- For our descendants' well-being (for our descendants to serve Heavenly Parent for eternity)

(6) Four-Position Foundations and Home Group Activities
- Organize four-position foundations by age (find measures to achieve goals)
- Call each other to say hello and get together for meals sometimes
- Form hobby groups
- Choir, Korean traditional music, Divine Principle education, health exercise
- Monthly meeting, collect fees, and hobby activities

Vision for 2020 as a Heavenly Tribal Messiah

(1) Community vision
1. We shall support all members of the tribe to become Divine Principle lecturers through worship services (family, church), a life of prayer (40 bows) and Divine Principle hoondok sessions (read the Divine Principle one-hour manual 100 times).
2. We shall become individuals and families who serve Heavenly Parent and True Parents and spread God's Will to the world.
3. We shall create a system with which to inherit True Parents' traditional culture.
4. We shall create an educational system for the future genera-

tions of our tribe.

(2) Tribal Vision

1. We shall mature ourselves through a life of faith and prayer, restore ourselves to the original state envisioned by God during the time of creation, and fulfill the duty and responsibility of Cheon Il Guk citizens.
2. All members of the tribe shall express their individuality in looking out for their neighbors with concern and care and shall convey the word of Heavenly Parent and True Parents to them.
3. Group communities shall make the most of their unique characteristics and take part in local events if needed.
4. We shall spread the hyojeong culture by performing in choruses, Korean traditional music and dance events held by the tribe, church and local community.
5. We shall experiment with Korean farming methods using Korean seeds and establish an agriculture and food company in Kalasin Province, Thailand.

I walk out of the front door early in the morning every day to meet new people or the families in my tribe. Although I may be inadequate in many ways, there are still many people in this world who need my help. It is a blessing to be needed by more than 430 families. They are my brothers and sisters who have been brought together by God through blood lineage. True Parents said that what you must leave in this physical world is your record of loving others.

You can live happily in the afterlife by bringing that record of love to the spirit world. Everything I obtained in life was a gift from Heavenly Parent and True Parents. Thank you very much.

Chapter 6

Collaborating with the National Government and Public Agencies

Chatibut

Person giving Testimony	Husband's Name	Region	Nation
Chatibut Choopojcharoen	Lluis Babi Picolo	South Europe	Andorra
Blessing Information	Number of Children	Spiritual Children (couples)	Number of Families Attending Church
6,000 Couples	5 children	440 couples	2 couples

Blessed Are the Poor in Spirit, for Theirs Is the Kingdom of Heaven

"

Once we understood the direction of the providence that True Parents were pursuing, my husband and I lived each day praying earnestly to be able to fulfill our responsibility. Since we joined the church, my husband and I always have responded to the call of True Parents whenever there were mobilizations for God's providence, and this has helped give us a foundation to overcome the opposition from our families and from my husband's country.

Then one day, we heard that True Mother had announced Vision 2020 and that at least seven nations must be restored. We understand clearly the two main things that True Parents expect from us: to bring the Blessing to all the 7.1 billion people on the earth, and to liberate and bless our ancestors to 420 generations. The part they are calling each of us to do is to bless and educate a minimum of 430 couples as our tribe and liberate 420 generations of our ancestors, who are our spiritual tribe which will help to expand the kingdom of heaven and push away the evil world until it disappears.

"

I Stand Here Because You Have Called Me

I am Chatibut, from Thailand. My husband's name is Lluis Babi Picolo, and he is from Andorra.

I majored in business administration and finished my studies in 1979 in the United States, after which I helped out at the hotel and restaurant run by my parents. My elder sister, who had finished her studies in London and had sent me a letter telling me of her plan to come and visit me in the United States, suddenly contacted me to say that she was not coming. The reason she gave was that she had joined the church in London.

I decided that I should meet my sister and find out what kind of church it was. When I think about it now, I believe that my ancestors were pushing me to visit her so that I could join the church too. Though I was in a situation in which it was not easy to get away and visit my sister, I decided to go to London right away. As soon as I arrived in London, my sister took me to a two-day workshop, where I heard about the Divine Principle. During the two-day workshop I realized straightaway that the Divine Principle was the truth, so I stayed and completed the seven-day workshop, and in the end I joined the Unification Church on October 14, 1979.

When I joined, it was not easy for me to leave behind not only my parents' business and my friends but also the travel agency my parents and elder brother had established for me. However, the call of God had a much stronger pull on my heart. Without knowing what I was getting into, I had gone to London as if someone had pulled me there.

Through these experiences, I came to realize that God does exist and that the Divine Principle is the solution for changing the world. While studying in the United States, I had dreamed of becoming the prime minister of Thailand so that I could transform it. I wanted to eradicate corruption, help the poor, and make Thailand an ideal country. God and True Parents gave me the mission of changing my country through love and the Divine Principle. It was a task that could not be completed through any of the things I had studied in the past—politics or economics—or any other field of study, for that matter.

In 1982, I was matched and received the Blessing. Though it took a long time for my family, including my parents, to accept this fact, they began to change their way of thinking about the church. I keenly felt that the spirit world was indeed working on them from behind. I began to follow True Parents even more devotedly. For three and a half years I worked on a mobile fundraising team (MFT) in Britain, and for another three and a half years I toured across the United States together with the International One World Crusade (IOWC) to carry out witnessing activities.

While walking down the path of the providence together with my husband, I have undergone many experiences. In particular, during my 38 years of church life, I have met God frequently. Whenever I was in a difficult situation, He comforted me and personally showed me His great love. In addition, I have experienced how close the spirit world and our ancestors are to us, and how much they are endeavoring to help us. I also had the great honor of meeting True Mother in person. I also have met True Father spiritually and could feel the amazing love he has for us.

Beginning Our Mission Work in Andorra

Ever since my husband, Lluis, and I joined the church, in 1975 and 1979 respectively, we have lived our lives as missionaries. From 1985 to 2008, Lluis was the president of the church in Andorra, a small nation with a population of 70,000 people. After True Father proclaimed the era of women and instructed that women be entrusted with more responsibilities, since 2008 I have been the national leader for Andorra, and Lluis has been in charge of UPF.

We are trying to do what we can in this small Catholic nation. However, even though it is a small nation, we have been unable to

A "Family is the School of Love and Peace" Blessing ceremony in the Picolo–Chatibut heavenly tribe (March, 2017)

bring all the people of Andorra to receive True Parents' Blessing, and we are sorry that we could not fulfill this responsibility.

To find our spiritual children, we began witnessing in the traditional way by approaching people on the street and going from door to door. When we try to teach people about the truth, they ignore it because they are not prepared to hear it. They are interested only in living a comfortable life. In Andorra there is still a lot of persecution and negative news about the church, so many people refuse to listen to us if they so much as hear the name "Unification Church."

Witnessing to our relatives was also quite difficult for my husband and me. Because there is so much negativity about the church in Andorra, Lluis' family refused to accept anything about the church for a long time. In my family, my parents could not understand why three of their daughters had joined the church and thought we should work at my father's hotel and restaurant. But two of my other sisters were more open-minded, and they helped us out financially in the mission to liberate and bless our ancestors. Finally, after years of prayer and jeongseong, with the cooperation of the spirit world, we were finally able to bring two couples from among my husband's family to participate in the 40 million couples Blessing. We are truly grateful for that.

Returning to My Hometown in Thailand and Beginning the Heavenly Tribal Messiah Mission

Once we understood the direction of the providence that True Parents were pursuing, my husband and I lived each day praying earnestly to be able to fulfill our responsibility. Since we joined the church, my husband and I always have responded to the call of True Parents whenever there were mobilizations for God's providence, and this has helped give us a foundation to overcome the opposition from our families and from my husband's country.

Then one day, we heard that True Mother had announced Vision 2020 and that at least seven nations must be restored. We understand clearly the two main things that True Parents expect from us: to bring the Blessing to all the 7.1 billion people on the earth and to liberate and bless our ancestors back to 420 generations. The part they are calling each of us to do is to bless and educate a minimum of 430 couples as our tribe and liberate 420 generations of our ancestors who are our spiritual tribe, which will help to expand the kingdom of heaven and push away the evil world until it disappears.

In 2016, I decided to return to my hometown in Thailand to carry out the 430 couples mission as a tribal messiah. Though I was very hesitant at first, because I had never worked in my hometown before, I resolved to carry out my work with faith in God and True Parents and their support, and I was determined to invest all my jeongseong and resources into completing the blessing of 430 couples. I offered lots of internal jeongseong, and Thai members also teamed up to help me tackle witnessing to local leaders and officials.

Then heavenly miracles began to take place. They began to occur especially in Kalasin Province, which is located in the northeast part of Thailand, and as our foundation began to solidify, we became connected to public officials from other districts within the province as well. In a short amount of time, thanks to the assistance of Dr. Ronnachit Puttala, county governor of Kalashin Province, we were able to hold three Blessing ceremonies and complete the blessing of 433 couples. There were other miracles, too, as the governor himself also received the Blessing and helped us bless other citizens in the province.

In the end, my husband and I, together with our leader Sangkom Netsopa, were able to bless 433 couples in Kalasin Province through three Blessing ceremonies held within one year. We blessed 60

A heavenly tribal messiah Blessing ceremony in the Picolo–Chatibut tribe

couples on June 17, 2016; 130 couples on July 8, 2016; and 243 couples on March 15, 2017. We have continued to carry out activities in my hometown in Thailand and have achieved amazing success. In particular, many families have come close to us.

When the Blessing Was Given, Villages Opened Up and People Came Flocking (Heavenly Tribal Messiah Activities)

We were really fortunate in that Kalasin Province in the northeast part of Thailand already had a strong, solid foundation. The governor, in particular, is a blessed couple, and he truly understands the value of True Parents, so he wanted to assist in blessing all citizens within the province. We no longer had to carry out one-on-one witnessing; we were witnessing to the official leaders in charge of a province *en masse*. The highest leaders invited employees working under them to attend the Blessing ceremony; and as long as the date of the Blessing ceremony did not conflict with any of their own religious events, most of those people came to attend the Blessing ceremony in response to the guidance of their leaders.

The governor introduced us to a particular mayor in the district who was ready to receive the Blessing. We visited that mayor and discussed the Blessing ceremony with him. We chose the date and requested the use of a room in the city hall to use for the ceremony. We also showed an introductory video about the Blessing at a monthly meeting where all local leaders working for the city were gathered and handed out FFWPU pamphlets and invitations to the Blessing ceremony. Moreover, an official notice was sent out to every head-of-district office in the province, asking them to cooperate in inviting people to the Blessing ceremony.

After that, we sent out official notices from heads-of-district offices to every village headman under their jurisdiction, inviting them to bring the heads of townships and neighborhoods within their districts. There was one district with 111 villages in it, and we visited the head of every village to check and make sure that everything had been communicated clearly. A few days before the Blessing ceremony, we called all the leaders once again to confirm that they were coming to attend it with their spouses.

At the beginning, we didn't even have a car to use when we went to visit the leaders. Three members telephoned people to invite them; and three full-time members worked together in a district and contacted social leaders and local government officials. Then they began inviting the people belonging to that district to the Blessing ceremony.

On the day of the Blessing ceremony, one of the church leaders gave a lecture titled "Becoming a Blessed Central Family" using PowerPoint. The governor also gave a short lecture under the title "The Family as the School of Love." It was a lecture using simple words, and it complemented the atmosphere of the Blessing ceremony and touched the hearts of the participants.

Next, an introductory video about the Blessing was shown. It showed the ever-expanding activities of the Unification movement, particularly the Blessing and the Pure Love Movement. After that, the Blessing ceremony itself started with the benediction of three religious leaders. One of our senior blessed couples served as officiators in the position of True Parents, leading the holy wine and holy water ceremonies and the affirmation of Blessing vows. The Blessing ceremony concluded with a video of True Parents' giving the benediction prayer. After the ceremony was finished, we explained to the participants that they should observe the 40-day separation period, starting from that day, and invited them to participate in the indemnity stick ceremony.

It is truly amazing that we were able to complete the blessing of 433 couples as tribal messiahs at these three Blessing ceremonies within one year. The first one was held in a small place called Meung Na (subdistrict), on June 17, 2016, with 60 couples in attendance. The second ceremony was held in Nong Kungsri (near the district center) on July 8, 2016, and 130 couples took part in it. The third one was held on March 15, 2017, in Kamalasai, one of the eighteen districts, with 243 couples participating.

About 20 members came to assist in the preparations on each of the Blessing ceremony days, even though they had to travel five hours by car or eight hours by bus. These ceremonies were fruit born of support from Heaven and the spirit world as well as the jeongseong and efforts of the local members. With their help, we were able to fulfill our heavenly tribal messiah mission of blessing 433 couples.

A week or two before the 40-day separation period was to end for the newly blessed couples, we contacted the head of the district office and requested permission to use the lecture hall in the district office to hold a seminar on the three-day ceremony. We also gave him a list of the couples who had received the Blessing 40 days earlier and asked him to invite them all to attend the seminar.

At the seminar, we repeated the "Becoming a Blessed Central Family" lecture, which had been given on the day of the Blessing ceremony, to remind the newly blessed couples. After that, we instructed them on how to carry out the three-day ceremony. We also handed out three-day ceremony packages to all the participants, containing portraits of True Parents, holy handkerchiefs for the husband and wife, holy candles, holy matches and holy salt, and instructions on how to perform the three-day ceremony.

The couples who had not carried out the indemnity stick ceremony yet were asked to do it that day. Also, the couples who had failed to observe the 40-day separation period were instructed to begin the 40-day separation from that day and to carry out the three-day ceremony afterward.

Because a large number of people had received the Blessing, it was not possible for them all to attend the three-day ceremony seminar on the same day. Therefore, we once again contacted the leaders, concentrating on those from the smaller districts. First, we requested the leaders to invite those in their districts who had attended the Blessing ceremony to take part in the three-day ceremony seminar. We set up a system so that the newly blessed couples would be educated and guided by the leaders until they had completed the three-day ceremony. Once they have done so, they are divided into home groups in which they receive ongoing education.

Guiding Spiritual Children and Establishing Tribal Traditions

We have a record of all the couples who have received the Blessing. The record contains information on the couples' participation in the Blessing ceremony, indemnity stick ceremony, the 40-day separation period, seminar attendance, and completion of the three-day ceremony. Most of those blessed couples are local leaders who live within those smaller districts. We find and establish 12 good, Abel-type leaders from each tribal district who can manage the people in their district. Then we contact the blessed couples who are also local leaders and have them form home groups and hold meetings. In carrying out home group education, they are asked to follow the method of Dr. Gil Young-hwan. People are invited to lunch. Following the meal, they sing songs and recite the Family Pledge together, after which they are taught how to hold a hoondokhae meeting. They also study other church traditions. The participants discuss what they have learned with one another and receive feedback, and then they pray together for those in the group who ask for prayer support. After that, they encourage one another to bring new guests, talk about their news, and discuss how they can help one another.

Hoondokhae Family Meetings and Tribal Meetings

We use two books on church traditions for our hoondokhae meetings. They are Volumes One and Two of *Basic Traditions for the Blessed Family Model*, which were written by a member who works as a lecturer in our province. He plans to write even more such books to supplement the existing ones.

Everyone comes together at the leader's home, where they are taught how to hold a hoondokhae meeting using a book for new members on church traditions, which was especially written for tribal education. The tribes also are taught about True Parents' words, internal guidance, and so on. In the beginning stage, the leader studies the scriptures together with the participants and asks them to summarize what they have read together. They also carry out several activities to develop their relationships with others. This is repeated until enough leaders who can lead home groups have been trained, after which those leaders step up and organize home group meetings and lead the members of their own groups. The leaders are always present at the meetings, and couples who have received the Blessing become connected to them and are educated by them. When a home group grows too big, it is divided into smaller groups. The members and community leaders are in charge of leading this process and training the group leaders.

Solving Financial Problems

When we started our work to bless 430 couples in 2016, we actually had no money. All we had was a determination in our hearts to complete the mission of heavenly tribal messiah as quickly as possible, by 2017 at the latest. Because we were unable to handle all the expenses with my husband's salary and the income from our small business, we got a loan from the bank and we also borrowed money from our friends. The three Blessing ceremonies and the seminars that came after them cost a total of about $30,000. It was a tremendous sum for us. We are doing our best to pay back our debts now, little by little, but we are not done yet.

A Family is the School of Love and Peace family education meeting in the Picolo–Chatibut tribe

However, we believe that when we follow True Parents with absolute faith, absolute love and absolute obedience to fulfill the responsibility they have given us, we will find ways to get money when we need it and also to pay back any debts we incur, because those debts were incurred not for any personal expenses but to accelerate the providence of Heavenly Parent.

In our province, the blessed couples who already have completed the 430 couples mission work together as a team. The team members help with the education of other tribes. They also carry out activities to collect donations, such as setting up donation boxes in public places like central business districts. Some members organize teams to go out fundraising and also make items (soap, multipurpose detergent, etc.) for all tribes to use in raising funds. Tribe leaders donate a certain amount each month, which is used in educating and guiding tribe members. Since we carry out a wide variety of activities for all the tribes in our province, we are always in need of more funds.

However, we need to endeavor to help the blessed families reach the stage of settlement, in which a center can be established and making donations can become a part of their daily lives. That is all the more reason to continue to educate and train them as people of the Divine Principle.

Overcoming Difficulties and Limitations as Heavenly Tribal Messiahs

We need more lecturers who can guide the blessed couples within a tribe. Since many people are being blessed at the same time, we also need many members who can guide and educate them. They wish to be educated, but there are limits to carrying out effective ongoing educational programs for them. Most members also have day jobs, so there are not that many members who have been trained as professional lecturers to give Pure Love Education lectures to the teenage children of the blessed families.

Money is important in educating people and helping them to become true blessed families who follow True Parents. We may be able to carry out such a task with little or no budget, but in that case our work will progress very slowly. Our nation of Thailand has a high possibility of becoming Cheon Il Guk, because we have a good connection between the leaders at the top, the leaders in the middle, and the people in the local areas, and God's Will has been communicated to them all. Moreover, many of them have responded positively and have become blessed families.

Many government heads and social leaders have become blessed couples, and the leading class of our society also is in favor of giving our Pure Love Education to the youth. What that means is that we can branch out into elementary, middle and high schools and even colleges, and that even teachers, government officials and parents are ready to accept and support our teachings.

If we have enough funds, we will be able to train teachers who can give lectures on the Blessing and the Pure Love Movement to many people. Though we are making efforts to find and train people from blessed families who can educate others, we are facing many difficulties because it takes time to create professional-level educational contents and training facilities.

Visions for the Community

The visions for our community are: first, to train many Abel-type leaders who can lead other people; second, to increase blessed families by blessing our family members, relatives, friends and acquaintances; third, to teach people to have a sense of community to build a better society; fourth, to become connected to affluent people to carry out social projects that can assist the community, such as creating schools and homes for the aged and assisting the disabled and the poor; fifth, to build educational centers within tribal communities with the cooperation of community leaders; and sixth, to make a program through which young members from abroad can come to spend time with the members of our tribes and carry out social activities together.

Centering on the visions of our community listed above, we hope to educate blessed couples so that they can complete all the stages and become true blessed families. We wish to make this society into a society of goodness that has the clear purpose of realizing a world of peace centered on True Parents.

Blessed families, who are the leaders of society, must lead it well and make it a model society. Until people can realize the importance of following True Parents and living together with them, blessed families, the leaders of society, must thoroughly educate those entrusted to them on both the regional level and the national level.

Rev. Kamol Thananopavarn

Person giving Testimony	Wife's Name	Region	Nation
Kamol Thananopavarn	Huang Shu-Chiung	Asia	Thailand
Blessing Information	Number of Children	Spiritual Children (couples)	Number of Families Attending Church
360,000 Couples	1 son, 1 daughter	430 couples	430 couples

Cheon Il Guk Can Be Realized by Accomplishing the Heavenly Tribal Messiah Mission

"

Our strategy is not interreligious. Yet, it is only when we transcend religion that we can embrace all religious traditions. I also hope that this is as effective in Muslim countries. When a person tries to give a religious explanation by interpreting religious doctrines, it will be difficult to avoid conflict, since many people already interpret their teachings in a certain way. However, when you approach people based on true family values, which are rooted in the universal value of the cosmos, many religious people will be able to accept it from their heart, support and follow it.

"

The Salvation of the World through Heavenly Tribal Messiahs

I cannot find any word to express our gratitude for True Parents who have given the mission of heavenly tribal messiahs to me and all blessed families and members in Thailand. The success of heavenly tribal messiah activities in Thailand has raised hopes that the Unification movement is going to grow even more, internally and externally. Moreover, we feel that True Father in heaven is substantially carrying out this tribal messiah work with us. We are also directly experiencing that the doors to the spiritual world have been opened wide by the True Parents so that good spirits can cooperate with heavenly tribal messiah activities and we experience the glory and blessings of this.

At present, our movement in Thailand is working on establishing the traditions of blessed families through True Parents' teachings and has been recognized as an organization with effective projects that can tackle the problems of immorality which inflict great agony on society throughout the country. The Thai government also is working with our headquarters with great expectations that True Parents' teachings will guide families and young Thais toward the right path and save the local communities, society as a whole, and the entire nation.

What I wish to tell you here is also a testimony of my life as a heavenly tribal messiah. As the national leader of FFWPU-Thailand, I am guiding the Unification movement based on the various strategies established to build Cheon Il Guk in Thailand. We are conducting heavenly tribal messiah activities with the great guidance of Dr. Yong Chung-sik, our beloved regional president, and Dr. Lek Thaveetermsakul, Cheon Il Guk special envoy, who is also the first person to fulfill the heavenly tribal messiah mission.

You Have Called and Led Me

I grew up in a middle-class family with a Chinese background in Bangkok City Center and studied at a private school under a Presbyterian foundation. In the immaturity of my youth, I aspired to become successful and wealthy. I studied hard and entered the faculty of engineering at Chulalongkorn University, the most prestigious university in Thailand.

I did a lot of volunteer work from the age of 18 to 20, going even to the remote countryside to do so. I felt the deepest happiness when

A heavenly tribal messiah Blessing in the Thananopavar-Hwang tribe

I served others and was able to deeply love the people I met. While in university, I participated in over 20 volunteer activities with four clubs and led some of those volunteering projects. After graduation, I asked myself a lot of questions about my life, purpose, and value, as I found I had created a self-identity that no longer had anything to do with becoming wealthy. I had come to clearly see the limits of capitalism and how wealth made people more egoistic, and this has been the main culprit behind the destruction of nature and morality of the world. I want to be part of a movement that would build an ideal kingdom of love in which people could love one another, live for the sake of one another and love nature.

Influenced by my new convictions, at the age of 21 I entered graduate school and decided to study environmental engineering.

At the time, I felt alienated and lonely. I studied different ideologies and philosophies, including Buddhism, and communism and sought for the meaning of life in nature. I also did volunteer work at a few non-governmental organizations to conserve nature.

During this time, I came across the Divine Principle by chance in 1994. While listening to all the Divine Principle lectures, the part that touched me the most, of everything the lecturer said, was "One must unite the body and mind centered on true love, form a true family and society, and thereby establish the kingdom of heaven on earth that expands from ideal families." I was impressed by the goal of this new truth.

This felt different from Buddhism, which only teaches levels of self-discipline and mercy. I could feel great sympathy with these teachings, which focused on the value of the family and how the expansion and multiplication of that value takes place through true love.

Yet, I still had not been convinced of God's existence. Godism was a concept I did not understand. Back in university I would turn down Christian evangelists because they only focused on belief and could not explain the root cause. Christian clubs at the university were very stubborn and would disregard other religions like fanatics.

One day, during a midnight prayer on December 31, 1994, I had a personal experience with God for the first time in my life. This was a time when we were welcoming the year 1995. We offered prayers of repentance and determination. I could feel God coming to me, accepting my prayer of repentance, and expressing His warm and great love to me. This was a phenomenal experience, one that I never had before in my life. I always remember how God revealed His suffering heart to me and asked me to work for Him to liberate the suffering of all humankind.

Following this experience, I began to study the Divine Principle very hard in order to understand the Principle and True Father from various new perspectives and angles and to find the answers to the various questions I had. I especially tried to understand the Principle and True Parents from the viewpoints of rationalism, humanism, sociology, and empiricism. It was fortunate that my spiritual father, Mr. Jakrin Iamsamang, is someone who deeply understands various philosophies and religions. My spiritual father would give answers or make suggestions to my questions from humble perspectives from humanism and rationalism and helped me realize that True Parents and the Principle broke through narrow-minded Christian perspectives that interpreted everything with only the Bible and belief. Later on, I began to actively participate in outreach activities on campus with my spiritual father and members of the Unification Movement who were attending Chulalongkorn University.

Cooperation with Government and Entrance of the Era of Group Outreach through the True Family Movement That Goes beyond Religion

First, I would like to testify about the progress and development of the heavenly tribal messiah movement in Thailand from the strategic point of view for realizing Vision 2020 and the restoration of Cheon Il Guk.

Heavenly tribal messiah activities have opened the era of group outreach in Thailand. This became possible through the cooperation and joint effort of the Thai government and FFWPU Thailand. The heavenly tribal messiah movement was a bold step in challenging the problem of how to carry out the Unification movement in Thailand. Furthermore, it was a decisive time for the Thai headquarters, particularly with regard to how the Thai government and local communities recognize our projects and whether we can become established as an organization that is needed by them.

True Parents' teachings and the Principle began to influence the mainstream society of Thailand through heavenly tribal messiahship. It is accepted as the teachings of mainstream society which provided solutions to issues regarding teens and young people rooted in the drug issues that Buddhism, the main religion of Thailand, schools and universities could not solve.

People who received the Blessing through the heavenly tribal messiah movement began to accept the 40-day separation period and the three-day ceremony as a sacred procedure to obtain forgiveness for past sins and start anew. The local community understands the Blessing Ceremony as a blessing from Heaven for couples to re-establish their relationship and form happy families.

As I carried out the heavenly tribal messiah movement, I realized that the mission of heavenly tribal messiahs applies to not only our

Rev. Kamol Thananopavar and his wife officiating a heavenly tribal messiah Blessing

organization and our members, but it also applies to leaders in the government and society as well. These leaders are interested in spreading substantial peace, unity, and happiness, which manifests from the family, throughout their communities and their nation. Recently our activities have involved hundreds of government leaders and we are educating them to have this sense of mission and ownership. Thanks to the heavenly tribal messiah movement, the government and local leaders have become strong supporters of our movement.

Most people in Thailand believe in Theravada Buddhism mixed with Hindu beliefs. However, when we teach True Parents' teachings and offer the heavenly tribal messiah blessings in local communities, we hope that many people will live according to True Parents' teachings in their families and communities, after experiencing how their lives have changed through This is because our Principle and the traditions of blessed families are rooted in the fundamental thought of family values which is universal.

The focal point of our goal is always to establish a community of Blessed families which are the model ideal families of the Family Federation. The government and many community leaders, therefore, are eager to study more of True Parents' teachings in order to lead their communities to be transformed into the ideal.

Since September 2017, we have held three-day Divine Principle workshops and home-group seminars at local sub-district government offices for government officials and community leaders on the topic of ideal family values. The results have been very meaningful. Many people are recognizing and regarding True Parents as leaders they respect the most or as the victorious parents of humanity. They have come to realize true love and to experience God's grace; they are now aware of Satan's identity and activities, and clearly understand what they must do to be saved. In order to create the blessed families' community model within their jurisdictions, they are volunteering to become home group leaders and conducting family gatherings every week to study True Parents' teachings.

What we now need most urgently is to raise up new Family Federation public leaders who can lead worship services on a home group and village community level. If we can raise leaders in a short time, we can increase our membership to 100,000 soon.

Educational Strategy for Heavenly Tribal Messiah Activities

- Introduce universal principles based on the ideal family.
- Go beyond religion and accept current existing religions, traditions and cultures from a parental standpoint.

Our strategy is not interreligious. Yet, it is only when we transcend religion that we can embrace all religious traditions. I also hope that this is as effective in Muslim countries. When a person tries to give a religious explanation by interpreting religious doctrines, it will be difficult to avoid conflict, since too many interpretations already exist within one religion. However, when you approach people based on true family values, which are rooted in the universal value of the cosmos, many religious people will be able to accept it from their heart, support and follow it.

- Declare the value of True Parents ourselves from the perspective that True Parents are the parents of humanity who achieved the ideal that the first human family failed to achieve and completed the ideal True Parents' model.
- Focus on raising leaders and regular members who tithe and donate, practice the traditions of blessed families, and live a life of attendance True Parents. Raise new heavenly tribal messiahs and new Family Federation leaders who can work in the mission similar to pastors who take care of the FFWPU ideal family community through leading hoondokhae counselling,

and organizing blessing and outreach activities.
- From the viewpoints of political science which is the foundation of mainstream society, we will reach out to millions of people using that same platform. We will continue to develop heavenly tribal messiah programs, lectures, hoondok gatherings, and life of attendance in a way that government and leaders in society can understand, accept, and apply on a community and national level.

A Great Shift in Our Explanation from a Christian Perspective and Realization of the Original View of the Principle

While learning about the Divine Principle, I was able to reach beyond the Christian frame and perspective of the Divine Principle and grasp the core of the Divine Principle and what True Parents are really trying to accomplish. I remember what I said to my spiritual father at the beginning of 1995:

> "The Divine Principle and True Parents' goals have very fascinating and attractive and are so powerful that I have never experienced anything like them in any other philosophies or religions. This movement has a principle that centers on true love and ideal families in building the kingdom of heaven on earth. This is greater than Buddhism or any other ideologies I know. However, the method by which the Unification movement explains about

the Principle and True Parents is not effective at all. It must be customized based on the needs of the client and must be market-oriented."

Thai people cannot understand the Principle when it is taught based on Christianity. Furthermore, if they feel the Principle is essentially a Christian-based teaching, our movement will be stopped and a big barrier will be put in place, blocking True Parents.

I thought a lot about how we can make Thai people become members without feeling negative about the Principle, or how to teach Principle-based education more efficiently.

If we were able to do so, we would have the opportunity to recruit tens of thousands and millions of people and True Parents' movement would change this world to an ideal world of true love on earth. This was a movement that I had earnestly sought for and even thinking this way gave me deep inspiration. Although I believed that explaining the Principle from a Christian perspective was difficult and ineffective, at the time I continued to actively participate in outreach activities and church programs.

In August 1995, as part of the 360,000 Couples Blessing, I received the Blessing with my loving wife, Huang Shu-Chiung, and afterward received the mission from my CARP center leader to become head of witnessing at the center and take on the responsibility of MC for Sunday services. I continued to live a life of faith and after I completed my master's degree, I determined to become a fulltime member. The motivation for this determination was my desire to give joy and glory to Heavenly Parent and to fulfill True Parents' wish to build the substantial heaven on earth. I considered this my goal and the meaning of my life. Once I became a fulltime member, I did fundraising, and from 1998 to 1999, I was a Divine Principle lecturer at the national education center.

In 2002, I graduated from Unification Theological Seminary (UTS). I then joined the ILTP / STF fundraising team in the United States led by Mr. Ittetsu Aoki. Through my training on the front line in the US, I went through many experiences that dramatically changed my life—I grew spiritually and gained conviction in my faith.

Since March 2004, I have been a CARP center leader, the vice chair of World CARP for outreach. In October 2005, I was appointed as W-CARP Thailand president and vice national leader of Thailand. In 2010, my mission changed to director of public relations and Universal Peace Federation. Since May 27, 2012, I have been serving as the national leader of Thailand.

We are currently examining our outreach system and hope to create a new "group outreach" system that meets the needs of the new era and enter mainstream society. If we achieve this, we can receive support from the government and we will be able to further expand a movement for ideal families. Through this, I believe we can restore Thailand and realize Cheon Il Guk in our country.

Carrying Out Heavenly Tribal Messiah Activities for the Era of the Firm Settlement of the Substantial Cheon Il Guk

In April 2012, three weeks before I became the national leader of Thailand, I went to the southern part of Thailand near Malaysia. It was in the Hatyai city and Songkhla province areas, where frequent conflicts arise between Muslims and Buddhists. I was instructed to prepare an International Leadership Conference and a Blessing ceremony at which participants from more than 20 countries could participate together. The goal was to bless more than 3,000 couples. I knew that we could achieve a Blessing ceremony of such a scale only with the cooperation of the national and local governments. It was during this mobilization period that I heard of True Father's ascension. The news was such a shock; however, upon hearing of True Father's last wish, I made an even stronger determination to build the substantial Cheon Il Guk on earth. With this determination, I began to prepare lecture presentations and educational video materials for the Blessing ceremony that the government would be able to accept based on FFWPU and the Original Substance Divine Principle.

Carrying Out Heavenly Tribal Messiah Activities for the Settlement of the Substantial Cheon Il Guk

The heavenly tribal messiah movement began in October 2012 after the Blessing ceremony and International Leadership Conference were conducted. All the leaders and members in Asia united with Dr. Yong Chung-sik, the regional president, and we all began conducting extensive heavenly tribal messiah activities in accordance with True Parents' directives.

What I am most proud of is that we once more changed from being the Unification Church to the Family Federation and began referring to God as Heavenly Parent. When I received this official memo from the International Headquarters, I felt a strong stirring in my mind. Furthermore, True Parents had instructed us to break the existing frame we had as a church, embrace all religions and cultures, and extensively carry out the Blessing movement so that many people could be grafted into the true lineage regardless of their background. This was a huge leap forward and a great development. We now could show people that the era of indemnity had come to an end and that we had entered the era of the settlement of Cheon Il Guk.

In other words, the fact that we transitioned from God to Heavenly Parent as a standard way of calling God in the Family Federation was truly amazing in itself. I thought that this concept could transcend religious barriers and was the way to become mainstream. In the same stream of thought, I worked together with Dr. Lek to find ways to solve, through the heavenly tribal messiah movement and the transcending concepts of the Divine Principle teachings, the social problems that the government and public institutions were finding difficult to resolve. We also were determined to act in a manner acceptable by the Thai government and thereby become a mainstream organization. We created video presentations on heavenly tribal messiah projects, the Blessing and FFWPU. Furthermore, we hoped to not only conduct Blessing ceremonies through the heavenly tribal messiah movement but also to educate and care for the couples so that they could complete the three-day ceremony, following which, we also hoped to guide them to practice the blessed family tradition, thereby becoming regular members. Then, from among them, we would select good people and raise them as new FFWPU leaders.

We could implement this activity from early 2013. On January 21, 2013, the first group of Dr. Lek's heavenly tribal messiah activities—34 couples in total—completed their three-day ceremony during a Divine Principle workshop period. This gave us a chance to see whether the meaning of the three-day ceremony could be universally accepted or not. It is for this same reason that I can never forget this particular date.

True Family Movement Results in a New Blessed Family Wave

I decided to invest myself fully in Dr. Lek's heavenly tribal messiah activities. As the national leader, I was the head of the Organizing Committee and emcee for all blessing ceremonies from 2012 to 2015. I would educate and motivate new blessed families, and actively guide them in their lives. The response we received was amazing. There was little to no opposition or any kind of religious struggle. The heavenly tribal messiah providence generated a positive response and received support wherever we went. In addition, those couples who completed the three-day ceremony had miraculous experiences. Everything simply was so phenomenal that it became obvious why the Thai government and community leaders were involved with heavenly tribal messiah activities and why they were loving, respecting, and following True Parents.

I have listed some of their reasons for doing so:

1. They feel that True Parents gave them the greatest of blessings to them.
2. They that True Parents' Blessing can sanctify them and that they can receive forgiveness for past mistakes made on the individual, family, and public levels.
3. They can receive clear teachings, guidelines, encouragement, and a clear vision as to how to lead a successful life, marriage, and family.
4. They can have hope for and receive clear guidelines to establishing an ideal model FFWPU blessed family community. They are inspired to joins hands and work together with FFWPU to realis this dream especially through home group activities, family gatherings (worship services), and hoondokhae meetings.
5. They feel deep happiness and gratitude for the liberation of

past family hardships since their teenager years, to marrying, as couples, parents, or grandparents. They are really impressed with the Divine Principle, particularly by the four great realms of heart and three kingships, the three great blessings, the meaning of true love, hyojeong, and building ideal families. When we organize programs to teach the Divine Principle in communities, some grandfathers and grandmothers testified that they had never felt this happy in their whole lives.

6. They can see hope for their children and the other members of their extended families, as well as their communities and the nation. Local people in communities that our heavenly tribal messiahs are active in deal with serious issues such as drug abuse, sexual immorality, violence, crime, lives without purpose, and suicide among young people. When these people come in contact with True Parents' teachings and pure love projects, they feel comfort and hope and they guide their young people with vision and conviction.

7. Whenever I have a chance to visit my heavenly tribal messiah community in the areas of Buriram and Mahasarakham, they welcomed us with love, honor and respect. It is just like meeting relatives I have not seen in a long time. We truly miss and love one another.

Raising Intermediate Leaders and the Expansion of Faith Communities of Blessed Families

Our aim through the heavenly tribal messiah activities that we have planned since November 2012 is to establish a foundation for Cheon Il Guk. We are seeking to raise members who practice the blessed family traditions and to bring members together in blessed families' faith communities. We wanted to create a model of a peaceful community in accordance with True Parents' teachings.

Across Thailand we hosted three-day Divine Principle workshops as well as workshops on the traditions of blessed families. We conducted these workshops for blessed families in the Phutthaisong District, Buriram Province, Baan Pao Subdistrict, Kammuang District, Pone Subdistrict, and the Lup Subdistrict of Kalasin in Callahan. In September 2017 we held one of these workshops in the Kalashin area, and the results were amazing.

Through the three-day workshops, participants were able to realize True Parents' value and Satan's identity. They were moved by Heavenly Parent and the Divine Principle, and they were guided in finding their identity as filial sons and daughters of Heavenly Parent and True Parents.

The education was well received by the government and by the newly blessed families as it is similar to the traditional culture that has been passed down for thousands of years in Thai society. We are preparing presentations and handbooks for the three-day DP workshops and the blessed family traditions workshops to raise up hundreds of lecturers within a few months. Then we will be able to expand this education and guide new blessed families, VIPs and high-level government officials in their life of faith. Our next goal is to be able to do home group activities everywhere in the country. This task will be undertaken by potential leaders who have completed the three-day Divine Principle workshop. Through a Heavenly Tribal Messiah Leader School, I believe I can raise thousands of leaders by 2020 in Thailand's heavenly tribal messiah movement. We will be able to realize Vision 2020 by restoring millions of members and supporters in this way.

Testimony of Life and Conviction for the Establishment of Cheon Il Guk

I am truly grateful to True Parents for giving me life and a family as a blessed family and the great mission of heavenly tribal messiahship. Through my heavenly tribal messiah mission, I could see our potential to give hope to the Thai people and to the nation. My wife and I are very grateful. The heavenly tribal messiah mission allowed my young children—my 14-year-old son, Kamolpat, and 12-year-old daughter, Manatsaporn—to be confident and proud of their parents and the Unification movement.

We are equipped with teachings based on true family values that transcend religion and culture. Thailand has been suffering from several social problems, and the arrival of the true family movement centered on heavenly tribal messiahs was not only timely but also the perfect principle for Thai society, as it is rooted in family values. When we look at the expansion of the providence in Thailand, it is only a matter of time until Cheon Il Guk is established. No one opposes our movement now. We have begun creating a model community starting from the village level to the provincial level. I believe that we can request support from the central government and I believe that the central government of Thailand soon will become our main sponsor. On that basis, I believe that in the near future we will be able to plan projects that will affect tens of thousands of people, successfully increase the number of regular members, and receive donations and tithing from them. We now are creating a system for data management, including training courses. It will take time to set up these systems and expand to the scale of leadership, skilled officers and financial resources in Thailand to have an impact on hundreds of thousands or millions of people but where there is a will there is a way.

I am truly grateful to Dr. Yong Chung-sik. He gave us so much faith, conviction, vision and encouragement to work together as a movement united with hearts of filial piety. I am also grateful to Dr. Lek and Mrs. Vipa Thaveetermsakul who are full of conviction in vision of heavenly tribal messiahship and have worked so hard to achieve it. I am so grateful to all the leaders, blessed families and members who have supported and sacrificed for one another, especially the 21 leaders who were imprisoned for 21 months and underwent persecution in the court for 21 years.

I believe in the True Parents' vision for heavenly tribal messiahs and FFWPU. Once again, I cannot find any word to express my gratitude to True Parents for their sacrifice and indemnity that they paid to open the gateway to the settlement of Cheon Il Guk. I can feel that True Parents have prepared everything and fulfilled their portion of responsibility already. It is up to us to have absolute faith, absolute love and absolute obedience in order to realize the substantial Cheon Il Guk on earth.

I totally believe that the Thailand heavenly tribal messiah education and methodology that I have thought of since 1995 and continue to develop step by step since October 2012. I have conviction that Thailand will become Cheon Il Guk in only a matter of time! We want to liberate and bring the greatest joy to True Father in spiritual world and True Mother on earth. This is a life and death commitment which is crucial for all our descendants who should be able to see and be allowed to live in Kingdom of Heaven in the near future. I believe we can do it. This is my life testimony for our most beloved and respected True Parents.

Sangkom Netsopa

Person giving Testimony	Husband's Name	Region	Nation
Sangkom Netsopa	Chaiwat Netsopa	Asia	Thailand
Blessing Information	Number of Children	Spiritual Children (couples)	Number of Families Attending Church
360,000 Couples	1 son, 1 daughter	430 couples	430 couples

3

Find and Establish God's Nation in the Very Place Where You Are Standing

"
After True Father's Seonghwa, I dreamed that I was at Cheon Jeong Gung, participating in a women leaders' event with women from all over the world. In the dream, True Mother and I were in the same group. Before the end of the event, I saw True Parents standing there, so I went up to greet them. True Father gave me three different kinds of fruit, and True Mother encouraged me with a warm smile. When I woke up, I prayed to find out what the dream meant. I realized that I must plant and nurture the seeds of the fruit. I thought that I must produce all the seeds and spread out their seedlings everywhere. Then I determined that I would fulfill my mission of tribal messiahship to realize True Parents' dream.
"

God Has Raised Me with Dreams and Hope since My Youth

My name is Sangkom Netsopa. I am 46 years old, and I am from Thailand. My husband is also from Thailand. I have been a member of the Unification Church since October 1991. My husband and I were blessed in 1995 in the 360,000 Couples Blessing. My parents also received the Blessing the same year but they didn't complete the three-day ceremony. My father passed away 13 years ago. So my mother did a spirit world – physical world three-day ceremony. My parents-in-law did the same ceremony as well and they all count in the 360,000 Couples Blessing. My husband and I have liberated both sides of our parents up until the 277th generation.

When I was young, I had the opportunity to lead youth teams from CARP, YFWP and SFP and ICEF Marine Plan which support the Ocean Providence in Thailand. Heavenly Parent and True Parents gave me the opportunity to educate young people and gain experience while working with all sorts of agencies, government organizations and NGOs. I was always thinking about how to witness to the people in the local community.

As I read the book *Home Church*, I began to offer sincere jeongseong. This book gave me great hope and inspiration that we can save many people through our tribal messiah activities. While I was reading this book, I talked to my parents and relatives about the Blessing, and my grandchildren received the Blessing. My husband's parents also participated in the Blessing.

Meanwhile I was determined to liberate and bless my ancestors up to 210 generations, and I began offering jeongseong. I have more than 12 spiritual children. Whenever I have the opportunity, I go to CheongPyeong and write wish papers for them. My husband and I continuously did 21-bow conditions. After fulfilling a certain spiritual condition, we heard the continental director's words saying that everyone should fulfill the mission of tribal messiah, which left a deep impression on us.

You Are My Motivation and My Life; I Will Respond to Your Call

I cannot forget the final prayer that True Father offered before he ascended. True Father proclaimed that True Parents already had accomplished everything. He said that the only thing left is for us to become tribal messiahs.

An Interfaith Peace Blessing in the Netsopa heavenly tribe

Fortunately, before True Father ascended I had participated in the 10thSpecial Workshop which was the last workshop that he led. Father looked and smiled at us with love which we were listening to his direct guidance. No one knew that that workshop would be the last memory we had of him.

After True Father's Seonghwa, I dreamed that I was at Cheon Jeong Gung participating in a women leaders' event with women from all over the world. In the dream, True Mother and I were in the same group. Before the end of the event, I saw True Parents standing there, so I went up to greet them. True Father gave me three different kinds of fruit, and True Mother encouraged me with a warm smile. When I woke up, I prayed to find out what the dream meant. I realized that I must plant and nurture the seeds of the fruit. I thought that I must produce all the seeds and spread out their seedlings everywhere. Then I determined that I would fulfill my mission of tribal messiahship to realize True Parents' dream.

I discussed this with my husband, so that we could take immediate action. We decided that we first would raise 12 spiritual children and then get their help to do tribal messiah activities in our hometown. From that time, we began offering jeongseong for our guests as well as a relative who was a parliament member at the time. Furthermore, we prayed for the leaders of each region's cities, provinces and counties. I asked my ancestors for help. I went to my hometown to find righteous people to create an environment for outreach.

God's Grace in Preparing a Member of Parliament and a Chief District Officer to Work with Us

My relative who was a member of parliament organized a meeting at his house with the chief district officer. Through this meeting I saw great hope and potential. Dr. Ronnachit Puttala, who was a district leader of the Khao Wong district in Kalasin at the time, attended the meeting. I officially announced the project, and we created teams to work with the leaders of six local subdistricts and 71 villages. The project called "Thai Families, Loving and Unite" was to introduce the Blessing to international religious leaders and to organize Blessing ceremonies. Next, we would establish blessed families as models for the community. The chief district officer announced this project and sent out an official letter to all village leaders, inviting them to attend a one-day workshop with their spouses so that they could understand the meaning and importance of a principled life. In the one-day workshop we spoke about the principle of monogamy and fidelity in marriage. Dr. Ronnachit, the Khao Wong chief district officer, attended the workshop and received the Blessing together with other government leaders and people in his district.

In my hometown in Khao Wong District we have a particular ethnic tribe called Phu Thai. Our ancestors migrated from southern China and passed through Vietnam and Laos to settle in Thailand. Therefore, we have our own traditional clothing, language and culture. The Blessing ceremony was beautiful, with all the participants wearing traditional clothes. It was also a special day because I had a chance to see all my relatives who are leaders of the community. My husband's relatives also participated. It was truly great that because of God and True Parents this could take place. It was such an occasion of joy for our ancestors and salvation for our tribe.

From Roi-Et Province, 25 couples who were my husband's relatives participated and received the Blessing. During the Blessing ceremony we explained the indemnity stick ceremony and the 40-day separation. We had the blessed couples sign a contract and go through a separation period of 40 days to restore all wrongdoings from the past and be reborn. And we had a one-day workshop with other important lectures to prepare them for the three-day ceremony.

It is very important to establish spiritual conditions every time we do this kind of work in the field. My husband and children continuously did 21-bow jeongseong every day. We had been preparing in advance with spiritual conditions for years and it was very important for our family to do hoondokhae every morning. We used our home as the main center for gatherings and meetings. My mother, who was staying with us, helped us a lot. Every morning at dawn we prepared for the lectures. With the help of our new members, we united as one and fundraised, gave lectures and organized Blessing ceremonies.

We received a warm welcome at the places that we visited, depending on the level of jeongseong we offered. The more we visited them, the more warmly they welcomed us. Every time I met people who had finished the three-day ceremony, I felt they were truly like my relatives and family. As time went by, there were more and more blessed families, and we established the house of the head of the village as a church center. We put up True Parents' picture in that center.

We organized two Blessing ceremonies so that all the people in the Khao Wong District could receive the Blessing. My spiritual children, blessed families and the HQ Family Department helped enthusiastically in putting on these Blessing ceremonies.

Then I consulted with the district chief, Dr. Ronnachit, about how we could expand this Blessing work to other areas. We worked together even more earnestly in order to achieve our goal, and through this we became even closer. I invited Dr. Ronnachit to meet my mother in order to do the adopted child ceremony. Following a local Phu Thai tradition, he became my mother's son and I became his younger sister. We thus became siblings, and I could more freely ask him for advice.

I invited Dr. Ronnachit twice to participate in a three-day Divine Principle seminar for VIPs. He then was appointed as an ambassador for peace and he also was promoted with responsibility over 12 districts and 113 villages. He established the policies and directions for workshops and Blessing ceremonies to be prepared in all the districts. He believes in our work because he saw the sustainable and positive change in the leading families of the Khao Wong District, where we formerly worked.

I Will Put This Place in Your Hands, So Bless It like the Stars in the Heavens (John the Baptist Mission)

After receiving the Blessing, many of those who participated became better husbands and, in some serious cases, they could overcome the temptation to visit prostitutes, realizing more deeply the importance of family. They began new lives, made their wives happy, and their families became harmonious. Many people stopped smoking and drinking. As this virtuous cycle was established, Dr. Ronnachit actively supported our team. We organized activities and Blessing ceremonies continuously, supported members and educated newly blessed couples. At the same time, the government officers promoted our foundation to other organizations in the region and supported us in our activities.

A good point is that all the subdistrict directors became closer.

Gil Young-hwan and Professor Yoon Do-young with the Netsopa heavenly tribe in Thailand

While staying at the center (my mother's house), our team members worked hard until all the citizens of the districts received the Blessing. After that, Dr. Ronnachit was promoted to a bigger area: Kalasin County District, which has 17 local districts with 180 villages. Now, instead of supporting us by sending out official letters, he personally participates in meetings for organizing each Blessing. Every time he was done with one task, he would be busy moving onto the next mission. When I think of this, I have great respect and am very moved by him. His wife also supported these efforts greatly.

Not only heads of villages but also the chairmen of subdistrict administrations, subdistrict heads, permanent secretaries of each subdistrict, administrative leaders and local politicians participated. They all cooperated and earnestly participated in the Blessing ceremony. This was all possible due to the hard work and dedication of the district leader, who has a good moral influence on the people around him. He laid this foundation, and even after he brought many people, he continued to reach out to other district chiefs in Kalasin Province so that they would conduct similar activities in their areas. Thanks to this, we were able to give lectures and hold Blessing ceremonies in other subdistricts as well.

In this way, in 2016 we expanded to 16 of the 18 local districts in Kalasin Province. Asia's continental director encouraged the district chief and government leaders of Kalasin to meet True Mother. When we visited Korea, True Parents' support became a source of great strength. Before traveling, Dr. Ronnachit called all the leaders to participate in a three-day workshop to lay a deep foundation to understand True Parents' vision. He checked on the participants one by one and ensured that righteous people would receive this grace.

Amazing Miracles in Families That Received the Tribal Messiah Blessing

During this time, many leaders participated in workshops and received a lot of inspiration. None of them will never forget meeting True Parents at CheongPyeong. All those who participated said that True Mother was very beautiful and the greatest saint. They wanted to meet True Mother's children also. After meeting True Mother, they worked even harder and supported the Kalasin tribal messiah team.

In June 2017, during the inauguration in Thailand of Youth and Students for Peace, 1,000 blessed families and the young people from Kalasin had the opportunity to meet True Mother. They said in their reflections after that meeting True Mother was like going to Heaven. After coming back home, we translated True Mother's words from the workshop into Thai, and our family has been reading it for hoondokhae.

I work at the Thailand Headquarters as the director of the Blessed Family Department. While I was working in Bangkok, I started teaching our family values to Thai Muslim families and many people completed the three-day ceremony. I realized that the door to the kingdom of heaven is open, no matter what your religion or denomination is, and that True Parents' Blessing and vision are spreading. I told all families that they should have a picture of True Parents and use holy candles and holy salt. I told them that every time the family gathers and before leaving home or after returning home, they first should offer a bow to True Parents. I told them that the husband and wife and children should revere True Parents and respect each other. Parents should teach their children about living a life of sexual purity.

Many families established these kinds of traditions, and when they did, they began to meet True Parents in their dreams. I told them that it does not matter what religion they believe in; they were all created to be Heavenly Parent's children. They began to realize that these traditions are not just religious but that they should be practiced in every family universally.

Thailand is a Buddhist country. That is why when we give Divine

Principle lectures, we do not use the term "God." Instead we use the terms "Heavenly Father and Mother," introducing them as the first parents of all humankind. This is in line with the Thai tradition that considers the king as the nation's parent. Therefore, we naturally can explain the position of True Parents as "the True Parents of all humankind." They can easily understand this.

Among my husband's relatives, there is a family who received an award from the government. This family has testified about the change in their family that was made possible through the teachings of True Parents. One thing that happened is that their children passed the university exam. The husband himself changed as well, after seeing how much his family changed. When there were difficulties and trials, they lit their holy candle and prayed to Heavenly Father and Mother. When this family received the award, they were wearing FFWPU scarves and holding True Parents' picture. This is recorded on video. He testified that it was because he put into practice the principles taught by True Parents that he was able to receive this award.

Plan for Guiding and Developing the Tribe

We have not established a center in this region yet, so our next mission is to figure out how we will guide and take care of all the blessed families. I have to create a plan for families to take care of other families. The Asian leaders have used the home group strategy and established regional leaders and a family leadership school. We also are planning to train 43 leaders and put that tradition into practice. We start with a small group of three people, who together invite guests and make them into members. We also do hoondokhae and family meetings.

Apart from holding these family meetings at the center, we also hold mobile family meetings at the house of each leader. Tribal representatives in Thailand and overseas take turns to visit their tribe. They create an online group using the Line software on their phones and exchange activities and news regarding True Parents.

Recently the Thailand Headquarters gave us the funds to open our own center in Kalasin and provided us with one vehicle and one full-time member. We will have to prepare the funds for other expenses as well, but we want to be financially independent.

We are continuously educating people about donations, tithing and special donations. As a result, some new families have begun tithing, even though they have a small income. Among these families, there are those who are farmers and have donated rice and food.

Furthermore, we have been able to witness to government employees who are unmarried and they have begun tithing and even bring us their single Blessing candidate application. At the same time, we also are preparing lectures on the principle of true love as well as principled education for young people in the region, including children of blessed families. Everything is progressing smoothly. We also have retired teachers who want to work with us.

We are helping not just our tribe but also other tribes and people to be successful and bring results as tribal messiahs. We are hoping to hold Blessing ceremonies soon in at least three other provinces, but we first have to establish the model in Kalasin. In Thailand there are a total of 77 provinces. If we can restore at least seven provinces, this can become a basic condition for the restoration of Thailand by 2020. To achieve this, we have set up a few guiding principles.

1. Have blessed families stand as home group leaders, establishing 43 families per tribe so that each family can take care of ten families.
2. Establish a young successor under the tribal messiah and raise young people and committed members who can help with the work.
3. Create funds and encourage everyone to practice the tradition and tithe consistently.

When establishing the foundation for heavenly tribal messiah activities, it is not easy to create funds or raise leaders. However, we have True Parents' vision and blessing, so I believe we will have many results. Dr. Ronnachit Puttala, the chief of district, and his wife have been helping us to resolve misunderstandings or difficult issues with other members. We are so blessed that this kind of Johnthe Baptist leader has been established for us. I believe that when we participate in tribal messiah activities, many ancestors are working with us. I never would be able to accomplish this without the help of Heavenly Parent, True Parents and the good spirits. Thank you.

Saito Hajime

Person giving Testimony	Wife's Name	Region	Nation
Hajime Saito	Jarurin Saito	Asia	Cambodia
Blessing Information	Number of Children	Spiritual Children (couples)	Number of Families Attending Church
360 Million Couples	2 children	445 couples	34 couples

4

Change of Lineage in Jerusalem, and in All Judea and Samaria, and to the Ends of the Earth

> I sincerely pray that as time passes, an amazing miracle will happen through our heavenly tribal messiah activities: that the whole population of Cambodia will receive the Blessing and change their lineage. We could not show True Father the substantial establishment of Cheon Il Guk. Therefore, I cannot escape the fact that I am an undutiful son. Now I think we should be children who accomplish this will and give our atonement and joy to True Father who already has gone to the spirit world. True Mother said that for us to establish Cheon Il Guk, we must restore heavenly sovereignty, heavenly land and heavenly people. To restore heavenly sovereignty, we have to have parliamentarians complete the heavenly tribal messiah mission through IAPP. In order to restore heavenly land, we have to expand the territory of the heavenly tribal messiahs where God can settle. We will do our best to have all Samarian lands (mentioned in the Bible) and all Cambodian citizens receive the Marriage Blessing and become blessed families.

Do You Believe Me?

I started to study the Divine Principle in 1994 and entered the Unification Church in 1995. The words of the Divine Principle inspired me, and I had no difficulty in understanding and accepting it. However, I still was not sure about the Messiah. In the middle of 1995, there was a brothers' workshop for church leaders at the Central Training Center in Guri (Korea). Although I had not prepared my heart at all, I was given the chance to attend the workshop.

As soon as we entered the training center, there was an announcement calling us to come to the auditorium right away because True Father had just arrived. I had a desperate need to use the men's room before I went in to sit down, so I ran to the nearest restroom. However, there was a long line of people, and I could not hold it. Finally, I had no choice but to urinate in the shower room; then I headed to the auditorium.

When I entered the auditorium, True Father already was speaking. I wanted to take full advantage of this opportunity to understand Father clearly, so I sat right next to the aisle where Father was walking back and forth and listened attentively. As True Father passed by, he looked at me and said in Japanese, "You pissed in the shower room," and then kept on walking. A little later, he came back and repeated the same thing, "You pissed in the shower room." This was a very strange and surprising experience. Since that moment when I met True Parents and realized that they know every move I make, I have never had any doubt about them. I became convinced that True Parents are the Messiah, the Savior, and the True Parents of all humankind.

After True Parents' Wishes Became My Dreams, a Person in the Position of John the Baptist Appeared

On May 30, 2015, I was having dinner with the Asian regional president, Dr. Yong Chung-sik, after a performance of Hyo-jin nim's band in Las Vegas. Dr. Yong told me very specifically about True Father's final prayer and instructions at Geomundo Island. The conclusion was that the lineage needs to change. This is the way that we, the heavenly tribal messiahs, have to walk. At the end of his talk, he looked at me and said, "Hajime, what are you doing?" Although Dr. Yong didn't say more than that, this became a big turning point for me.

A heavenly tribal messiah Blessing officiated in the Saito heavenly tribe

    I had thought about the final instruction of Jesus Christ, who was the first Messiah, "It is not for you to know the times or dates the Father has set by his own authority. But you will receive power when the Holy Spirit comes on you; and you will be my witnesses in Jerusalem, and in all Judea and Samaria, and to the ends of the earth." [Acts 1:7–8] This made me wonder about the meaning of the last instruction of True Father, who came as Christ at the Second Advent. It seemed the message was: "We have to convert all human beings who were taken away by Satan back into the lineage of God and re-create them as original children of God." I thought further and considered what the instruction of True Mother, who came to the earth as the only begotten daughter, would be. Since True Mother is perfectly united with True Father, I thought she must be focused on actualizing Father's direction. That's why True Mother had declared the Vision 2020 project and directed that we work as heavenly tribal messiahs to restore at least seven nations. After my conversation with Dr. Yong, I decided that from now on my mission was to complete the heavenly tribal messiah mandate. This had become my mission, whether I liked it or not.

On the 13th day of the first lunar month, 2013, Foundation Day arrived. At that time, I reaffirmed by goal by asking myself, "Where am I going to build Cheon Il Guk?" I replied to myself, "I'm going to build it in my mission area, in Indochina (Cambodia, Myanmar, Laos, Vietnam)." Then, "How will you do that?" I immediately stood up.

Since then, my prayer has become like this: "Please help me to restore even one of the four countries in Indochina and devote it to Heaven!" Then I remembered a wish True Father wrote in his autobiography. Father said, "I want to live even for one day in Cheon Il Guk, where the nation of God has been realized." As I recalled what he had written, I couldn't help regretting my lack of dutifulness, that I had not been able to achieve it during his lifetime on earth.

After long thought and through my sincere prayer at the holy ground at CheongPyeong, after the Foundation Day ceremony on the 13th day of the first lunar month, 2013, I decided to restore at least one of the four nations in Indochina during True Mother's lifetime. Of course, it is not easy to restore even one country in Indochina. This is because if you look at this group of countries, you can see a communist country, a socialist country, and a country under military rule. Although Cambodia has a certain foundation of blessed families, our church foundation in the other three countries is very weak.

I was reminded of the Bible verse again, which I had previously thought about: "In Jerusalem, and in all Judea and Samaria, and to the ends of the earth." I adapted God's word into my own situation like this: "In Phnom Penh, Cambodia, and to the ends of the Battambang." I made up my mind to start the local missionary activities that I had been thinking of for a long time but had not been able to execute yet. At the time of 2013, the Battambang area of Cambodia was the only place where we had established local churches. I went to Battambang Church to start my journey.

Rev. Hut Hen, the pastor of Battambang Church, is an enthusiastic person who has led the growth of the Battambang area from a pioneer area to an established church district. As a result of his successful activities, the providence there has developed greatly. Making this my central base, I started to work in the area. We have conducted a lot of character education seminars in Battambang-area schools. Since Rev. Hen has experience as a classroom teacher, he made good progress in establishing a foundation in the schools.

At that time the Asian region was planning a youth assembly in Indonesia. We took this opportunity to invite five principals who were close to us to our youth assembly. There, the participants received a three-day Divine Principle workshop. After that they became one with us completely. After returning to Cambodia, they had a meeting and said that they would like to put these great words into action. We set up a cooperative system with the Ministry of Education of the Battambang government. In addition, in June 2015 we held a youth assembly, with the cooperation of the Ministry of Education, which was attended by 3,000 young people. This was a breakthrough achievement that I couldn't even imagine.

The next month was July. Parents of the young people we had educated were invited to receive the Blessing, and we held a 700 Couple Marriage Blessing. Then we held a Marriage Blessing of 500 couples in Phnom Penh. When I saw the daunting speed with which the providence was progressing, it really made me think. God already had prepared everything. It was clear that the speed of this work was the result of His urgent heart to love humankind.

Concerns about Missionary Life and Witnessing

It is usually not too difficult to restore 430 families. I had not been a missionary for a long time, but after 14 years it was time to move to a new stage. I first came to Indochina in 2003 and spent about 14 years in Cambodia, including three years in Myanmar. Even if we conduct the Marriage Blessing ceremony with a large group and Divine Principle education through the heavenly tribal messiahs, the basis of witnessing must be one to one.

For example, when a mother gives birth to a baby, she usually gives birth to one or two at most. When a baby develops in the womb, these months should not be either too short or too long; otherwise that baby will have a problem. I think it is also the same in evangelism. The base of witnessing is a one-to-one relationship, and it is necessary for spiritual children to spend at least 10 months to grow up in a mother's "womb" 24 hours a day. During that period, a mother must invest everything in her baby and be careful. Without such sincere jeongseong, a baby will not be born. This process is the basis of witnessing, and people who newly join our church can be reborn into people of principle through this process.

In this manner, my own philosophy of witnessing is to make life and re-create people. Therefore, you must invest with a desperate heart in order to produce a baby in the womb. Even though witnessing is a one-on-one love relationship … how can we give birth to and raise 430 families at the same time? This was my concern about witnessing.

There was one more thing to consider about witnessing. There was a period when I was working in the United States of America in 1999. At that time, Hyo-jin nim spoke at a gathering at Pasadena House, in Los Angeles, and the title of his sermon was "The Four-Position Foundation Is the Network of Heart." It was a sermon addressing the kind of situation in which witnessing could be achieved, and his answer was that when the object partner becomes the absolute object partner in front of the subject partner, witnessing can be done. In other words, there is the position of the subject partner (Abel) as well as that of the object partner (Cain); when the object partner can accept absolutely what the subject partner wants, their union can be created and the child can be born there.

I tried to think carefully about these words, applying them to the heavenly tribal messiah mission. "True Mother, who is standing in the position of our subject partner, told us to complete our mission as heavenly tribal messiahs. Then, as the object partner, all I have to do is to just follow the will of my subject partner and become one with her; so what am I worrying about? There is nothing for us to be concerned about, so just think simply." I altered my thinking in this way. I thought, "If group witnessing and individual care and guidance cannot be managed at the same time, in that case it means my philosophy of witnessing is wrong."

I concluded that if I faced a limit, Heaven would give me better alternatives. From now on, I would offer jeongseong, pray hard and try to become one with True Mother, and then I surely would get the answer. This is what it really means to have absolute faith, absolute love, and absolute obedience in the Family Pledge that I swear by every day. I concluded if I offered jeongseong and prayed desperately, Heaven surely would open the way for me to help people settle.

Even If One Has the Strength to Move a Mountain, One Cannot Move Even Dust without Faith

Dr. Yong Chung-sik, the regional president for Asia, always has emphasized that when we work on a great providence, we should not think that we will do it by ourselves. However, we always have to be motivated by the Will of God and True Parents. He also told me that we must find someone who is ready to fulfill the role of John the Baptist and put him in the forefront. With this motivation, we have been holding Asian Leadership Conferences (ALC) for VIPs from throughout the entire Asian region, once a month.

These conferences primarily have been held in Bangkok, Thailand, which is relatively close to Cambodia. It is convenient that Thailand is geographically close to Cambodia, but another advantage is that Cambodians do not need visas to enter Thailand, so I have been using these conferences in my witnessing work. The airfare is usually less than $250, which is not such a heavy burden for me, so it seems like a good fit. In addition, the Battambang area of Cambodia is geographically close to Thailand, so I can even travel there by car. Sometimes I feel that the ALC exists just for Cambodia. Also the best instructors on the Asian continent are fully committed to the ALC. Another reason why I like the ALC held in Thailand is that Thailand has successful models of heavenly tribal messiah activities. We can learn from those successful cases, analyze their strengths and weaknesses, and reduce trial and error. Hearing about these victories when we are in Thailand has really helped the Cambodians. After visiting Thailand, most Cambodian members say, "We can do it too!" and go on to say, "We can do it better!" Another reason is the similarity of the cultures. Thailand has many similarities to Cambodia in both culture and religion. Their languages also use the same alphabet.

VIPs in Cambodia attend the Blessing ceremony after the ALC Divine Principle workshop at the same location. After they hear explanations about the 40-day separation period and the three-day ceremony from the best lecturers in Asia, those VIPs who attend the ALC are so inspired that they all start the 40-day separation period without fail. This kind of amazing phenomenon is happening. Since those VIPs already have started with such experiences in Thailand, when they return to Cambodia, all we have to do is just let them testify about what they have learned in Thailand and teach people in local areas where blessed VIPs are living. That's why Thailand is a much respected brother nation for the providence in Cambodia. We are very grateful to Thailand!

The Reason Why Cambodia's Hope Was Created

We began to create many vision statements through the youth events in Indonesia and the two marriage Blessing ceremonies. In addition, the Divine Principle education for VIPs inspired them to hold ongoing Divine Principle workshops in their own communities. Gradually they also added explanations about the 40-day separation period and the three-day ceremony. The next step was to create a community of blessed family members. As this foundation expands, we are trying to create a vision statement by using the wholesome qualities that are characteristic of the Cambodian people.

First, we are trying to work with the special character of the Cambodian people. Between 1975 and 1979, Cambodia suffered from a civil war. Many of the people who were not able to receive an education during those years are attending school now, even though they are much older than school age. It might be hard to imagine this situation in other countries. If you visit a school, you can find a lot of already married blessed couples among the student body.

Second, Cambodian people have a very pure nature. They experienced a lot of pain during the communist era, so they have a culture of helping each other to ease their pain. Recently, with materialism coming into Cambodia, their culture has changed a bit, but most local regions other than the metropolitan areas still have this culture. Fortunately, this country already has a strong cultural tradition of virginity before marriage; they feel it is common sense.

Third, the government is cooperating with our heavenly tribal messiah activities. Many VIPs have attended the VIP workshops and the ALC conferences held in Bangkok, and those participants who learned Divine Principle have helped us to expand that foundation. Once VIPs in Cambodia listen to the Divine Principle lectures of Dr. Yong, Dr. Robert Kittel, and special envoy Ursula McLackland, they are very inspired without exception. They are transformed into active supporters of heavenly tribal messiah activities. Because Cambodia has these three factors, the stage is set for the heavenly tribal messiah activities in this nation with healthy cultural traditions that correspond to the Principle and the true family activities we pursue.

Prepared John the Baptist Figures Are Transforming This City into God's Territory

We have to not only give birth to children but also nurture them. That's why we have conducted one-to-one witnessing for VIPs who were educated at the ALC. Although the level of those VIPs who attended the ALC workshops is governor and parliamentarian, we have encouraged them to become our members. I was very lucky because H.E. Suon Bobor, a vice-governor, attended the three-day Divine Principle workshop held by ALC, participated in the Divine Principle lectures of our church many times, built a standard of learning tradition, and finally was promoted to the position of governor. He became a great help and is now supporting everything our local leaders are doing. He actively participates in our education for local people and citizens of this nation. Because Cambodia is still a socialist country, if the leader gives an official direction, people in the organization will follow it.

How to Organize and Guide Family Hoondokhae Gatherings

I always find it challenging to manage local areas and organize blessed families. That is a question of how to guide blessed people well so that they become true blessed families. When I was concerned about this problem, Professor Gil Young-hwan, who had practiced home group and organization management for a long time, came to Southeast Asia. Professor Gil's management method applies a very good system that is used in Cambodia. Since Cambodia was a communist country in the past, there is still a system of organizing groups of five in order to manage people. We utilized that organizing method in Cambodia and incorporated our educational contents to the management method we created.

The detail of this method is that we appoint 43 leaders to manage 430 families, and we help each leader to take care of 10 families. However, first those 43 members have to receive leadership training. Therefore, we have to find and educate 12 core leaders in order to train 43 leaders, and before that, we have to create three top leaders to nurture the 12 core leaders.

If you study the words of True Father in the earliest times, you will find that Father frequently mentioned the Blessing trinity. This implies that there is a method to create and manage organizations by making three top leaders a Blessing trinity, nurturing 12 core members on the foundation of three top leaders, and expanding it to and managing 430 families. You also can read about these methods in *Cheon Seong Gyeong, Pyeong Hwa Gyeong,* and *Chambumo Gyeong.* The way we educated leaders through ALC was already taught by True Father during his lifetime on earth. However, we came to discover that truth only after we had realized, practiced and succeeded with it. After all, I think that in order to succeed, we must follow the foundation of True Parents' life course. There is a revelation, a will and a way of Heaven, and this is what I have felt through my missionary experiences in the field.

Heavenly tribal messiah Saito and staff with the special emissaries

When I Create and Organize 12 Tribes, I Have to Feed and Dress Them (Financial Independence)

Of course, my missionary areas are four countries, including Cambodia. I completed the goal of 430 families in Malai County, Bantey Meanchay State, Cambodia, where I concentrated on my heavenly tribal messiah activities. This area is the city where I started to teach English at a school in Banteay Nienchei during the earliest times of my mission in Cambodia. One day I went to the Malai area for a seminar. At that time, the local military officer attended, and thus the heavenly tribal messiah activities began. Our first concerns were financial. After a lot of prayer, I decided to contact my spiritual children for financial support first. As a result of the hard work in that area, we fulfilled the goal of 430 families. Of course, this meant only a numerical achievement, a Marriage Blessing ceremony, the indemnity stick ceremony, and the first Divine Principle education. Now we are continuing to educate tribe members so they can complete the 40-day separation period and the three-day ceremony. We form small groups from those who have finished the three-day ceremony, and we conduct continuous education and hoondokhae gatherings. As a result, we were able to receive donations from small group meetings and 430-family general gatherings, so that our community could attain a degree of financial independence.

Moses, Moses, Why Did You Call Us?
(Hardship and Vision of a Heavenly Tribal Messiah)

No matter what activities we are engaged in, there are always conflicts and difficulties, aren't there? There are always problems in human relationships, financial issues, and ongoing limitations in management and education. However, as the Divine Principle says, all we can do is just believe and follow. The truth I learned from my mission is that when I become the absolute object partner in front of the subject partner, spirit world will. Therefore, the conclusion is that no matter what happens, spirit world will work only if we attend and are absolutely one with Heavenly Parent and True Parents.

At the Global Assembly of the International Association of

Parliamentarians for Peace (IAPP) in February 2017, True Mother told members of parliament that they should do heavenly tribal messiah activities. I thought, "Why did she tell new participants to do it, when even blessed families have not done it?" But I was wrong. I realized that it was our responsibility to lead the IAPP members of parliament to participate in heavenly tribal messiah activities. True Father has said that if 12 families complete the mission of the heavenly tribal messiah, that nation will be restored. I have thought about a different interpretation of this message. I think that if 12 parliamentarian families who represent their country complete the heavenly tribal messiah mission, that nation can be restored. This is because those parliamentarians have their own local area, and if 430 families among the local people receive the Marriage Blessing and unite with their leader, legislation can be made centering on local issues. In addition, the moral values of Cheon Il Guk can be settled there by the local people. That is why in Cambodia we began to pray with our members for three parliamentarian families in 2018, seven parliamentarian families in 2019, and 12 parliamentarian families in 2020, to complete the heavenly tribal messiah mission. By that time, we will firmly establish a foundation for all citizens to receive the Marriage Blessing and declare Cheon Il Guk on the anniversary of Foundation Day, 2020. That is my dream, the vision of our members, as well as the mission and goal of FFWPU-Cambodia.

    I sincerely pray that as time passes, an amazing miracle will happen through our heavenly tribal messiah activities: that the whole population of Cambodia will receive the Blessing and change their lineage. We could not show True Father the substantial establishment of Cheon Il Guk. Therefore, I cannot escape the fact that I am an undutiful son. Now I think we should be children who accomplish this will and give our atonement and joy to True Father who already has gone to the spirit world. True Mother said that for us to establish Cheon Il Guk, we must restore heavenly sovereignty, heavenly land and heavenly people. To restore heavenly sovereignty, we have to have parliamentarians complete the heavenly tribal messiah mission through IAPP. In order to restore heavenly land, we have to expand the territory of the heavenly tribal messiahs where God can settle. We will do our best to have all Samarian lands and all Cambodian citizens receive the Marriage Blessing and become blessed families. Thank you very much.

Watcharin Kaewlamsak

Person giving Testimony	Wife's Name	Region	Nation
Watcharin Kaewlamsak	Boontawee Kaewlamsak	Thai	Thailand
Blessing Information	Number of Children	Spiritual Children (couples)	Number of Families Attending Church
360,000 Couples	1 son, 2 daughters	1,200 couples	430 couples

5

True Parents Have Come and the Gates to Salvation Have Begun to Open

> It is true that we often face various difficulties in heavenly tribal messiah activities, but we cannot give up our mission. I think the reason why True Parents gave us that mission is because they want to give us a way to grow as parents. We truly pray that we can restore a nation as True Parents wish, by inheriting their dream, planting the seed of true love, and expanding it to our family, tribe and nation. It is as though the water in Moon River has become higher, creating a bigger river, and someday it will create a big ocean. I have no doubt that the time will come, without fail, when we rejoice together as one family under God.

My Lifelong Desire Has Been to Follow True Parents' Will

My name is Watcharin Kaewlamsak, and I was born on September 3, 1973, and my husband is Boontawee Kaewlamsak, born on December 25, 1972. We are both Thai, blessed in 1995, and have three blessed children. Our first daughter is 12, our son is nine, and our second daughter is now three months old. As heavenly tribal messiahs, we have blessed 1,200 families.

In 1995, when I was in my third year of study, majoring in educational technology at Kanchanaburi Rajabhat University, I met my spiritual parent, and I participated in the 360,000 Couples Blessing later the same year. When I joined the Unification Church, my situation was not very good. My friends and professors labeled the church a cult and ostracized our members. I was fully involved in church activities and also had to study, so time passed quickly. I wanted to bring my faith and study to a successful conclusion, so after lots of effort, I graduated and became a schoolteacher.

Due to my firm determination to become a heavenly tribal messiah, I gave up teaching at school despite efforts by the people around me to dissuade me. Then I went to the church headquarters in Bangkok and fundraised for two years while doing accounting work.

In 1997 True Parents set the goal for us, which was to become tribal messiahs by blessing 180 couples. We returned to our hometown in order to witness to our relatives and neighbors. There were about 1,000 families in my neighborhood, and I went from door to door to give out holy wine to bless the people in my neighborhood.

During these activities, I witnessed to Prasit Yodlee, a schoolteacher. Though he didn't quite understand our goal, he gave me lots of help. My parents participated in the Blessing ceremony held at Queen Sirikit Center in Bangkok in 1997. After that, I went to the United States to fundraise for our Thai headquarters from 1999 to 2004. When I came back to Thailand, my husband had been in the International Leadership Training Program (ILTP) for one year. Soon I became pregnant with my first daughter, and three months after her birth I started doing witnessing activities again. From 2006, we started to hold major seminars about families using True Parents' Peace Messages.

Finally, 12 couples from my tribe participated in the Blessing ceremony held in Bangkok in 2009. My hometown of Tha Tum in Surin Province is about a seven- or eight-hour drive from Bangkok, but perhaps as a result of my long-term offering of jeongseong, they

An Interfaith Peace Blessing officiated by the Kaewlamsak heavenly tribal messiah family

traveled all the way to Bangkok for the Blessing, marking my first success as a heavenly tribal messiah. We were only a small group of blessed families, but we had a truly happy time. I felt as if all my difficulties disappeared as I watched the Blessing ceremony. My first spiritual son, Prasit Yodlee, participated in the Blessing ceremony held at Sun Moon University in October 2010. He handled the Blessing expenses by himself, felt honored to see True Parents directly and became very inspired. After his Blessing, he offered his reflection on the Blessing, saying that he himself wanted to become a heavenly tribal messiah. It was an amazing moment for me. His dream was to convey the truth to our entire village. Even now he is helping me in activities and working hard to become a heavenly tribal messiah.

When You Reach the Place I Told You to Go, You Will Find Someone Who Is Prepared to Help You

We are so inspired by True Father's last prayer, which he offered before he passed away in 2012. He prayed that all the blessed families could become heavenly tribal messiahs. After True Father's Seonghwa, Dr. Yong Chung-sik met me in particular and asked me to fulfill this mission. After that, we as a couple set a 40-day period of jeongseong and started to read the book called *Home Church*. This book contains all the words of True Father on home church given from 1976 to 1982.

When I was in the United States, this book was given to me by someone at the New Yorker hotel after they had been cleaning out a storage room, and I have been using it ever since. This book teaches all about the mission of the tribal messiah, and through True Father's words, I was inspired by the purpose and the importance of the home church providence.

I was quite surprised by the reactions of the people around me when I told them about my determination to complete the mission of heavenly tribal messiah. I thought they would encourage me, but instead they robbed me of my energy to go forward. They brought up the difficulties, saying, "That is not easy. How can you do that? How can you finance it?" However, I was not so concerned about what they said, because I was determined to go forward, placing my trust in God's Word, True Parents and my Abel figure. Then I started to pray seriously.

What I realized was that it is important to find a John the Baptist figure first. Right after I received that inspiration, I went out to see the county director and the city mayor, and I showed them the introductory video about True Parents. They were greatly moved and promised to help us in our activities and to create a partnership with the true family movement in my hometown. We sent an invitation letter to 165 villages, inviting 12 couples from each village. The mayor helped us by letting us use the best event hall in the region.

Even though the county had send out invitation letters, we visited the leaders in each village. Doing this helped us to connect with many people and to become very close to them. Then I was put through a test. While preparing for the Blessing, I had a miscarriage. Yet I continued, without stopping my activities.

I had a dream of True Father during that time. True Father came to me and said, "Don't worry, the mindset of the people in Tha Tum is ready to listen to God's Word." Then he disappeared.

We had many difficulties while preparing for the Blessing. This ceremony was the first event in the county. Coupled with our lack of experience, we underwent much trial and error. Though we received help from more people than I expected, it would have been much easier if we had people who were experienced with this kind of ceremony. Another big problem was our lack of funds.

I decided to talk with the president of FFWPU-Thailand about this. I was working at headquarters and also doing tribal messiah activities, so I asked him to advance me six months of my salary. Also, I asked various organizations for donations.

Heavenly tribal messiah Boontawee Kaewlamsak explains the significance of True Parents' birthday to members of his tribe (2017)

More than 1,000 people came to participate in the Blessing ceremony on December 6, 2012. I couldn't believe what I saw that day. It was obvious that God had made an amazing miracle. Then I also realized that we had done it not on our own but with True Father's support and help. I cannot forget what happened that day. It was the moment when I engraved in my heart True Father's words: "Sincerity moves heaven."

Become a Parent to Your Relatives and Your Village (Organization and Care)

After the Blessing ceremony we continued Divine Principle education so that those who had been blessed could understand the importance of the 40-day separation and three-day ceremony. We had worked for three years to reach the goal of 430 blessed families fulfilling those two conditions, but I was just at the beginning stage of restoring my tribe.

My husband and I started to visit the blessed families one by one. My husband served as my driver and lecturer. Sometimes we had to go to a village hall early to clean up before an event. People began to be inspired, seeing us working so hard to help the events go well, and at some places government officials volunteered to provide tea, coffee and fruit for participants. Others spent extra time setting up our meeting rooms very neatly.

We visited the first three blessed families to whom we had witnessed and spent time developing our relationship with them. We gave each family a framed photo of the Blessing ceremony and an FFWPU flag to hang on the wall in their homes. Our heavenly tribal messiah area is a seven- or eight-hour drive from Bangkok, but we were ready to go there at any time. When we arrived, we rented a room and stayed for several days before returning to Bangkok.

Every day we left our room early in the morning, and sometimes we stayed out until 8 or 9 p.m., or even later, explaining the three-day ceremony to people. For the sake of supporting them to fulfill the three-day ceremony, we went out even in a storm to keep appointments we had made, in order not to lose spiritual foundation that had been laid. We offered jeongseong as we prepared lectures and True Parents' words to love the people when we visited them. These efforts started to move people's hearts, and we realized that they trusted us because we were more sincere and unchanging than the people they normally met. They became fond of us, began listening to our words respectfully, and started to put them into practice. Furthermore, people were agreeing to do the 40-day separation and the three-day ceremony even without knowing their meaning. To avoid any problems that could arise from a lack of understanding, we advised them to participate in a one-day seminar.

There were two reasons why we encouraged them to participate in the seminar: first, to educate them, and second, to witness to and bring them to the heavenly side. Through this process they could grasp True Parents' vision, which also gave them motivation to unite and work together with us. We saw that those who received the education and fulfilled the 40-day separation and the three-day ceremony wanted to do more. Little by little they were becoming wholesome blessed families.

Now, when I enter the homes of the blessed families who have held the three-day ceremony, I see True Parents' photo. They have become families who can return joy to God and True Parents. How joyful this is in the eyes of God! Now when we visit elderly couples, they treat us like their grandsons and granddaughters. When we leave their homes, they give us rice, fruit, or vegetables they have raised. Some couples send their children, asking us to give them Divine Principle education.

Without our knowing it, those who completed the three-day ceremony became Abel-type families and went on to the next stage, in which we educated them on family tradition, worship, and making donations. Some of them had worried that they would have to abandon their religion and convert to the FFWPU. Then a very interesting thing happened. A county director, who had been blessed earlier, educated them in place of us. He told them, "True Parents' vision is to form a community of peace that reaches beyond the barriers of race and religion." He explained the ideal world beyond religion.

It was very fulfilling to visit all 430 families every month but also very difficult. Sometimes we found ourselves crazy for the mission of becoming successful heavenly tribal messiahs, but think about it: It is quite natural for parents to be crazy about loving their children. If they aren't, they are not parents. When we truly love the people in our tribe, they can become our spiritual children.

From time to time, some people oppose and persecute us, saying they do not agree with our vision. They are primarily worried that we will convert them to a new religion. When we are confronted with religious barriers and limitations, we pray more for these people, and we learn how to love and embrace different kinds of people. Through this process we have come closer to True Parents' heart, understanding that they want us also to be parents. We cried our hearts out when we felt their heart, which we hadn't known until that moment. We came to believe that filial piety in a true sense means that we form our tribal foundation to console our Heavenly Parent and True Parents.

Members of the Kaewlamsak heavenly tribe gather to celebrate the 57th Anniversary of True Parents' Holy Wedding (2017)

Where the Will Is, You Will Find the Path and Blessings Will Come

Heavenly tribal messiah activities cost a lot of money. We spent our salaries every month and borrowed money from the bank, but the situation was getting worse. But one day the regional president, Dr. Yong Chung-sik, told us, "Where the Will is, money will come," which really encouraged those who had no money due to their witnessing activities. Every single day, we prayed and were grateful. I am not sure I would be able to have the same attitude if I had a personal business and it was in debt; but every time we had this kind of difficulty, God helped us financially, through someone.

Sometimes non-Unificationists helped us. In Surin Province we had serious financial difficulties, especially when we became more active, and then True Mother helped us through headquarters. I shed tears more than on any other occasion. Other blessed families also collected money to help us.

To expand our activities to neighboring areas, we are planning to raise funds by selling high-quality local products. We are preparing a foundation to raise a dedicated member who can be in charge of 12 counties. We hope to have 430 blessed families in each county of Surin Province. We plan to fund our activities without relying on the church. We pray the time will come when we can provide financial support for local churches.

Those Who Receive the Blessing Are Revived as People of Heaven

Both my husband and I work at the national church headquarters. Often we need to balance our work there with our activities as heavenly tribal messiahs. We also frequently have to ask other members to take care of our children. My mother came to stay with our children, but the most joyful time for me was when we could take them with us to visit our tribe on weekends.

Through our heavenly tribal messiah activities, many changes and miracles have been happening in our tribe. One person was cured of cancer after the Blessing ceremony. There are many couples who came to have better conjugal relationships after they stopped smoking and drinking, something they had not been able to control till then. We are obtaining a good reputation among local people who see that through the Blessing ceremony, husbands and wives come closer and take care of each other more.

In this kind of atmosphere, we visited CheongPyeong together with representatives of different communities, and we met True Mother at Cheon Jeong Gung. The representatives who came with us were all very moved, because finally they could see her with their own eyes. After they came back to Thailand, they wrote in their reflections: "True Parents are the king of kings." They testified about True Parents in all parts of their village. Recently when True Mother came to visit Thailand, 450 members of my tribe from Moon River in Surin Province felt so honored at the chance to meet her in their homeland. They are still happily talking about their experiences that day, saying they saw the queen.

It is true that we often face various difficulties in heavenly tribal messiah activities, but we cannot give up our mission. I think the reason why True Parents gave us that mission is because they want to give us a way to grow as parents. We truly pray that we can restore a nation as True Parents wish, by inheriting their dream, planting the seed of true love, and expanding it to our family, tribe and nation. It is as though the water in Moon River has become higher, creating a bigger river, and someday it will create a big ocean. I have no doubt that the time will come, without fail, when we rejoice together as one family under God.

Chapter 7
Interreligious Peace Activities

Rupsingh Bhandari

Person giving Testimony	Wife's Name	Region	Nation
Rupsingh Bhandari	Divine Binawe Chanas Bhandari	Central Asia	Nepal
Blessing Information	Number of Children	Spiritual Children (couples)	Number of Families Attending Church
400 Million Couples 5th Phase	3 children	700 couples	70 couples

The Moment I Met You Was a Miracle in My Life

"
I think heavenly tribal messiahs are pioneers who make a great contribution to the providence by establishing a new historical hometown and lineage for their families during their lifetime. We ourselves are the very pioneers of our tribe, and we need a strong will and detailed plan to complete our mission. Therefore, we are preparing ourselves for the future by not only taking care of current tribe members but also sending their children to 21-day workshops, 40-day fundraising campaigns, or Top Gun workshops. Furthermore, in order to accomplish our ultimate goal, which is to establish God's nation, we will continue to make efforts to influence and be connected to the local society, government and mass media.
"

Return to Your Hometown and Lead Your Relatives and Your Father

I joined the church in 2000 when I turned 17. Soon I became a full-time member. I served at the National Training Center for two years, I was part of an international fundraising team for one year, and then spent three years in the witnessing center again before going to India, where I pioneered in local areas. I did pioneering witnessing in the Sikkim area for two years and the Chitwan area for one year. Then I returned to Nepal. I pioneered the witnessing center in the city of Nepalgunj and did public work there for six years. Since 2014, I have been serving as the president of CARP-Nepal and director of the Nepalese Training Center.

My wife and I were part of the first group of 12 couples selected by the national leader to complete the heavenly tribal messiah mission in Nepal. After receiving this directive, I realized that from then I should work not only for my family but also for my tribe and nation.

I prepared to hold a Blessing ceremony in the western area of Nepalgunj, where I had been working for six years, which was actually my hometown. Furthermore, it was also a place where I had planned and conducted many programs for students and young people. I had some VIP contacts there who were connected to our movement and had a positive image of us. The foundation I had made served well for my completing the heavenly tribal messiah mission there.

What Is Your Will in Raising Me as a Pioneer?

During my college time before I joined the church, I agonized over my future path. I was influenced by communism then, and I had never considered having faith in God. This was because believing in God could be possible only if I denied everything else I believed in those days.

When I first studied the Divine Principle, it was really hard for me to digest religious concepts and theories. However, in the process of putting what I learned into practice through my life of faith, I gradually understood about God, True Parents, and the spirit world. It was after I became a full-time member and experienced difficulties that I could be reborn as a true believer. Also, it was when I went to India as missionary that I could actually feel the

A heavenly tribal messiah Blessing officiated by the Bhandari family

heart of Heavenly Parent and True Parents. That was because my pioneering area was a place where I had to begin and conclude everything in conversation with God. Having led such a life for years, I found myself to have changed, which amazed me. Heavenly Parent and True Parents, without my noticing it, had entered into me and worked through me, even though I had been a communist during my college years.

After a time, I came back to Nepal, and I received the direction from the national headquarters that we all must become heavenly tribal messiahs. In the beginning I worried how I should do it. Financing the activities was one of the biggest issues, because at the time I had nothing. As a missionary, however, I had to obey the direction. In January 2015 my wife and I decided to set some conditions to make a foundation, so we headed for my hometown, Kathmandu. After arriving there, my wife and I offered a serious prayer. We determined to bring the Blessing to our relatives who live in different areas of Kathmandu.

My wife, who came from the Philippines, could not speak Nepali fluently. It was a big task for her to learn Nepali, a complicated language. But she studied the language desperately every evening. Her learning Nepali was not just as a necessity for life but came from her enthusiasm to witness. Though she did not become fluent, she learned enough to have regular conversations with people.

When people saw how much effort my wife made to speak to them in her poor Nepali, they were drawn to treat her more warmly. When I look back on those days, I felt both sorry and grateful to her.

When We Started Our Activities, the Time Was Already Ripe

There was nobody in my hometown to support us; hence, there was no other choice but for the two of us to do everything. That is, the only way was to meet people and give them DP lectures ourselves. In the beginning, I visited house to house with my motorcycle and brought people to the center. My wife, on the other hand, presented our educational program to them in their homes. It was very difficult in the beginning, but we focused on this, day and night, without thinking about anything else. Such sincere efforts and total investment on our side impressed our relatives, who had sat back and watched. Later, those who had come to our center once started to come back again, bringing other people with them.

True Father emphasized the importance of the heavenly tribal messiah mission in his last prayer, so I believed that we should try to accomplish it even at the risk of our lives. When we began to have too many guests, finally other church members and VIP contacts began to support us. In the beginning, the ambassadors for peace were hesitant to help us, but after listening to the lectures and understanding our vision, they started to actively support us. Later, they became so active that they organized and ran the programs for the people from their local areas.

For example, Mrs. Lata Sharma, an ambassador for peace who is the organizer for a women's group in our area, was interested in our program, so she worked together with us. She told members of her women's group to join our program and receive the Blessing. But it was not easy to educate and persuade the women's husbands to participate in the Blessing. Also, though some of the women wanted to participate, others raised some questions about the Blessing. It was not easy for them to understand and accept the 40-day separation and the three-day ceremony. But we completely devoted ourselves to loving and counseling them so that they could understand and participate in all five stages of the process. As a result, we started to influence the whole community in my hometown.

Saving My People with the Truth by Utilizing Mass Media

I invited the local press to our program, since I thought it would be really great if they understood our teachings and reported on the Blessing. I thought this was a good strategy to create an external environment of support.

The media reporters who participated in our event published amazing reports on the Blessing. They introduced our work by posting photos with captions like "430 couples who promise each other never to part" and "Promising to create healthy families." This generated a great and positive change in the local people. There were some delicate conflicts among religions, but people started to realize that family is more important than religion. Good articles by the media became a heavenly message to those who had refused to participate in our events or were still confused about our activities. Those who had a lukewarm attitude started to participate in the Blessing after they heard the news of the Blessing ceremonies that had taken place in other areas. Newly married couples and senior couples joined the Blessing together, which made our event truly beautiful.

Blessing participants shed tears of gratitude. All of them said that they had never heard such wonderful teachings on the ideal family. They publicly promised to become one as husband and wife. Some were a little regretful, feeling that they could have been better spouses or parents if they had heard such lectures before they married. Following this, our educational and Blessing programs became an important social issue among the media and the local people. The media wanted to interview us, which meant that we could convey True Parents' teachings through local radio and TV broadcasts.

The participants truly liked our program. Furthermore, our educational programs on the value and importance of proper sexual relations greatly influenced them. They believe in Hinduism, which has been influenced by secular culture, and they welcomed without hesitation our teachings on sex.

Our program was a great way to expand the true family culture and the Blessing ceremony, yet there was a limit in reaching people who had other religions. Still, we believe our sincerity and truthfulness someday will move their hearts without fail.

The True Family Movement, an Amazing Program Transcending Religions

We went to neighboring villages to promote our activities. They were actually difficult areas to witness in, since many Muslims live there and religious conflicts are more serious than in any other part of Nepal. Politically speaking, the area has a strong communist inclination. It also has the hottest climate in Nepal. The political, religious and natural climate there made it more difficult to hold a Blessing ceremony. But we laid out a plan and didn't stop meeting people.

It was slow going, since the communist and traditional cultures are so intertwined there that many people aren't interested in religious events of any kind. The Hindus in the area did think our movement was right, but at the same time, they were sensitive over their own religious identity. Before agreeing to join our program, they didn't hide their doubt in us. In fact, some even threatened us. But after joining and experiencing our program, they were greatly influenced by it and sincerely apologized for doubting us. We heard later that our program had become a hot issue and was discussed every evening in each household. Through this process, their thoughts started to change and our true family movement and the Blessing ceremony could settle there.

All Barriers Fall for Those Who Dedicate Themselves to Loving Their Neighbors

In promoting our activities in rural areas, we often had transportation problems. But our members volunteered to help us whenever necessary, even if it meant driving back and forth several times to get people where they had to go. Members often stayed up all night to set up the venues and help with the events, making it possible for us to accomplish our goals. Many times, their whole families, including their children, worked together to prepare the events.

Another difficulty we had was politics, simply because politics actively influences people everywhere. Before we started our heavenly tribal messiah activities, politicians were suspicious of us. We avoided making any direct political statements. As a result, instead of criticizing us, people actively participated in our Blessing ceremonies, regardless of their political platform, and then helped us host them.

Our educational programs gradually became popular among the local people. People with family problems who lived in other areas also began to visit us. Most of those who had received counseling from us until then were now able to lead better lives. Our activities became a good opportunity to convey our teachings and heart to people. I believe all of this was possible only because we had received such great love from our Heavenly Parent and True Parents.

One of our problems was how to visit homes that were very far from our area. Some members would go house to house, with their children on their back, to follow up with couples after the Blessing. They also offered the utmost sincere jeongseong in order to unite with the local people. It was difficult for each member, but their hard work filled the area with love.

Heavenly Tribal Messiah Activities Transcend Religious Denominations

Finally, we set the Blessing date for September 1, 2015. Our tension rose with this decision, and we became absolutely determined to complete our mission. From then, we visited my relatives whom we had not seen in six years. They welcomed us, and my uncle's family in particular understood our mission and actively helped us.

Among my relatives, some understood our movement, but they had a limitation in actively helping. This was because the people in the area are so sensitive regarding religious activities. Buddhism is the state religion, while Hindu tradition has settled into the culture. When my wife and I first invited our relatives to gather for a meeting, many of them were afraid to listen to the contents of our program. I continued to meet them one by one, eventually persuading them with truth.

My spiritual daughter Balmoti Chaudhary earnestly helped us bring people from her area. When I went out to meet and talk with people, they happily agreed to come to the venue which was far from the city. It took about one hour by bus, and many people came. Later, being so impressed with the program, they helped us to hold three programs in their area as well.

In our witnessing activities, we faced several difficulties, but we overcame them with the help of many local VIPs, my relatives, our full-time members, and home-group members. In spite of the difficulty, all the necessary preparations for the Blessing ceremony were completed. During the ceremony, we invited representatives of the major religions to the stage. In my area, the representatives of Islam, Hinduism, Buddhism and other religions were together on the stage, and each offered their respective convocation. This was a first for my area, and at first it was rather awkward for them. The Blessing ceremony and our interreligious teachings on the family were amazing enough to allow the various religious leaders to go beyond religious barriers and spend some time together. They were invited to participate in the ceremony of appointment for ambassadors for peace, and this encouraged them to work to realize a culture of true love.

The Blessing ceremony was truly wonderful. VIPs from the area participated, and, through the ceremony, all those who had joined our educational programs felt its value.

Our Next Challenges: Expanding Our Home Groups and Plans for Establishing a Center

The issue we have been facing is encouraging the people who received the Blessing to become our members. This has been a difficult task. Though they watch our services on television, it is still a challenge to connect them to the church as regular members.

People know the movement we have been promoting, and our broadcasting programs, which offer updated information connecting them to us, gradually have become popular in this area. But we have not been able to meet them and spend time with them to build heartistic relationships, so we need to consider what to do about this point.

Similar to PeaceTV, our programs convey the news and our worldwide activities. We understand broadcasting to be a tool to connect with and educate people; but most important is creating good personal relationships with them. While expanding the Blessing ceremony through our home group activities in all sectors of the local society, we need to connect with them personally as well. Actually, before we started the Blessing ceremonies, we had started our home group activities as heavenly tribal messiahs. During the Blessing ceremonies we gave True Father's autobiography to many people and asked them to read it, but it takes time to educate them in our church traditions, for example, donations, which are an important foundation in our life of faith. Those who have become connected with us are still in the beginning stages of their life of faith, so the work has just begun.

It is really difficult to teach tithing to people of our nation, because of its strong Hindu tradition and culture. Therefore, much investment of time and education is necessary for them to become core members and truly understand God's providence. My plan is to gradually expand home group activities, through which we can change their perception and start their lives of faith.

The most urgent issue is to establish a center where we can educate people. In order to convey True Parents' teachings, we need a place where those who have been blessed can meet. As of now, we visit their homes as much as possible, encourage them to become leaders for their families and tribes, and broadcast sermons on TV.

Some home groups have found places where they can meet locally, and they hold weekly services there. We know they truly wish that our organization will keep expanding. However, in reality we do not have sufficient financial resources to set up a center yet, and thus we now are planning a family business.

In conclusion, I think heavenly tribal messiahs are pioneers who make a great contribution to the providence by establishing a new historical hometown and lineage for their families during their lifetime. We ourselves are the very pioneers of our tribe, and we need a strong will and detailed plan in order to complete our mission. Therefore, we are preparing ourselves for the future by not only taking care of current tribe members but also sending their children to 21-day workshops, 40-day fundraising campaigns, or Top Gun workshops. Furthermore, in order to accomplish our ultimate goal, which is to establish God's nation, we will continue to make efforts to influence and be connected to the local society, government and mass media.

David Earle

Person giving Testimony	Wife's Name	Region	Nation
David Earle	Patricia Earle	Europe	United Kingdom
Blessing Information	Number of Children	Spiritual Children (couples)	Number of Families Attending Church
6,000 Couples	1 son, 3 daughters	430 couples	202 couples

The Heavenly Tribal Messiah and Eternal Life

> While doing tribal messiah activities, we understood the torn-apart heart of God and the love of True Parents. We are committed to be a blessed family that fulfills its responsibility and to become people that are needed in the providence of God. While there are people who grow up well as spiritual children, it is so incredibly sad when someone gives up on their faith and leaves without saying a word. I believe I now understand the heart that Heavenly Parent and True Parents feel toward us. Going through these trials has made us firmer in our determination to live as children of Heavenly Parent and True Parents. It also gives the motivation to continue with our providential activities.

Receiving Heaven's Call

Both of us met the Unification movement in 1977. We were matched in Camberg, Germany, in 1981 and were blessed in Korea in the 6,000 Couples Blessing in 1982. We have one son and three daughters, all of whom work in the UK. It is unusual for four children from one family to work in the same professional field, but what we are particularly proud of is that our children all have chosen to work in the field of health and social services.

Since 2008, we have been conducting public Interfaith Peace Blessings every year. More than 500 couples of different religious, cultural, national and ethnic backgrounds have attended, reflecting the diversity of the city of Birmingham, where we live.

My Lifelong Desire Has Been to Practice His Teachings (The Mission Path)

There were some similarities in our lives before we joined the church. Both of us had narrowly escaped death. Patricia contracted paratyphoid in Lebanon, and I was in a traffic accident that completely demolished our car. Also, we both come from Christian backgrounds—Patricia from a Catholic family in Belgium, and I from a Methodist family in England. Though we both had good, close relationships with our parents, we both were disinherited by our parents, who were naturally worried and concerned for our future, when we joined the Unification Church.

When Patricia joined the church, she was working as a pharmacist in Brussels, and she was kidnapped by her parents, together with some Catholic priests and the organization ADIF, and they tried to deprogram her to get her to leave the Unification Church. She managed to escape, but members of her family keep following and watching her, until she moved to London in 1978 and joined the International One World Crusade. Her direct spiritual experiences with God helped her to keep her faith through those difficult times.

In my case, my parents came to Aberdeen to persuade me not to join the Unification movement, and they also asked Christian ministers and friends to speak to me. I had many dreams during that time, often with True Parents, who gave me advice and helped me to understand the right thing to do.

Since 1991, we have been particularly interested in interfaith activities and working with women. These activities have been the foundation for the development of our work and the contribution we have tried to make to God's providence. Interestingly, these two kinds of activities combined in giving the opportunity to go to India in 1998, where we established an orphanage called "Interfaith Children's Home" near Hyderabad which then opened the door into the Indian and Asian communities back home in Birmingham.

Going to My Homeland
(Original Hometown and Heavenly Tribal Messiah Activity)

In July 1991, we had a profound experience while sitting on the grass in Belvedere and listening to the words of True Parents. Father suggested that we should return to our hometown, if we felt called to do so. We both felt strongly that we should do that. It was not easy to decide, especially since we finally had been given permanent residency in the United States after two years of legal and financial battles.

After much prayer and soul-searching, we arrived in Birmingham with three small children in November 1991 to start our new mission. The strong calling that we felt has been at the heart of all our efforts and activities since then, and we have never thought of abandoning the mission.

Patricia has always had a dream to have a house where she could invite people, and miraculously, less than a year after returning to

An Interfaith Peace Blessing officiated by heavenly tribal messiahs David and Patricia Earle

our homeland, that dream came true. Her father had visited us in the United States and was inspired by the type of work we were doing in the community. He was also impressed by meeting the people around us and hearing their stories. This changed his feelings toward us and toward the Unification movement. He even bought a house for us and continued to provide financial support, which allowed us to work fulltime in the movement. My parents also became more positive over time, especially through seeing our children and the practical work we were doing in society. Now, even though our parents are in spirit world, we still feel their continued love and support.

Spiritual Children Help Us to Feel the Heart of Heavenly Parent and True Parents

Patricia faced many difficulties in witnessing in the early days of the Belgian church. These became very special experiences to her. Just before leaving to go to England in 1978, she met a wonderful young woman on the street in Brussels. Patricia had had a dream that she would meet someone that day. She witnessed to her, but then had to leave to go to London. The young woman joined but also found it difficult in the church there and eventually left. However, she and Patricia kept in touch, and eventually she came back and received the Blessing. This was the result of persistent effort.

Recently in Birmingham, Patricia met a very nice Jamaican

A home group meeting in the Earle family's heavenly tribe

woman in the city center, who then attended the two-day and seven-day workshops. She joined the movement and came to church regularly every Sunday. However, she suddenly disappeared and would not answer her phone, and we have no idea what has happened to her. Patricia would find herself constantly looking for her, expecting and hoping to see her. After some months, Patricia met another woman from the Caribbean, very similar to the one who had disappeared, and she came to study the Divine Principle with us and became a member.

We have been able to meet so many good people in the last 25 years. We tried hard to find a way to bring them into a deeper relationship with God, to bring them closer to True Parents, and finally to bring them to the Blessing. There is a story to tell about each of them, an internal story of struggle. We could feel the aching heart of God and His longing to bring each of His lost children back home.

While doing tribal messiah activities, we understood the torn-apart heart of God and the love of True Parents. We are committed to be a blessed family that fulfills its responsibility and to become people that are needed in the providence of God. While there are people who grow up well as spiritual children, it is so incredibly sad when someone gives up on their faith and leaves without saying a word. I believe I now understand the heart that Heavenly Parent and True Parents feel toward us. Going through these trials has made us firmer in our determination to live as children of Heavenly Parent and True Parents. It also gives the motivation to continue with our providential activities.

Life with Them as My Children
(Substantially Restoring the Authority of the Elder Son)

When Patricia arrived in London in 1978, she could hardly speak English. She was doing home church activities in the district south of London. One day while she was witnessing, she heard a woman's voice speaking French, and she stopped to talk to her. The voice belonged to a woman named Margaret. She was not interested in God or religion, but Patricia was able to touch her heart and original nature. Gradually, Margaret began to study the Principle, and she was able to discover God within her life. In time, she became the most faithful and the most trusted among our spiritual children. She became part of our family and helped us greatly. She never hesitated to do any kind of work for God's providence and even offered devotions for the matching and blessing of our children. Our efforts as a couple did play a role in her transformation, but I believe it was all thanks to God's care and love. We also treated her as family without reservation, and she was completely open and willing to become part of our family. We concluded that this was exactly what the relationship of a spiritual parent and spiritual child should be like. The impact of how one loves a child in the Cain realm ultimately returns and affects one's physical children in the Abel realm.

In recent years there was a couple who moved to Birmingham from Rwanda. They lost their father in the 1994 tragic genocide, and their eldest son, Eugene, became like a member of our family, like our own son. Their younger son, Jonathan, is involved in the Unification movement with deep respect for True Parents and the Blessing. He is someone on whom we can always depend, whenever we need help with anything.

We met a truly beautiful couple, Lord Tarsem King and his wife, Mohinder, while working on a fundraising campaign. I met them in the middle of a difficult situation helping a Sikh Christian women's organization. We became very close friends. He attended all the UPF meetings in the British Parliament as a member of UPF and had a great love for True Parents. In September 2012, Lord Tarsem King was chosen as one of the two official speakers who read the memorial speech messages for True Father's Seonghwa ceremony.

The conclusion I reached from doing heavenly tribal messiah activities, and when witnessing to my spiritual children, is that I must love the children in the Cain realm just as much as I love my own children. In other words, witnessing is just the same as adopting our spiritual children into our family. This is no easy task, but I experienced that this results in great blessings. As mentioned in True Parents' teachings, the Fall caused Adam and Eve's family to be divided into Cain and Abel, with one side (Abel) representing goodness and the other (Cain) evil. God, who is the subject of goodness, could receive Abel's sacrifice but not Cain's. That is because God must remain in the realm of good. If God relates with evil, He becomes a God who also creates evil.

Hence, the only way for Cain to offer his sacrifice to Heaven was through Abel. In order to establish such a standard, you have to raise your Abel children and your Cain children to become one. As I understand it, when they become one, the authority of the elder son is restored and the authority of the parent is also restored for the spiritual parents. We have experienced this directly in our heavenly tribal messiah activities. It is not easy to realize a family in which the restoration of the eldest son's authority has been achieved between the spiritual children and the physical children. However, once this is achieved, Heaven's fortune and blessings will unfold.

Characteristics of Our Own Tribal Messiah Activity

Since 1996, we have had the privilege to work full time as a couple representing UPF, WFWP and FFWPU in the city where we have now lived for more than 25 years since returning to our hometown in 1991. This gives us a way to touch the lives of almost every kind of person in the city. We have tried to involve as many parts of the community as possible in our tribal messiah and outreach work. We are not focused just on our tribal messiah work; rather, we see it as part of something much bigger than our family. We have always tried to offer our efforts upward, hoping to bring inspiration to those in the church who are shouldering greater responsibilities than we, and of course to Heavenly Parent and True Parents. Behind the scenes, we also offer prayers and other devotions, especially for those who are preparing to participate in the Blessing, which is often a spiritual battle. So many times on our journey we have felt God's help and the support of many in the spiritual world.

Our hometown of Birmingham is a small city with a population of about one million, but it is an incredibly diverse community. There are people of every religion, race and culture living here, as evidenced by several hundred churches, more than 160 mosques, three synagogues and numerous Sikh *gurdwaras*, Hindu temples and Buddhist *viharas*! In the past ten years, the combined numbers of ethnic minority children have grown to exceed 50 percent, first in the primary schools and now also in the secondary schools. The Muslim families in the city now make up almost 25 percent of the population.

When we arrived here in 1991, we made a point of learning about other faiths, taking a course in Interfaith Relations, and we began to make friends with people of all faiths and visit their places of worship, which laid the foundation for many of our future activities. However, even more importantly, we realized that we needed to radically change our mindset and motivation toward others. We had to shift from a results-driven agenda, in which we were trying to achieve certain goals, to a different focus that would allow us to work gradually, to love people, building genuine friendship and trust.

This is a long-term rather than a short-term approach. The age of indemnity, when we had to focus on fulfilling certain providential goals and numbers, has passed, and we are working to understand the best way of working in this age of Cheon Il Guk. We also took Father's declaration of the Age of Women very seriously. For us, beginning in the early 1990s, it meant that the age of the couple and the family had arrived, and we had moved forward from the previous period of the individual and the church. Patricia began a Women's Peace Meeting in 1993. This has continued regularly for the past 24 years and has been a wonderful way to involve our friends of all faiths. This is been one key axis of our activities.

In recent years, the average number of women coming to the Peace Meetings has been well over 100. From 2000 until 2008, we invited many of our friends to European UPF and WFWP conferences, events in the UK Parliament, True Parents' speaking tour events and Middle East Peace Initiative events. These experiences helped to build great trust for our activities in the community.

The Women's Peace Meetings have resulted in many practical outcomes and projects, including an Interfaith Children's Home in India. The home provides education for orphans from the disadvantaged class. These practical activities have given people great confidence in us and in our movement, because they provide hard evidence that we practice what we preach.

As a result, many people want to study the Principles of Peace behind these activities, and many people also have become interested in participating in the Blessing. Since 2008, we have tried to hold Family Evenings every week to impart the Divine Principle, as well as an Interfaith Peace Blessing once a year. It has been very challenging to keep the meetings going consistently. People have come to attend the meetings through a variety of different routes—through street witnessing, from the Women's Peace Meetings, and from UPF and other organizations with which we are involved.

When friends come to hear the Principle for the first time, we always begin with a short summary of our activities, partly to build confidence and partly to give value to the teaching that follows. We always try to make our presentations relevant to people's day-to-day life experiences and to the things that are happening in society and the world around us. The other major aspect of our work is trying to consistently care for people. We try to present all the education, including presentations about our activities, True Father's autobiography, and information about True Parents' life course, with love and sincerity. This requires consistent small acts of kindness.

These include things like visiting people when they are in the hospital, sending birthday cards, giving Christmas presents and telephoning people to stay connected. Every year we visit our closest Muslim friends during Ramadan, taking something for them to eat when they break their fast, and during the Christmas season we visit as many of our Christian friends as possible, taking a small gift and our year-end letter. The letter reports on our activities during the past year and invites people to join the Blessing coming up in February the following year. As a result, people get a little experience of true love and what an ideal family would be like. Results naturally follow, as people want to come and participate in our activities and attend the Blessing.

We have held an Interfaith Peace Blessing every year since 2008. We have held the Blessings in various locations in Birmingham, including Christian churches and a Hindu temple. They have been attended by people of all faiths, and from the top to the bottom of society, usually with some prominent figures present, such as religious leaders and city council members who give credibility and substance to the occasion. We are hoping that soon we can begin to hold Blessings for specific communities, such as individual churches or mosques. In February 2017, many more people than we anticipated came to the Peace Blessing, including groups of people from a mosque, a Hindu temple and an Iranian organization.

It was very exciting to see this. The door was opening to a new era at a new level, and we could feel True Mother's heart of longing to give the Blessing to all the world's people, as she expresses to us so often. At the same time, we felt that what we can do is just a drop in the bucket, and there is so much more to do. When we bring a couple to the Blessing, for us it is the beginning, not the end, and we feel that we are committing ourselves to go on a journey with them and their family, that together with them we will create a better future for all our children. We are making an eternal commitment to each person and each couple.

Our Family

As I mentioned earlier, Patricia was kidnapped by her family soon after she joined the movement, and my parents tried strongly to dissuade him from joining, and we both were disinherited by our families. However, after returning to our hometown, we were able to gradually restore the relationships with our parents, and then with our extended families, through our children's influence, friends of different faiths testifying to our family, and all the practical work and projects we have been involved with, particularly the Women's Peace Meetings. It has developed to the point where Patricia's sister and a group of her friends, including Catholic priests, meet in Brussels to pray at the same time as we hold our Peace Meetings in Birmingham, which is very moving and inspiring. Our whole family gathered in 2014 for a public celebration of our eldest daughter's Blessing, followed by a larger celebration in Birmingham for all our friends of different faiths, races and cultures.

Development of Blessing Activities and a Vision for the Future

We have thought a lot about how to develop our existing foundation with couples who have taken part in the Blessing, how to build deeper relationships with them, how to help them share the Blessing with their extended families and communities, and how to organize them in such a way that we can have a bigger impact on our society together.

We want to develop a Blessed Family Association with many of the couples, offer marriage enrichment programs and opportunities to study the Principle in more depth, as well as opportunities to gather for social activities. We want to make a good balance between sharing the Blessing with many more couples and at the same time deepening the understanding of the Blessing among those who already have taken part.

We are very small, and the task before us is so big, but with God's help, the invaluable vision and example which our True Parents have given us, and the support of those in the spiritual world, we feel there is nothing we cannot accomplish. We want to continue on this journey toward sharing the Blessing with every person we meet.

We personally chose to accept the responsibility of the tribal messiah mission. It is much more than just something we have been asked to do. It is a calling from God. The intimacy of this calling means that God needs our urgent help at this particular time in history. We hope that every one of our members can also feel this calling, each in their own unique way. It is a serious and gloriously joyful opportunity.

From this perspective, the Blessing is not simply an event at a certain moment in time, but the beginning of an eternal journey that we make with each participant. The nature and scale of the problems we face in our modern society are such that we can tackle them only with others. We must solve them together, and the Blessing gives us the opportunity to gather together like-minded people with shared values. We can encourage and empower each other as we build and maintain God-centered families, and we can make a shared contribution toward a better future for all of our children.

> "These lessons have to become our way of life such that, when we go out anywhere in society, we see the elders in society as our grandfather and grandmother, and our elder brother and sister. When this kind of heart and this kind of family become universal, the world will be the Kingdom of Heaven. The person who lives in such a way can go everywhere without any opposition. Wherever he or she is, God will be there. He or she will never be alone and will never perish."
>
> *True Father's words, November 21, 1971*

"If you follow the path until you become old and still have not fulfilled the mission, and then you die, you still have to keep going. Since it is the path for the sake of the world, it goes on eternally. God is everlasting, therefore the path of the Will centered on God has no end. Even after death, still you should keep going."

True Mother's words, October 26, 2014

"Not all of us can do great things, but we can all do small things with great love."

Mother Teresa

Joyce Suda

Person giving Testimony	Husband's Name	Region	Nation
Joyce Suda	Hideo Suda	Europe	United Kingdom
Blessing Information	**Number of Children**	**Spiritual Children (couples)**	**Number of Families Attending Church**
1,275 Couples	1 son	452 couples	30 couples

3

Making True Parents' Wish My Own, by Becoming a Tribal Messiah

(UPF-Centered Activities and Completion of the Heavenly Tribal Messiah Mission in Africa)

> I always form close relationships with my spiritual children and become friends with them, offering daily prayers and jeongseong for them. Whenever possible, I prepare gifts for them, and I try to move their hearts continuously by taking a constant interest in them and giving them love and care. By doing so, I continue to guide them to God, but I do not hurry them, so that they can approach God at their own pace, step by step.
>
> I also teach them how to lay their foundation of faith and instruct them about the basic ways of witnessing to others and practicing a life of faith. I educate them with the Principle and encourage them to experience the heart of God through prayer. After my spiritual children receive the Blessing, I instruct them to give tithes and donations for the providential goals and projects to keep developing, and for God to live and dwell in their families and homes. Some of them attend Sunday service to continue to develop their faith, and also witness to others and study the Divine Principle in small groups in their homes.

My Life before Joining the Unification Church

My name is Joyce Suda. I come from a Catholic background, and I currently reside in England.

Before I joined the church, I was a certified nurse, midwife and family care practitioner, and I was working in that field. I visited many homes in the district where I was in charge and formed deep relationships with the people I met. However, as time passed, I realized what was happening around us: Families and societies were crumbling, innumerable problems were increasing day after day, with many broken families, teenagers becoming pregnant and becoming single parents, mental problems caused by drug abuse, AIDS and sexual promiscuity, violence and crime. Though a home may look peaceful from the outside, when I went inside the home I saw how serious the situation actually was. I saw that this phenomenon was spreading and was leading good people to destruction.

At present, nations and governments are working to resolve these problems in some ways, through education, and religious organizations also are trying to make programs for the same purpose in different ways, but it seems all their efforts have their limits. Now the society we live in has lost the core moral values and basic principles that people should uphold.

So I started prayed earnestly to God, asking Him to guide my life so that I could transform this suffering world and bring peace to the earth. Before I joined the church, I loved Jesus with all my heart. I implored him to help me become a person who could comfort the heart of God and change this world.

I also studied the Bible and other religious scriptures and prayed and fasted. I actively participated in seminars and retreats, trying to find the meaning of life. During that time I heard about a place where, they said, if you offered profound prayers at the shrines, you would be given an answer. It was Fatima in Portugal. I made a pilgrimage to pray deeply there.

However, even after going through this period of spiritual exploration, I encountered only more suffering in my life. I continued my spiritual search, and finally after seven years I received an answer to my prayers. Now, when I look back upon that time, I think that it was a period in which I experienced God's suffering heart through the suffering I endured in order to find my way to true love, true life and true lineage. One day my brother Robert guided me to a new understanding of the purpose of life and how to solve humanity's problems. He had known about the Unification Principle and knew

I was searching for answers. I came to realize that the Divine Principle clearly explains the meaning of life to the people of this age, and how to solve the fundamental problems of humanity. I also learned that Jesus had already bequeathed his incomplete mission to True Father to spread the Divine Principle on earth to all people.

After Joining the Unification Church

After I heard the Divine Principle, my life changed. Though I had a very good job and earned good money, the course my life was taking did not allow me to continue that life anymore. I donated the house I owned to the church and began my life as a full-time member of the Unification Church.

My missions in the church included witnessing, fundraising, interreligious and intercultural dialogue and educational programs, as well as work with Christian pastors. We organized programs and seminars for resolving conflict and bringing about reconciliation. These were carried out in England and other countries. I also participated in a wide variety of activities, including projects for supporting pioneer work in foreign mission fields and service projects for peace in the Middle East region.

I traveled and worked in Japan, the United States, Korea, Bulgaria, India, Germany, France, Nigeria, Israel, Jordan and England. All the work I carried out was to help people, live for the sake of others and realize world peace, as has been taught by True Parents.

A meeting of Hideo and Joyce Suda's heavenly tribe in Zambia

My Mission Now in the UK

I have been working for the Universal Peace Federation (UPF) for the last 12 years. UPF is an NGO in consultative status with the United Nations Economic and Social Council, and it is working in all fields of society to break down the walls that divide people. UPF is elevating the values of reconciliation, dialogue and cooperation, and sponsoring service and youth programs and projects for peace. It also conducts programs to strengthen marriage and character development in families. It highlights humanitarian service and human rights awareness. We host these kinds of events every month, and some of them are held in the British Parliament and in other countries.

Witnessing Activities, My Strong Point

No matter where I am, I try to talk to people I meet with a joyful heart, whether it is on the street, bus or train, or even when I am out shopping. If there are people about, I try to form a connection with them, as God and spirit world can send me someone in any situation.

I am always inviting guests to the many UPF events we host. Through the Internet I can find other peace groups, interfaith or women-related meetings hosted by other organizations. I then attend these meetings and network, connecting with new people whom I can invite to our UPF events.

I regularly send my guests, contacts and other organizations the reports and newsletters of our UPF activities and conferences, keeping them informed about our activities for world peace.

When I meet new contacts, I introduce them to FFWPU, WFWP, UPF or other church-affiliated organizations, depending on their needs or interests. Every chance I get, I pass on information about our events. I exchange contact information with people I meet, so that I can invite them to educational programs, and once I have made a connection with them, I start thinking about what programs I can invite them to. In this way, I have been able to invite many people through the UPF route to study the Divine Principle and receive the Blessing. I have traveled to Korea with several of my guests and ambassadors for peace to participate in the Blessing ceremony personally officiated by True Parents. It was one of the happiest moments of my life.

From among those people in the community who carry out many activities to serve and care for others, do service projects, community cohesion and interfaith activities, I selected 120 people and presented them with ambassadors for peace certificates, commissioning them to do greater work for peace. They also come to recognize the value of UPF activities, and many work in partnership with us.

I have taken ambassadors for peace to other countries to attend events like the European Leadership Conference and the International Leadership Conference, and often I was in charge of helping and taking care of them. After attending such events, ambassadors for peace come to understand True Parents' vision for world peace and some begin to take an active part in our movement. When I see that, I feel so rewarded and encouraged that I become more eager to continue the work I am doing. After reading True Father's autobiography and gaining a deeper understanding of our Unification movement, some of them take on central roles. There was a time a few years ago when we had a chance to bring many ambassadors for peace who had formed deep relationships with us to Cheon Jung Gung in Korea, in the original holy ground, where they had the precious opportunity of meeting True Parents in person.

At UPF we hold two educational meetings a month on subjects related to the Divine Principle, character education, living for the sake of others, and UPF activities. I invite my acquaintances and guests to these meetings. I believe that our UPF activities and successes were possible because we had the cooperation of Heavenly

Parent and the spirit world.

In my local area, I carry out some activities with my husband. We hold two meetings a month in an Elderly Care Home, where the residents have the chance to receive a massage, practice yoga, do meditation and receive Principle education. Through these meetings we gradually educate them, and later they can receive the Blessing.

Regarding financial issues, when participants register for seminars we have them offer a small donation that we use to cover event costs and for refreshments. Yet even though we don't have a perfect financial strategy, God always gives us the money we need in the most miraculous ways. I have always had faith in these miracles when we hold events.

The Driving Force behind My Work and My Method of Offering Jeongseong

Today, as always, I began my day by offering jeongseong. Every morning and evening I do hoondokhae, conversing with True Parents through their words and renewing my determination. I also share the words I find deeply meaningful with the people to whom I have witnessed and the people with whom I have formed connections, via mobile messenger and email. Sometimes when I meet a stranger, I begin talking to them about the words that I read that morning. This habit is a great way of preparing a spiritual foundation centering on True Parents and not myself. I also invite people to our UPF events which are held two or three times a month. I challenge myself to witness to at least one person a day.

In addition to following the divine commands of Heavenly Parent and True Parents, it is important to receive the help and cooperation of our ancestors in actually carrying out our work. That is why I completed the liberation and blessing of my ancestors, and those of my husband, to a level higher than the official one set by the church. I encourage my spiritual children to do it as well since many of them have not. In addition, I distributed 460 copies of True Father's autobiography, which I believe is also a very important kind of jeongseong. I do not just hand out books; I start out by giving someone a copy of the autobiography and exchange contact information with them. After that I try to meet them so that I can listen to their impression of the book and hold a more profound conversation with them, while explaining the value of True Parents in more detail and guiding them to attend a seminar. In these small seminars we share our reflections and give feedback to one another so they can understand more about True Parents' lives and contributions. I plan to continue introducing people to our movement through True Father's autobiography as one of the ways of my outreach work.

Another good way to offer jeongseong entails going to CheongPyeong holy ground as often as possible to purify ourselves, since CheongPyeong is the place that True Parents found and established after prevailing in the fight against Satan and setting the conditions for spiritual and physical victory. I believe it is the restored garden of

Eden of the original homeland, the place where we can fundamentally separate ourselves from Satan and resentful spirits.

When I give tithes, and holiday offerings, I realize how important the condition is for separation from Satan. It is only when I set the conditions by which Heaven can work through me that I gain an understanding of the position in which I stand and can establish a greater vision for the providence. Only then can I break through my own limitations and receive the cooperation of Heaven. I also think that, by so doing, we can achieve developments in the providence and receive material blessings required for attaining our goals. My husband and I are both working for the Unification movement, and I believe the blessings as well as the income we receive, which helps us to run our home and family life, are a result of leading such lives.

My Attitude toward Raising My Child

We have a son, Toby, who is a blessed child. In the matter of educating him, I have taught him to offer prayers and attend hoondokhae every morning and evening, and I sent him to participate in all kinds of Divine Principle workshops, so that he could make friends with other second-generation blessed children. We have a tradition of attending Sunday service together every week. I also educated him about practicing a life of living for the sake of others. Rather than thinking that he is my child, I try to look at him as a special child of Heaven whom I have been allowed to guide and care for as part of my spiritual growth, just as I do with my spiritual children. When I received the heavenly tribal messiah award from True Mother in February 2017, my son accompanied me to CheongPyeong.

Three Spiritual Children Won amid Opposition and Ordeals

I have met much opposition not only from Christians but also from my relatives and other people. The persecution was very intense and caused difficulties both for me and my guests. At the same time, they constantly tried to persuade and brainwash us to convert to their way of thinking.

Many of my witnessing contacts could not overcome this trial, and in the end they lost faith and disappeared. Such ordeals were very difficult for me to surmount, and they were repeated again and again. I cannot even describe the pain of losing a spiritual child. It broke my heart, and there were times when I stayed in my room and cried all day. I still prayed for them with a heart of forgiveness similar to that which Jesus had for the Roman soldiers who crucified him, stabbed him with their spears and ridiculed him. I even took the time to reflect upon myself and repent. At such times, I was reminded of True Parents' sorrowful heart, which in turn made me concentrate more on my witnessing work and offer more jeongseong. Such ordeals continued most strongly from 1979 up until 2000, and it was truly a long, arduous journey. Our Unification movement was also negatively portrayed and severely criticized on a massive scale,

Participants in a heavenly tribal messiah Blessing in the Suda tribe in Zambia

via mass media, the Internet and all kinds of bad press. When my witnessing contacts came across such information on the Internet, they started having doubts. I, however, did not give up and had even greater determination that I would stand my ground and never back down, just as True Parents taught me to do. In fact, during this period of trials in the 1980s, I went out to witness on the streets with even more passion. I guided the guests to the video center to study the Divine Principle and had them attend Divine Principle workshops. As a result of such struggles, three of my spiritual children joined the Mobile Fundraising Team (MFT), a fundraising course run by the church, where they worked devotedly for three years. They continued carrying out witnessing work for several years until they received the Blessing.

I trust my spiritual children, and I have continued to work together with them. However, there were some spiritual children who left the church a few years after joining it. Witnessing is not easy, but I feel that God is training me as a parent through it. It makes me understand more clearly that our Heavenly Parent is also a parent who experienced that pain before me.

My Special Method of Training Spiritual Children

I always form close relationships with my spiritual children and become friends with them, offering daily prayers and jeongseong for them. Whenever possible, I prepare gifts for them. I try to move their heart continuously by taking a constant interest in them and giving them love and care. By so doing, I continue to guide them to God, but I do not hurry them so that they can approach God at their own pace, step by step.

I also teach them how to lay their foundation of faith and instruct them about the basic ways of witnessing to others and practicing a life of faith. I educate them with the Principle and encourage them to experience the heart of God through prayer. After my spiritual children receive the Blessing, I instruct them to give tithes and donations for the providential goals and projects to keep developing, and for God to live and dwell in their families and homes. Some of them attend Sunday service to continue to develop their faith and also witness to others and study the Divine Principle in small groups in their homes.

I also visit their homes and teach them how to use the holy salt and holy candles, discuss with them how they should raise their children and how they should pray together with their children, and I share my own experiences with them. And to safeguard their children, I recommend that they hold hoondokhae together and that the children should attend Divine Principle workshops during their vacations.

I also have visited the homes of my spiritual children during their children's holidays to hold home workshops, where I taught Divine Principle and principled lifestyle to their children. Of course, I also encourage them to attend other workshops run by the church, but I hold these home workshops too, because I want to create a deep rapport with them as their spiritual parent and teach them to practice the Divine Principle in their daily lives at home. Through these workshops I teach them about the traditions of Heaven and True Parents, the holy songs, developing a character of goodness, and living for the sake of others. I believe these family workshops, which are quite different from group workshops, have significant meaning.

Blessing 430 Couples as the Fulfillment of My Tribal Messiah Activity

For many years I have supported missionaries working in less developed nations such as Africa and the Philippines by sending them money to fulfill their activities. Using those funds, missionaries working in those countries were able to witness to candidates and bless them and take care of them both physically and spiritually. In addition, I also sent them copies of True Father's autobiography. In 2016, I heard that blessed families living in Europe could go and work in Africa to accomplish the 430-couple goal and become heavenly tribal messiahs. I think it is a precious and wonderful opportunity through which members in Europe can support their brothers and sisters on the African continent.

Since I already had been supporting the mission work in Zambia by sending money for the Blessings there, I was able to receive some of the couples as my tribe of 430 couples. These couples have been through the five stages of the Blessing process: They attended Divine Principle workshops, received the Blessing, participated in the indemnity stick ceremony, went through the 40-day separation period, and performed the three-day ceremony.

Some of the members of my tribe have not only attended Divine Principle workshops but also received continuous education from church leaders, chiefs and members of Zambia on True Parents' vision for peace and the value of the Blessing. A few of them have attended the seven-day Divine Principle workshop.

Their children also are being taught the Divine Principle in stages, through such events as the Top Gun Workshops.

I think that more Blessed Central Families should willingly step forward to complete their mission as heavenly tribal messiahs. I do not believe that there is any special method to fulfill tribal messiah activity. The most important thing is the will and desire to obey the command of Heaven and to "get it done." Then Heaven will find a way to help them achieve it. I plan to encourage families and to help them fulfill their mission, which includes:

Blessing 430 couples (five-stage process), guiding guests to attend Divine Principle workshops, offering 430 copies of True Father's autobiography for them to read and study, and holding meetings to get their feedback; connecting the 430 guests to FFWPU, UPF, WFWP and other providential organizations; and holding home study groups so that guests and spiritual children can participate regularly in small group meetings and receive more education.

Through my UPF mission and witnessing outreach activities, I will continue to connect people to True Parents' vision for world peace. I also will continue to carry out the work of educating even more people and guiding them to receive the Blessing.

We truly are living in an amazing age. I am really grateful to True Parents for inspiring us to convey their hope and vision for world peace to others.

Tomiko Duggan

Person giving Testimony	Husband's Name	Region	Nation
Tomiko Duggan	Dennis H. Duggan	North America	United States
Blessing Information	Number of Children	Spiritual Children (couples)	Number of Families Attending Church
2,075 Couples	1 son	450+ couples	

I Will Be There, Where Your Will Needs Me

"
True Mother laid the outline of our spiritual alignment and has shown a direction of steps that we should take.
I learned through the works of UPF and the tribal messiah mission that many leaders who are like-minded in government, civil society, faith communities and think tanks agreed that the conventional ways will have limitations and will not be able to bring solutions to the challenges we are facing. We need God in our families and communities, and we need to turn around from selfishness to unselfishness. Self-centered greed will not bring happiness and joy.
"

God Changed My Life

I joined the Unification Church in July 1964, when I was a high school student. My family was Buddhist, but I was a Catholic and loved Jesus. I started dreaming about Jesus, Mary, and the spiritual world six months prior to my first meeting with Mrs. Eriko Kagikuri, my spiritual mother. She came to my hometown, Toyama, as part of the first 40-day summer pioneering in the history of the Unification Church in Japan.

On the first day that I heard the Divine Principle from Mrs. Kagikuri, an Asian man who had appeared in my dream six months earlier appeared in my dream again and told me to stay in the Unification Church. In the dream there was an Asian man praying on a rock, and an angel who came down from Heaven with Jesus guided me to meet this man. A bright, beaming light from Heaven was over his head. Because of the dream that I had had six months earlier, I understood that the encounter with Mrs. Kagikuri was no coincidence. I later confirmed from a photo that the Asian man in my dreams was True Father. This is how my life in the Unification Church began.

I was invited to come to the United States in 1973. My mission in the United States started with fundraising. This was a blessing for me to meet American people by knocking on their doors one after another in Queens, Brooklyn, and the Bronx in New York City. I experienced the generosity and kindness of the American people, and at the same time it gave me the opportunity to learn English.

When True Father began the 32-city "God Bless America" speaking tour, I was selected to work with Teddy Verheyen's International One World Crusade (IOWC) team, where I came to work together with my future husband. We were on the same team, but I was fundraising and he was witnessing and on the public relations team. When we traveled by passenger van to the different cities, I always sat behind his driver's seat.

True Parents matched us in the ballroom at the New Yorker hotel in 1979, and we were part of the 2,075 Couples Blessing at Madison Square Garden in 1982. We have one son, 27 years old, who has studied filmmaking, which is his passion, and he is now working as a production assistant in the professional TV and movie industry.

After the "God Bless America" tour, among other activities I worked at the World Media Association for 17 years, which gave me the opportunity to travel to over 60 nations to help organize the World Media Conferences and fact-finding tours. Working with

Heavenly tribal messiah activities by the Duggan family

Larry Moffitt and under Dr. Bo Hi Pak from 1979 to 1996, I especially remember the 11th World Media Conference in Moscow and the events surrounding it. These were important providential events that contributed to the collapse of the Soviet Union and the end of the Cold War. This was the time when True Parents first met Mikhail Gorbachev, the head of the USSR and the leader of the communist world.

Working under Dr. Douglas M. Joo and with American sisters of the WFWP from 1995 to 1996, I was also responsible for all the logistic aspects of the many US–Japan Sisterhood programs that True Parents initiated as part of the 50th commemoration of the end of World War II. I was then privileged to travel to six cities in

Japan with U.S. President George H.W. Bush (41) and his wife, Barbara, assisting them during his speaking tour.

True Parents initially assigned me to represent Colombia during their visits to 100 nations around the world. I eventually became *boonbongwang* to Albania, where I came to know many wonderful Muslim believers and became acquainted with the former president of Albania, Hon. Alfred Moisiu, who welcomed True Parents in Albania when he was the president.

I am very privileged to continue working on the front line. Currently I work as director of public affairs of the Universal Peace Federation in Washington, D.C.

True Parents' Desire and My Desire—Heavenly Tribal Messiah Activities

I became serious to accomplish my tribal messiah mission when I heard that my spiritual son in Japan had become the third couple acknowledged to have accomplished the tribal messiah mission. At the Famicon (an assembly of Unificationists from across the U.S.) in April 2017, I also was very impressed and inspired by the testimonies of the Willett family, the Hoffman family, and Claudette Kambara, all of whom have fulfilled the goal of 430 couples. Their commitment and devotion to True Parents are extraordinary.

I had a spiritual experience during the Famicon. God told me how True Parents had guided me all these years. I thank Claudette, who gave me step-by-step guidance on how she approached people about the Blessing and what she prepared for the Blessing.

When we heard that True Mother was coming to speak at Madison Square Garden in New York City on July 15, 2017, I immediately felt that I must finish blessing 430 families to welcome True Mother, so that I can be useful to work for America. I felt I should welcome True Mother at least on a tribal messiah level, because True Mother is coming on the global level to bring a victory to America. This should be my gift and my offering for America and my welcome to True Mother.

I prepared a Blessing kit so that I would be able to meet and bless people anytime and anywhere. I determined to go out every day after work until I fulfilled the goal of 430 couples. I quickly learned how many women are single parents and how difficult it is to meet married couples on the street.

Since I organize so many local UPF programs, such as American Leadership Conferences, Japanese tea ceremonies, interfaith prayer breakfasts, etc., I decided to invite our local pastor to conduct the Blessing at the end of a UPF program as a special session and to encourage the ambassadors for peace participants to accept the Blessing.

The Treasure of My Life, My Spiritual Children

Half of my 430 couples were blessed by my spiritual children in

Japan. They are the fruit of the early period of my church life.

In those earlier days, I went out after school every day for street preaching. I was filled with joy and spiritual grace. While many people stopped and heard me preaching, they often persecuted me, and my high school teacher told me to stop because I was bringing disgrace to my school. However, most of my spiritual children were from that time, and they became 777 couples, 1,800 couples, and 6,000 couples.

I want to explain about some diverse witnessing experiences with my spiritual children. I was assigned to work at the Kanazawa Church in Ishikawa Prefecture in 1969–1970. One day, I had to prepare lunch for the Kanazawa CARP students who were organizing a "Divine Principle Exhibition" on the Kanazawa University campus. The exhibition was very successful. The CARP members could not speak to everybody who had come to hear about their Divine Principle exhibition panels, so even though I had gone to the university only to bring the CARP students their lunch, I ended up having to help explain the contents of the DP panels. Mr. Katsu Sakabe was one of the students to whom I lectured at that time.

Mr. Sakabe became a dedicated Unification Church member and was blessed in the 6,000 Couples Blessing. If I had not delivered lunch that day, I would not have met him. He and his wife together have more than 90 spiritual children and spiritual grandchildren. All their immediate families on both sides have been blessed, and most of their relatives are also blessed. They are an extraordinarily faithful couple. Four generations of their family—grandparents,

Some Japanese relatives from wife's side of the Duggan heavenly tribe

parents, he and his wife, and their children—all have received the Blessing. His father was an especially outstanding church member who offered everything he could for True Parents. His father offered their property to the church and continues to financially support God's providence. Their home became the Unification Church center in the city of Tsu, until the church was able to move to a larger building. They are an outstanding blessed family. God has brought them grace and made their faith deep and strong. Their dedication to God and True Parents never weakened, even when they faced external difficulties.

My husband went to Japan and Korea as a member of First Global Team. One of his spiritual children in Japan joined after he gave her one simple pamphlet. She became a powerful fundraiser, a local church leader, brought spiritual children, participated in the 6,000 Couples Blessing, and raised two daughters.

More than half of my husband's spiritual children, as well as mine, were witnessed to in Japan many years ago. To find the rest of the couples we needed to reach the goal of blessing 430 couples, we went out witnessing every day to talk to people at shopping centers and on the street, and we talked to our neighbors, to UPF ambassadors for peace, and the families, relatives and friends who came to our events.

The first couple I blessed after attending the Famicon conference in April 2017 had been my neighbors for 13 years, but I had never approached them. They are highly educated professionals who emigrated from Ghana. After they attended one of True Mother's events in Washington, D.C., I discovered that the husband had heard True Father speak at Yankee Stadium in New York City in 1976, when he was a young single man! When True Father's autobiography was published, I invited them to our home and we started reading it together. I also started giving Divine Principle lectures to each of them separately, whenever they were available—one hour or sometimes two hours, whenever we could spare the time. The wife has completed the Divine Principle, and her husband has completed it up to Abraham's family. They have two sons, who have graduated from university. Their entire family became ambassadors for peace. They always support our UPF programs and attended the Madison Square Garden rally in July 2017 to hear True Mother's message.

They invited me to meet the priest at their Ghanaian Catholic Church and to bless their congregation.

One of the ways we are working to expand the UPF work in the USA is through reaching out to patriotic Americans through their involvement in cultural and civic activities rooted in the immigrant communities. Dr. Zalfqar Kazmi and his wife, Tanvir, helped me to bless more than 50 couples from his Pakistani community and brought 500 guests from his Virginia Muslim community to the Madison Square Garden rally. His non-profit interfaith organization, The Common Grounds, has collaborated with UPF to organize an American Leadership Conference and Peace Forums. He now assists in promoting the importance of True Parents' work for peace and the Blessing as a foundation for peace in the Islamic world and for understanding between Christians and Muslims. Dr. and Mrs. Kazmi were one of the couples recognized during the recent Parents' Day program.

Connecting to People through NGOs and Bringing Them to the Blessing

At Famicon in April 2017, I learned how the Willett family, the Hoffman family and Claudette Kambara accomplished the goal of blessing 430 couples. Their model of commitment to accomplish the blessing of 430 couples is the most important element to begin fulfillment of the tribal messiah mission. The method can be uniquely guided by the foundation and ability of each couple.

I prepared a Blessing kit based on Claudette Kambara's guidance—a beautiful plastic box which contains holy juice, holy water, and forms to be filled out for follow-up. In addition to those basic holy items, I prepare flyers about future educational programs for their further understanding of True Parents. I give out an *origami* crane to express my appreciation for their accepting the Blessing—explaining the crane as a representation of True Mother's character.

When I am witnessing, I invite guests whom I have blessed on the street or in a shopping mall to UPF programs and appoint them to become ambassadors for peace. I continue inviting them to other programs such as American Leadership Conferences and cultural events.

I hold Blessings at the end of each UPF program. I offer True Father's autobiography to the participants to help them further understand the heart and mission of Rev. Moon.

After I attended Famicon, I invited about 12 Japanese and American Unificationists from the Maryland Family Church and the Washington, D.C., Family Church to hear my testimony and plan. They were re-inspired to finish their goal of blessing 430 couples. We set a goal for the Maryland church to bless 430 couples before the Madison Square Garden event, and we were able to do it. Now each of them is on their way to fulfilling their own goal of 430 couples. One sister blessed 330 couples as of December 1 and committed to finishing by the end of 2017. Two sisters completed 250 couples. We meet every Monday night at the Maryland Family

Duggan family tribal messiah activities at a UPF Ambassadors for Peace event

Church to discuss activities from the week, and about how we have found couples. Their testimonies are sometimes funny and sometimes tearful. They will invite their guests to a Japanese tea ceremony or an ALC program as a follow-up and an opportunity to care for their guests and deepen relationships.

Guiding Your Spiritual Children and Establishing Traditions for Your Tribe

The work of UPF has been my mission, and I hope that UPF will be a great institution to substantiate God's ideal in the world. Having completed my tribe, it is my aspiration to work and develop together with them, participating to make real changes in our community and build lasting peace in this world so that we finally can bring peace and happiness to God and True Parents.

Pastor Jim Boothby of Maryland Family Church has been very supportive in encouraging tribal messiah witnessing and establishing community prayer conditions to provide a foundation for these efforts. Several sisters of the church committed to finish their tribal messiah mission by encouraging each other to finish their goals. We know that one individual cannot do much, but when we help and work together, the result was more than we anticipated. God wants to help us where unity exists, especially when in pursuit of God's Will. Until we all finish our tribal messiah missions, we are meeting every Monday night to give honest reports about the experiences of the outreach efforts, and we conclude with a 21-minute unison prayer.

I still have a lot of work to do to educate my tribe to understand the true meaning and value of the Blessing. Currently, as director of public affairs of the UPF USA-DC office, I will continue inviting members of my tribe to the programs that UPF offers as personal follow-up meetings for them. I also encourage other Unificationists to bring their contacts and to use the UPF programs for further education. In 2018 we should challenge ourselves to set up a good education system that will become a template for many people to use. We should exchange good success stories from other parts of the world as well, to enlarge our ideas of how to work. Some examples are:

- Invite them to a Japanese tea ceremony
- Invite them to an American Leadership Conference
- Read True Father's autobiography together
- One-day Divine Principle seminars
- Three- or seven-day Divine Principle seminars at the International Peace Education Center (IPEC) in Las Vegas

My husband and I have been inviting neighbors and Japanese sisters to our home to deepen our friendships. However, I am quite busy with the work of UPF, and it is not always possible to find time to meet with them.

Future Perspectives and Strategies

"We look at this world and see unspeakable, inarticulate misery happening all around the globe. This is impossible to solve with mere human power. What should we do from here on forward? We should start a movement that once again attends God as the original owner of the universe in our families, countries, and world. However, the reality is that, although our hearts are eager to attend God, it's hard to practice in real life."

True Mother, Kennedy Caucus Room, US Senate, Nov. 30, 2016

"True Parents have invested more than 40 years in America. Now America should live for the sake of the world as the elder-son nation embracing all brother and sister nations. The left and right division in America needs to change. One nation cannot solve the problems. Because of religious conflict and the rise of terrorism, we live in fear as to when the next attack will happen. We must resolve this with True Parents. We should use our powerful weapons of goodness and not stand on weapons of destruction.

It's been a while since I've seen your faces, and I am so happy. Next time we meet, I hope you will have more people sitting next to you. This country has 50 states. I would like to hear that this person from this state restored the state. If you have a state that you truly love, do your best to restore that state and connect it to the restoration of the nation and the world. Next year, for True Parents' birthday celebration, I want to receive a report saying how many states have been restored in America."

True Mother, Manhattan Center, Dec. 3, 2016

True Mother laid the outline of our spiritual alignment and has shown a direction of steps that we should take.

I learned through the works of UPF and the tribal messiah mission that many leaders who are like-minded in government, civil society, faith communities and think tanks agreed that the conventional ways will have limitations and will not be able to bring solutions to the challenges we are facing. We need God in our families and communities, and we need to turn around from selfishness to unselfishness. Self-centered greed will not bring happiness and joy.

One person fulfilling the 430-couples heavenly tribal messiah mission will not create a big movement, but when we come together globally, I believe we can create "One Family Under God."

A GLOSSARY OF KEY TERMS

home church :

A style of community ministry that was emphasized in the Unification movement in the 1980s. Each blessed family had the mission to create a model home and family and seek to love and care for 360 families living nearby. Providentially the home church movement had the goal of restoring from Satan the authority of the eldest son.

tribal messiah mission :

The tribal messiah mission was the family ministry that followed home church. Starting in 1991, blessed families were called to return to their home towns and minister to their extended families and others in their home towns. Tribal messiahs worked to bless 160 couples to the Blessing. The tribal messiah age led to the restoration of the authority of parents.

family church / hoondok family church :

The age of hoondok family church was declared in 2005. From this time forward each blessed family was called to establish a hoondok family church, establish a strong tradition of hoondokhae in their families, and put into practice what they learned through hoondokhae in ministering to their extended families and neighbors. Through hoondok family church the authority of the king was restored.

heavenly tribal messiah mission :

The role of heavenly tribal messiahs was first introduced in March 2012, and True Father emphasized it again in his final prayer. Working in their hometowns or another mission area, heavenly tribal messiahs can shorten the time required for the complete restoration of their lineage from a vertical period of seven generations to as little as one generation, by liberating and blessing 430 vertical generations of their ancestors, and gathering and blessing a horizontal tribe of 430 families, with three generations of their families working together.

home group :

A small group of people, often organized around a few families, who gather regularly as a community of faith, to pray, study, fellowship and minister together. In heavenly tribal messiah activities, a home group sometimes serves as a local pioneer church center.

small group :

see "home group"

midsize group :

A community of faith formed by combining a number of small groups which are in the same vicinity, to work together and support each other, by organizing education programs or community events, for example.

large group :

A larger local church or center which provides opportunities for weekly worship, workshops, and other support services. Parts of the congregation might separate off into small groups and create new pioneer centers.

jeongseong :

An act of devotion, service or care offered to mobilize spiritual support and protection as part of a life of faith. Jeongseong can include prayer, bowing conditions, fasting, taking special care of people, cleaning the church, cooking a special meal, writing letters, and many other types of offering of heart.

"To offer jeongseong means to do your utmost internally and externally. You must offer everything, combining your words, your attitude, your mind and thoughts, all your actions, everything in the internal and external realities of your life." [CSG 11.1.2.1]

hyojeong :

A heart of filial devotion, love given by children in response to the love they have received from their parents, and the exchange of heart between humankind and Heavenly Parent, who also stand in a parent–child relationship. A heart of hyojeong is the starting point of a world that expresses the ideal of creation.

hoondokhae :

Hoondokhae is a meeting where people gather to read, discuss and understand the teachings of True Parents. It is also a time for offering jeongseong of the mind and the body. By engaging in hoondok reading with the whole mind and body, we participate in "hoondok mind-body purification jeongseong."

Cheon Il Guk :

Cheon Il Guk is the shortened name for "Cheonju Pyeonghwa Tongil Guk," which is the "Cosmic Nation of Peace and Unity." Cheon Il Guk is the kingdom of heaven on earth, which we build by practicing what we have learned about love and living for the sake of others.

Seonghwa :

In the Unification movement, the transition from life in the world of air to life in the world of love is call *Seonghwa* (成和: completion and harmony) The end of life in the world of air is nothing to be feared, but is a time of ascending nobly to heaven. When we gather for a Seonghwa Service after somebody has ascended, we celebrate their life up until now, and rejoice for their coming life.

BonHyang Won :

True Father's final resting place above Cheon Jeong Gung is called *BonHyang Won*, which means "garden of the original homeland."

weonjeon / Paju Weonjeon :

Weonjeon is the word used to describe a memorial garden where Unificationists have been laid to rest. The Paju Weonjeon is a special weonjeon in Paju, Korea, for members of the True Family and early church members.

supporters :

Already married couples who received the Blessing through Heavenly Tribal Messiah activities, or other active supporters of FFWPU and/or related providential organizations.

registered members :

Members who attend worship services or donate at least once every six months.

associate members :

Members who donate (tithe if possible) and attend at least two worship services every three months.

regular members :

Members who tithe twice and attend at least six worship services every three months.

Editors
Wonju McDevitt (Head Editor, Chief of Staff, Dr. Hak Ja Han Moon's Secretariat)
Yun Young-ho (Secretary General, FFWPUI HQ)
Yong Jin-hun (Director, FFWPUI HQ Heavenly Tribal Messiah Academy)

Writers
Yong Jin-hun (Director, FFWPUI HQ Heavenly Tribal Messiah Academy)
Cho Hyun-yong (FFWPUI HQ Heavenly Tribal Messiah Academy)
Lee Bok-jin (FFWPUI HQ Heavenly Tribal Messiah Academy)
Lee Gil-yeon (Korea University)
Park Ye-ran (Advisory Consultant)

Heavenly Tribal Messiah Collection 3 Life Skills
Life as a Heavenly Tribal Messiah

Published June 21, 2018

First edition © 2018
Layout by Sung Hwa Publishing Co., Korea
Published by Heavenly Tribal Messiah Academy
Printed by HSA-Books, New York, NY   June 2019

www.ingramcontent.com/pod-product-compliance
Lightning Source LLC
Chambersburg PA
CBHW060910300426
44112CB00011B/1411